STEM Programming for All Ages

About the Series

This innovative series written and edited for librarians by librarians provides authoritative, practical information and guidance on a wide spectrum of library processes and operations.

Books in the series are focused, describing practical and innovative solutions to a problem facing today's librarian and delivering step-by-step guidance for planning, creating, implementing, managing, and evaluating a wide range of services and programs.

The books are aimed at beginning and intermediate librarians needing basic instruction/guidance in a specific subject and at experienced librarians who need to gain knowledge in a new area or guidance in implementing a new program/service.

About the Series Editor

The **Practical Guides for Librarians** series was conceived and edited by M. Sandra Wood, MLS, MBA, AHIP, FMLA, Librarian Emerita, Penn State University Libraries from 2014 to 2017.

M. Sandra Wood was a librarian at the George T. Harrell Library, the Milton S. Hershey Medical Center, College of Medicine, Pennsylvania State University, Hershey, PA, for more than thirty-five years, specializing in reference, educational, and database services. Ms. Wood received an MLS from Indiana University and an MBA from the University of Maryland. She is a fellow of the Medical Library Association and served as a member of MLA's Board of Directors from 1991 to 1995.

Ellyssa Kroski assumed editorial responsibilities for the series beginning in 2017. She is the director of information technology at the New York Law Institute as well as an award-winning editor and author of thirty-six books including *Law Librarianship in the Digital Age* for which she won the AALL's 2014 Joseph L. Andrews Legal Literature Award. Her ten-book technology series, The Tech Set, won the ALA's Best Book in Library Literature Award in 2011. Ms. Kroski is a librarian, an adjunct faculty member at Drexel and San Jose State University, and an international conference speaker. She has just been named the winner of the 2017 Library Hi Tech Award from the ALA/LITA for her long-term contributions in the area of library and information science technology and its application.

Titles in the Series Edited by M. Sandra Wood

1. *How to Teach: A Practical Guide for Librarians* by Beverley E. Crane
2. *Implementing an Inclusive Staffing Model for Today's Reference Services: A Practical Guide for Librarians* by Julia K. Nims, Paula Storm, and Robert Stevens
3. *Managing Digital Audiovisual Resources: A Practical Guide for Librarians* by Matthew C. Mariner

4. *Outsourcing Technology: A Practical Guide for Librarians* by Robin Hastings
5. *Making the Library Accessible for All: A Practical Guide for Librarians* by Jane Vincent
6. *Discovering and Using Historical Geographic Resources on the Web: A Practical Guide for Librarians* by Eva H. Dodsworth and L. W. Laliberté
7. *Digitization and Digital Archiving: A Practical Guide for Librarians* by Elizabeth R. Leggett
8. *Makerspaces: A Practical Guide for Librarians* by John J. Burke
9. *Implementing Web-Scale Discovery Services: A Practical Guide for Librarians* by JoLinda Thompson
10. *Using iPhones and iPads: A Practical Guide for Librarians* by Matthew Connolly and Tony Cosgrave
11. *Usability Testing: A Practical Guide for Librarians* by Rebecca Blakiston
12. *Mobile Devices: A Practical Guide for Librarians* by Ben Rawlins
13. *Going Beyond Loaning Books to Loaning Technologies: A Practical Guide for Librarians* by Janelle Sander, Lori S. Mestre, and Eric Kurt
14. *Children's Services Today: A Practical Guide for Librarians* by Jeanette Larson
15. *Genealogy: A Practical Guide for Librarians* by Katherine Pennavaria
16. *Collection Evaluation in Academic Libraries: A Practical Guide for Librarians* by Karen C. Kohn
17. *Creating Online Tutorials: A Practical Guide for Librarians* by Hannah Gascho Rempel and Maribeth Slebodnik
18. *Using Google Earth in Libraries: A Practical Guide for Librarians* by Eva Dodsworth and Andrew Nicholson
19. *Integrating the Web into Everyday Library Services: A Practical Guide for Librarians* by Elizabeth R. Leggett
20. *Infographics: A Practical Guide for Librarians* by Beverley E. Crane
21. *Meeting Community Needs: A Practical Guide for Librarians* by Pamela H. MacKellar
22. *3D Printing: A Practical Guide for Librarians* by Sara Russell Gonzalez and Denise Beaubien Bennett
23. *Patron-Driven Acquisitions in Academic and Special Libraries: A Practical Guide for Librarians* by Steven Carrico, Michelle Leonard, and Erin Gallagher
24. *Collaborative Grant-Seeking: A Practical Guide for Librarians* by Bess G. de Farber
25. *Story-Time Success: A Practical Guide for Librarians* by Katie Fitzgerald
26. *Teaching Google Scholar: A Practical Guide for Librarians* by Paige Alfonzo
27. *Teen Services Today: A Practical Guide for Librarians* by Sara K. Joiner and Geri Swanzy
28. *Data Management: A Practical Guide for Librarians* by Margaret E. Henderson

29. *Online Teaching and Learning: A Practical Guide for Librarians* by Beverley E. Crane
30. *Writing Effectively in Print and on the Web: A Practical Guide for Librarians* by Rebecca Blakiston
31. *Gamification: A Practical Guide for Librarians* by Elizabeth McMunn-Tetangco
32. *Providing Reference Services: A Practical Guide for Librarians* by John Gottfried and Katherine Pennavaria
33. *Video Marketing for Libraries: A Practical Guide for Librarians* by Heather A. Dalal, Robin O'Hanlon, and Karen Yacobucci
34. *Understanding How Students Develop: A Practical Guide for Librarians* by Hannah Gascho Rempel, Laurie M. Bridges, and Kelly McElroy
35. *How to Teach: A Practical Guide for Librarians, Second Edition* by Beverley E. Crane
36. *Managing and Improving Electronic Thesis and Dissertation Programs: A Practical Guide for Librarians* by Matthew C. Mariner
37. *User Privacy: A Practical Guide for Librarians* by Matthew Connolly
38. *Makerspaces: A Practical Guide for Librarians, Second Edition* by John J. Burke, revised by Ellyssa Kroski
39. *Successful Summer Reading Programs for All Ages: A Practical Guide for Librarians* by Katie Fitzgerald
40. *Implementing the Information Literacy Framework: A Practical Guide for Librarians* by Dave Harmeyer and Janice J. Baskin

Titles in the Series Edited by Ellyssa Kroski

41. *Finding and Using U.S. Government Information: A Practical Guide for Librarians* by Bethany Latham
42. *Instructional Design Essentials: A Practical Guide for Librarians* by Sean Cordes
43. *Making Library Websites Accessible: A Practical Guide for Librarians* by Laura Francabandera
44. *Serving LGBTQ Teens: A Practical Guide for Librarians* by Lisa Houde
45. *Coding for Children and Young Adults in Libraries: A Practical Guide for Librarians* by Wendy Harrop
46. *Teen Fandom and Geek Programming: A Practical Guide for Librarians* by Carrie Rogers-Whitehead
47. *Comic Book Collections and Programming: A Practical Guide for Librarians* by Matthew Wood
48. *STEM Programming for All Ages: A Practical Guide for Librarians* by Chantale Pard

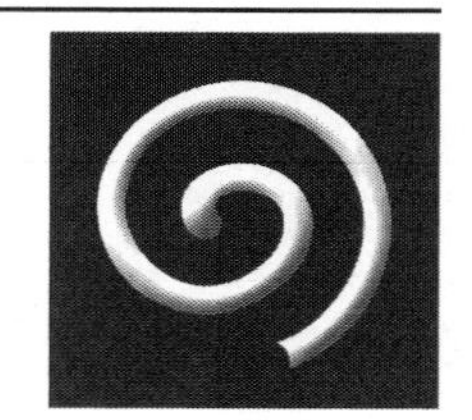

STEM Programming for All Ages

A Practical Guide for Librarians

Chantale Pard

PRACTICAL GUIDES FOR LIBRARIANS, NO. 48

ROWMAN & LITTLEFIELD
Lanham • Boulder • New York • London

Published by Rowman & Littlefield
An imprint of The Rowman & Littlefield Publishing Group, Inc.
4501 Forbes Boulevard, Suite 200, Lanham, Maryland 20706
www.rowman.com

Unit A, Whitacre Mews, 26-34 Stannary Street, London SE11 4AB

British Library Cataloguing in Publication Information Available

Library of Congress Cataloging-in-Publication Data Available

ISBN 978-1-5381-0816-1 (pbk. : alk. paper) | ISBN 978-1-5381-0817-8 (ebook)

∞™ The paper used in this publication meets the minimum requirements of American National Standard for Information Sciences—Permanence of Paper for Printed Library Materials, ANSI/NISO Z39.48-1992.

Printed in the United States of America

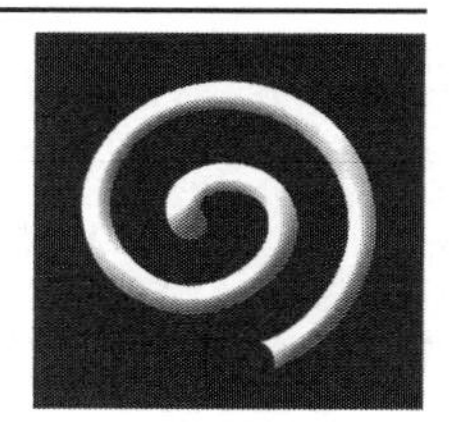

Contents

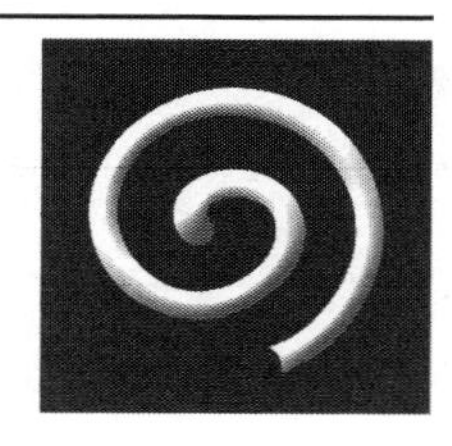

List of Figures

Preface

Welcome to *STEM Programming for All Ages*! Although STEM library programs have been a hot topic at public library conferences for some years now, when I started writing this book in early 2017, the market lacked any recent print materials on this important trend that only seems to be getting more and more relevant in both libraryland and communities today.

While there have since been other youth-focused STEM resources published for librarians, as a practical guide, *STEM Programming for All Ages* will be useful for librarians, staff, and students alike, due to its comprehensive coverage of STEM programming ideas for library users of all ages. Readers will learn why STEM skills are necessary for their communities, why the library is perfectly suited to help supplement them, and how to start implementing some of the simple and fun STEM-based activities in their own branches. Other important STEM topics covered in this book include gathering the necessary funds and supplies, creating partnerships, breaking down barriers for underserved populations, and quick and easy passive program ideas.

I first delved into the realm of STEM programming by way of the library maker movement in 2014. As a youth services librarian with Halifax Public Libraries, I had recently returned from the OLA Super Conference inspired by a session I had seen on Squishy Circuits and Makey Makeys. Due to my displayed enthusiasm, I was tasked with purchasing the necessary supplies for a regional Squishy Circuits kit and creating a program module for our fourteen branches, which then led to my leading of a regional STEM program training session at our annual Children's Services training day.

Even from the early days of my Squishy-Makey experiments with children, I have always been most excited about finding ways to pump up the excitement and engagement in these activities by finding ways in which to incorporate them into pop culture themes: Star Wars, Dr. Who, Minions, anime, and so forth (and I even saved the pictures, which you can see in chapter 5!).

About a year into my Squishy-Makey pop culture programming, I attended another local conference here in Atlantic Canada, and I was surprised to hear the following complaint at one of the Maker gadget sessions: "But this stuff falls out of fad so quickly! My community is tired of Squishy Circuits—people will only want to make a ball of playdough light up so many times." This was my call to action—I immediately started developing my own presentation for the following year, and in spring of 2017, "MAKE it POP!" taught APLA Conference attendees how to incorporate pop culture themes into their maker projects while reusing core materials like Squishy Circuits and Makey Makeys.

It was thus a natural extension to branch out into the wider area of STEM programming at large—maker projects can so often incorporate not only technology and engineering skills, but also scientific and mathematical elements. When I heard of the opportunity to write a book for Ellyssa Kroski's Practical Guides for Librarians series, I was immediately excited about the possibility, and honored to have the opportunity to write about developing STEM programs in libraries.

Writing this book has been an inspiring learning process. Although I continued to encourage pop culture inspirations for our youth STEM programs in the summer of 2017 (a mania after which some of our teen volunteers joked about never wanting to see another fidget spinner, slime, or unicorn again), I knew I needed to branch out past pop-culture- and youth-focused projects, and this thus required me to expand my repertoire. I spent many hours researching through our local library school databases and interviewing other librarians about their involvement in STEM programming for libraries.

How to Use This Book

Chapters 1, "STEM Programming in Public Libraries," and 2, "Getting Started," discuss our clear need for wider adoption of STEM skills, why the library is perfectly suited to support this goal, and how librarians can start the process of implementing these activities.

Chapter 3, "Budgeting and Gathering Supplies," discusses how to develop budgets and find funding to support library STEM programming. Chapters 4 through 8 discuss specific STEAM programs for all age groups including preschoolers, elementary-aged children, teens, adults, and even families, including examples from experienced librarians and their staff. Chapter 11 provides examples of passive STEM programming.

Chapter 9, "The Power of Partnerships," talks about the importance of creating relationships with local community organizations in order to draw upon their expertise to supplement STEM programming options at the library. Chapter 10, "Breaking Down Barriers: STEM Skills for Underserved Populations," informs readers about communities that have been traditionally underrepresented in STEM fields, such as newcomers, girls, and LGBTQ+, and suggests ways in which the library can help advocate for their STEM learning.

The appendix includes a list of must-access STEM resources such as websites, blogs, and must-watch YouTube series, as well as other library STEM titles to add to your professional collection.

STEM skills are vital to the success and development of all our communities. I hope that you find this book useful in ensuring that your libraries do all they can to supplement such integral learning opportunities in community members of all ages.

Acknowledgments

Many thanks go to Jennifer Evans, Eric Drew, Candice Blackwood, Heather Love Beverley, Ted Belke, and Trina Orchard for their invaluable thoughts and program ideas provided through their interviews submitted to this book. I was truly inspired and genuinely excited to start planning Keshen Goodman Public Library's summer 2018 programming roster while reading through all of their unique and insightful answers.

I am also constantly impressed by my creative and hardworking library colleagues I have met through library school, conferences, and particularly within the Halifax Public Libraries system. Seeing the spark of a STEM-filled passion ignite in a member of my community (regardless of age) is motivating on its own, but knowing I can then share and learn even further from my talented coworkers brings it to another level entirely.

I'd also like to thank my editor Ellyssa Kroski for her supportive feedback and incredible patience as I juggled writing this book and working full-time. I couldn't have done this without you. To my amazing family and friends, many of whom are eager to read this book, even though library programming isn't a part of their daily lives, except through their association with me. I hope that it might help them to discover a new STEM-related passion or hobby.

To all the children who have shared these creative and fun learning experiences with me—be it my young friends in-branch, my nieces, or any other children my friends and family have brought to me for these often messy activities. Thank you! I hope that you grow up to someday return to our branch as a professional in your chosen field, to teach me and our community even more.

Last but not least, to my work family at the Keshen Goodman Public Library, whose dedication to the developing of their community inspires me on a daily basis. Special thanks to members of my Keshen Goodman Youth Services team both past and present who've taught me so much. They've also contributed to the practical and creative sides to many of the programming ideas in this book. I look forward to the many more STEM programming adventures in our futures! And of course, to our LEGO-loving, explosion-making, screen printing guru, Kevin Croft: STEM programs won't be the same without you, but I endeavor to make sure that they are as exciting and educational as you would have wanted them to be.

CHAPTER 1

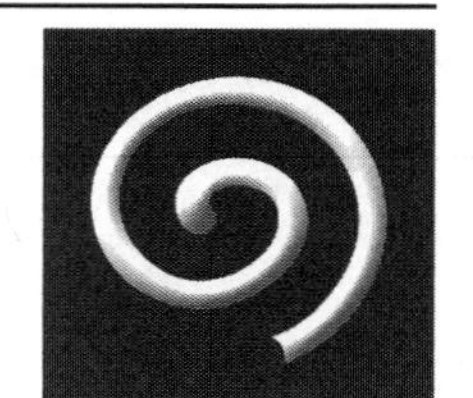

STEM Programming in Public Libraries

IN THIS CHAPTER

- ▷ What is STEM? Why does it matter?
- ▷ Does STEM belong in the library?
- ▷ STEAM: What's in an "A"? Is it inherent in library programs?

What Is STEM?

STEM IS A RECENT BUZZWORD that might call to mind plant structures or human embryo research, but ironically instead refers to the very educational skill sets needed to work with either of those materials. STEM is an acronym for Science, Technology, Engineering, and Math. It is generally used when one is referring to the grouped set of educational subjects or skill sets, in addition to their resulting employment fields.

Merriam-Webster says that science is the knowledge of the natural world based on facts obtained through experiments and observations. These tests are carried out using the scientific method—a set of procedures that involves recognizing a problem, collecting data through observation and experiment, and then formulating and testing a hypothesis.[1] Science has long been a common core subject in classrooms for all ages, all over the world. From early elementary school activities, all the way through to its post-secondary educational fields such as biology, chemistry, and physics, science is a commonly known subject area to people of all ages. A few of the more recognizable science-related employment options include doctors, forensic scientists, zoologists, astronomers, psychologists, and environmental scientists.

Technology is "the practical application of knowledge."[2] The emphasis in this definition is on the word "practical." By this, it often means the use of methods or machines in order to solve a problem or to invent a new tool. The word "technology" often conjures up images of people working on computers and other electronic machines, but it's important to remember that it also refers to the early, simple machines and tools such as the wheel or the hammer. The most popular technology-related fields are positions such as software developers, computer programmers, and web developers. Technical programs that lead to skilled trade employment can also fall under the area of technology too, such as with carpentry or construction, where students learn to use a variety of techniques and tools to solve the problem of creating something.

Engineering is defined as the design and creation of large structures or new products or systems through the use of scientific methods.[3] Engineers apply scientific and mathematical concepts to things like matter and energy in order to make them useful to people. Engineers are most commonly known for building roads, bridges, or large structures, and while the field of study is most often introduced to older, more studied learners, the practice of building design is one of the earliest games of a young preschooler. Toddlers using wooden blocks or DUPLOs to create their own imaginary skyscrapers, while basic, is the very beginning of one's use of engineering skills for design. Engineers design more than just infrastructure, however. Other common engineering roles include biomedical engineers who can design prosthetic limbs, or help to regenerate blood vessels, or chemical engineers, who work with pharmaceuticals, food processing, or even with textiles, where they help convert raw materials into products.

Mathematics is another common core subject that is introduced to even the youngest of elementary students. While plenty of teens can often be heard lamenting about the lack of real need to go to math class (When am I ever going to use *this* again?!), it is the study that explains numbers, measurements, and quantities, and how those relate to each other. It is thus applicable in daily life.[4] Post-secondary math studies seem to have the most publically unknown employment outcomes, but math careers do indeed exist. Some of these include statisticians, who work with data analysis, and actuaries, who use statistical analysis to calculate insurance risks. Both require higher education in the field of mathematics.

Combined Study

However, while each individual field of study within the STEM acronym is an important stand-alone educational skill set, STEM often collectively refers to the "combined study" of "one or more" of the core subjects of science, technology, engineering, and math.[5] In the 2016 issue of *Public Libraries*, Dilnavaz Mirza Sharma explains that STEM "signifies the unification of these individual disciplines" based on their "commonalities and interconnectedness."[6] Indeed, even in the brief individual overviews above, one can start to see the crossovers. Engineering and technology often rely upon math skills and the scientific method, while all four disciplines are routed in methodical ways to solve a problem. The shared practices and concepts found throughout this group of disciplines is what makes it such a well-rounded concept, which, Sharma argues, can be the most effective tool for solving problems. She emphasizes the need for students to approach "STEM disciplinary thinking as a collection of practice principles" in order to solve a wide array of contemporary problems.[7] This serves to reinforce the importance of STEM, twofold—both as individual areas of study, and through the collective practice.

Why Is STEM Important?

If STEM is society's best bet in training our future generation of modern problem solvers, it's no wonder that these skills are in the spotlight in today's "complex and uncertain global economy."[8] Countries are looking to maximize their "economic competitiveness and productivity," and as a result, "governments, policy-makers, educators, and business leaders are particularly concerned" with how well equipped their countries are "with the STEM skills needed to fulfil [their] labour market demands and promote innovation."[9]

In his 2011 presidential State of the Union address, Barack Obama told the United States that "this [was their] generation's Sputnik moment,"[10] referring to the need to elevate their levels of scientific research and development to great new heights as the Soviets had when they succeeded in sending the Sputnik satellite as the first nation into space, or as the US did, when we then turned around and were the first nation to land on the moon. He assured his country that by further investing new funds into STEM fields such as biomedical research, information technology, and clean energy, they would be able to "strengthen [their] security, protect [their] planet, and create countless new jobs for [their] people."[11]

The US Bureau of Labor Statistics released several different reports and spotlights on the future of employment projections for STEM occupations, which, according to its spotlight report, consists of one hundred different occupations including "computer, and mathematical, architecture and engineering, and life and physical science occupations," among others.[12] Looking at the data from the May 2015 Occupational Employment Statistics, one could conclude that the field has been doing well. This report saw 8.6 million STEM jobs in the US, which represented a total of 6.2 percent of US employment.[13] Additionally, ninety-three out of the one hundred listed STEM occupations had wages above the national average, and the national average wage for all STEM occupations was $87,570, which was "nearly double the national average for non-STEM occupations" as $45,700.[14]

The Bureau of Labor Statistics also predicts that the fastest-growing STEM occupation group from 2014 to 2024 will be in mathematical sciences (which includes statisticians and mathematicians), which should result in 42,900 new jobs over that period, which would mean a 28.2 percent growth (which is quite a bit higher than the projected growth for all occupations, at 6.5 percent).[15] The computer occupational group, alone, is projected to "yield over 1 million job openings" from that same 2014–2024 time period as well.[16] These statistics project a possibility-laden future for students looking to enter into the STEM occupational field.

STEM subjects are likewise seen as "critically important to the economic success" of the United Kingdom.[17] Engineering alone makes up 25 percent of the gross value added for the UK economy and, similar to the American statistics above, EngineeringUK predicts a healthy demand for STEM occupations from 2012 to 2022, noting that there will be demand for "1.82 million people in engineering occupations at all levels," including both the advanced technician and professional engineering levels.[18]

However, it's important to note that community STEM education isn't advantageous for the future STEM-related occupation growth alone. Science, engineering, and technology are said to underpin the entire UK economy, including "power generation and electricity distribution, utilities, the food chain, healthcare, and [their] physical, transportation and information and communications infrastructures."[19] STEM literacy can also simply equate to the ability to "work smarter" due to the universally relevant fundamental skills such as "problem solving, technological proficiency, and numeracy."[20] While they are obviously the "building blocks of more advanced and specialized STEM skills," they are also applicable to everyone, regardless of one's chosen career field.[21] STEM-qualified people can be found in a wide array of occupation types, including the "arts and entertainment sectors, sports, education and financial services," and plenty of employees in non-STEM roles are actually recruited "because of their STEM background."[22] A 2015 report from the Council of Canadian Academies argued that STEM skills can open doors to a "range of education and employment options," which means that they are thus "vital for all Canadians."[23] Their eighteen-month research study confidently concluded with their strong recommendation toward "high-quality investments in STEM skills; in both early education and in more advanced training," which they believe is "critical to Canada's prosperity."[24]

Clearly, STEM has an important place in our future. It is thought to be of critical value to governments due to its necessity to meet labor market and innovation demands, which thereby allow countries to remain economically and productively competitive. The statistics above show that STEM fields are indeed creating countless job opportunities, while STEM skills training alone can open up even further employment into non-STEM-related fields. On a basic fundamental level, STEM education will help all students to work smarter, giving them further problem-solving skills and technological proficiencies. Thus, in order to create enriched and successful communities, one of the next steps seems clear—helping community members to build and hone their skills in the areas of science, technology, engineering, and math. If only there was a perfect local meeting space that was dedicated to building and improving communities. . . .

Does STEM Belong in the Library?

Traditional library stereotypes often include a dark, silent building where one goes to quietly seek the permission of a cranky old lady in an attempt to find information through a rare book. More modern assumptions presume the library is simply a place where one can gain free internet access and DVDs—but, "doesn't *everyone* have internet these days?" While free computer and internet access are indeed still a much-required service, the public library has long since expanded into the perfect place to help build communities. A "third place" (a place that isn't home, nor is it work, and is yet still free from the pressures of consumerism, religion, or politics), the library should be that perfect, neutral space where all community members can meet, learn about, and inspire each other. If communities are requiring further learning and experimentation with STEM fields in order to enrich their lives and help their communities and economies succeed, the public library should be ready and willing to take on the task.

Community Developers

In fact, the library is indeed well suited as a place to help encourage the growth of STEM skills in community members of all ages. Libraries all across Canada and the US are continuing to further subscribe to the model of community development, whereby they are focusing their strategic goals on helping to build and support communities. Community development has been defined as the "planned evolution of all aspects of community well-being (economic, social, environmental and cultural)."[25] It is often a process whereby "community members come together to take collective action and generate solutions to common problems."[26] In the context of public libraries, this ideally results in library staff developing trusting relationships with the people in their communities (patrons, or better yet, underserved populations) so that community members will feel comfortable enough with asking the library for what it is they feel they need. Community members would then continue to help plan, possibly host, and definitely provide feedback into the resulting services and programs, in order to ensure maximum sustainability. Ultimately, the primary outcome of community development is "improved quality of life."[27] If your community has identified the need for STEM programming (and it is likely that it would, given the above research), the library is perfectly suited to step in and work with its local contacts in an effort to help solve this problem.

Rebecca Oxley, a librarian and tech teacher at Robert Goddard Montessori in Seabrook, Maryland, remarks that "modern librarianship and science education go together like bread and butter."[28] Her statement certainly reflects the trend in the STEM-in-libraries literature research, which consistently echoes that "STEM programming is a challenge that many libraries can and should accept,"[29] while insisting that libraries "can play a vital role in fostering creativity, curiosity, and a community of tinkerers."[30] Tinkerers—people who seek to repair or improve—should certainly find a safe and supportive place in the library learning environment, which, with all its "unique strengths and learning opportunities," has the potential to transform the international STEM education landscape. It can do this by ensuring that public libraries and their staff are sufficiently supportive and trained enough to deliver engaging, inspirational, and educational STEM programs.[31]

In fact, while schools would seem the obvious placement for educational initiatives, the library seems to surpass this suggestion as the "ideal platform for reaching national consciousness about the need for STEM."[32] Of course, the formal educational systems will continue to teach their core science, technology, engineering, and math courses, but the library is an ideal place to help inspire a looser, more creative experimentation or discovery of STEM skills due to its "flexible space," in contrast to more rigid school classrooms.[33] It's a neutral space where students can avoid "being graded on participation," yet still holds all the access to resources and information should any questions or curiosities arise from such experiments.[34] Heather Love Beverley, the Children's Services assistant manager at the Cook Memorial Public Library District, follows this same line of thought when she explains that libraries allow kids to "explore and learn in a risk-free environment" since library STEM programs won't be grading children on their experiments.[35]

Beverley adds that most important, libraries are an excellent place for STEM programming because it is fun: children can "build fantastic structures, make slime, play with LEGOs, create robots, learn about dinosaurs, extract DNA," and so much more.[36] There is thus a resulting "energy and creativity in STEM programming that is invigorating and refreshing," which helps to remind children that "the library is a place where they can have fun, explore, and learn."[37]

Even within formal education, "rote memorization seems to be becoming a thing of the past as the ability to do and to question becomes the modus operandi for the next generation of independent thinkers."[38] However, although some formal educational classes might be more open to adapting to the importance of flexible STEM skills and using the scientific method as a hands-on way to solve a variety of complex problems, there are still the "less affluent communities" whose schools may not have funding to offer 3D printers, LEGO robotics clubs, or Makey Makey kits, and the library could be the very key to filling that "major void."[39] The Martin Library in York, Pennsylvania, did just this in 2015 when they engaged in unique and inventive ways to help pursue bridging the STEM gap within a distressed school area that had recently experienced budget cuts.[40]

Eric Drew, the Youth Services librarian of Tantallon and J. D. Shatford Public Libraries, believes that providing STEM programming is important because it provides "opportunities that individuals could not easily provide for themselves" due to their required resources, space, people, or even the commitment to cleaning up a mess.[41] When reflecting on the importance of offering STEM programs to his community, Drew draws upon the dual nature of his role as a librarian: as a community provider, he feels it is necessary to offer entertaining resources and programs, while so too, as a knowledge provider, he sees the importance of offering educational resources and programs, and strives to achieve both of these goals in each of his programs "simultaneously."[42]

Trina Orchard, a customer service clerk in Children's Services at the Lethbridge Public Library in Alberta, reflects upon libraries' strange position as "centers of knowledge and information—but not necessarily centers of science."[43] Libraries, she says, have an opportunity to interact with people of all ages and provide exposure to concepts in a way that is engaging as well as non-threatening, and unlike formal education systems, they serve everyone, with no price of admission. In an age where science literacy is becoming more important than ever before, libraries thus have "the opportunity to be at the forefront, helping people understand the foundation of the science-based world in which they live."[44]

Whether a library is in an impoverished area or not, it is clear that it is well suited to provide STEM programs to its community. As a free, flexible space where patrons need not worry about being graded or scolded for any faulty memorization, libraries are an accessible, diverse place where neighbors can join to discover, learn, and experiment with a variety of different STEM skills. Their access to funding, and ability to develop partner contacts, may even allow them to introduce technologies that may not have been seen by some communities otherwise.

STEAM: What's in an "A"? Is It Inherent in Library Programs?

The STEM term has spawned evolutions into other incorporative acronyms, such as STEAM. The included "A" stands for "arts," and has become somewhat of a controversial topic. Experts argue that the "A" is implicit (and therefore unnecessary in the acronym), as skills from the collective group of arts are used within the design stages of engineering, or through the communication skills necessary in any discipline, for example. Others have argued, however, that leaving the "A" out is devaluing the importance of the arts.[45]

Debaters against the inclusive STEAM acronym, however, insist that the urgency with which we need to fill STEM employment roles (which thereby creates the need to amp up society's STEM skills in general) is nonexistent for arts professions,[46] and the acronym should thereby remain as is, in order to keep the heightened focus on this need. But what about fine arts? Within libraryland, fine art programs aren't unheard of. A fine art component in a program may still be unique enough to warrant some extra interest from library programmers, in the context of this book.

There is then even the evolution of STREAM—with an "R" for "reading."[47] Reading, of course, is certainly inherent in the work of libraries, who, for decades, have focused on developing and enhancing both literacy and pre-literacy skills in the members of their communities. They do this through the offering of free reading materials, storytimes, tutoring sessions, and the variety or other ways in which they constantly incorporate literacy skills.

Relevant Field Notes in Program Listings

And so, while some programs found throughout this book will indeed mark a fine arts inclusion, it will continue to refer to the collective educational skills sets by their original acronym of STEM. Because any of the categories of science, technology, engineering, arts, and math might be something that library programmers are specifically looking to develop within their branch programs, the following program plans suggested throughout this book will give any commonly associated individual STEAM subjects after each program listing. This should help to remind planners which particular area of STEAM is the focus of the program, while also allowing them to tailor their choices based upon a specific educational need if necessary. For the purpose of this book, it would be unnecessary to include a mention of every "reading" or "literacy" component (STREAM), as it would likely turn up throughout every listed program.

Key Points

STEM has a critically important place in our future. It is of value to governments because it allows countries to remain economically and productively competitive.

- STEM fields are creating countless job opportunities.
- STEM skills training can also open up even further employment into non-STEM-related fields.
- STEM education will help all students to work smarter, giving them further problem-solving skills and technological proficiencies.

The library is well suited to provide STEM programs to its community and by extension act as an advocate for the importance of STEM skills and the enrichment and success of its community members.

- It is a free, flexible space where patrons need not worry about being graded or scolded for any faulty memorization.
- It is an accessible, diverse place where neighbors can join to discover, learn, and experiment with a variety of different STEM skills.
- Its access to funding, and ability to develop partner contacts, can bring new materials and technologies to communities.

Notes

1. *Merriam-Webster*, s.v. "Science," accessed December 10, 2017, https://www.merriam-webster.com/dictionary/science.
2. *Merriam-Webster*, s.v. "Technology," accessed December 10, 2017, https://www.merriam-webster.com/dictionary/technology.

3. *Merriam-Webster*, s.v. "Engineering," accessed December 10, 2017, https://www.merriam-webster.com/dictionary/engineering.

4. *Merriam-Webster*, s.v. "Math," accessed December 10, 2017, https://www.merriam-webster.com/dictionary/math.

5. Dawn States, "Out of the Pickle: Promoting Food Science and STEM in Public Libraries," *Pennsylvania Libraries: Research & Practice* 3, no. 2 (2015): 102.

6. Dilnavaz Sharma, "Does STEM Education Belong in the Public Library?" *Public Libraries* 55, no. 2 (2016): 17.

7. Sharma, "Does STEM Education Belong," 17.

8. Council of Canadian Academies, Expert Panel on STEM Skills for the Future, *Some Assembly Required: STEM Skills and Canada's Economic Productivity*, 2015, p. xii, accessed November 27, 2017, http://www.scienceadvice.ca/uploads/ENG/AssessmentsPublicationsNewsReleases/STEM/STEMFullReportEn.pdf.

9. Council of Canadian Academies, *Some Assembly Required*, xii.

10. "Remarks by the President in State of Union Address," National Archives and Records Administration, January 25, 2011, accessed December 10, 2017, https://obamawhitehouse.archives.gov/the-press-office/2011/01/25/remarks-president-state-union-address.

11. "Remarks by the President."

12. "Nearly 8.6 Million STEM Jobs in 2015." US Bureau of Labor Statistics. Accessed December 10, 2017. https://www.bls.gov/spotlight/2017/science-technology-engineering-and-mathematics-stem-occupations-past-present-and-future/home.htm.

13. "Nearly 8.6 Million STEM Jobs."

14. "Nearly 8.6 Million STEM Jobs."

15. "Nearly 8.6 Million STEM Jobs."

16. "Nearly 8.6 Million STEM Jobs."

17. Royal Academy of Engineering, *The UK STEM Education Landscape*, May 2016, accessed December 10, 2017, https://www.raeng.org.uk/publications/reports/uk-stem-education-landscape.

18. Royal Academy of Engineering, *UK STEM Education Landscape*.

19. Royal Academy of Engineering, *UK STEM Education Landscape*.

20. Council of Canadian Academies, *Some Assembly Required*, vi.

21. Council of Canadian Academies, *Some Assembly Required*, vi.

22. Royal Academy of Engineering, *UK STEM Education Landscape*.

23. Council of Canadian Academies, *Some Assembly Required*, vii.

24. Council of Canadian Academies, *Some Assembly Required*, vii.

25. Flo Frank and Anne Smith, *The Community Development Handbook: A Tool to Build Community Capacity*, 1999, p. 12, accessed November 29, 2017, http://publications.gc.ca/collections/Collection/MP33-13-1999E.pdf.

26. Frank and Smith, *Community Development Handbook*, 12.

27. Frank and Smith, *Community Development Handbook*, 12.

28. Leila Meyer, "Higher Stem," *School Library Journal*, April 1, 2017, 28.

29. States, "Out of the Pickle," 106.

30. Meredith Farkas, "Making for STEM Success," *American Libraries* 46, no. 5 (2015): 27.

31. "Public Libraries and STEM: An Interview with Paul Dusenbery and Keliann LaConte," *Young Adult Library Services* 14, no. 2 (2016): 10.

32. States, "Out of the Pickle," 108.

33. Meyer, "Higher Stem," 28.

34. Farkas, "Making for STEM Success," 27.

35. Heather Love Beverley in discussion with the author, November 2017.

36. Heather Love Beverley in discussion with the author, November 2017.

37. Heather Love Beverley in discussion with the author, November 2017.

38. Shannon Peterson, "Sowing the Seeds of STEM," *Young Adult Library Services* 10, no. 2 (2012): 8.

39. Farkas, "Making for STEM Success," 27.
40. States, "Out of the Pickle," 107.
41. Eric Drew in discussion with the author, December 2017.
42. Eric Drew in discussion with the author, December 2017.
43. Trina Orchard in discussion with the author, November 2017.
44. Trina Orchard in discussion with the author, November 2017.
45. Anne Jolly, "STEM vs. STEAM: Do the Arts Belong?" *Education Week Teacher*, April 29, 2016, accessed December 10, 2017, https://www.edweek.org/tm/articles/2014/11/18/ctq-jolly-stem-vs-steam.html.
46. "STEM vs. STEAM: Why The 'A' Makes a Difference," Edudemic, January 21, 2015, accessed December 10, 2017, http://www.edudemic.com/stem-vs-steam-why-the-a-makes-all-the-difference/.
47. Amy Pietrowski, "The History of STEM vs. STEAM Education (and the Rise of STREAM)," *EdTech*, August 14, 2017, accessed December 10, 2017, https://edtechmagazine.com/k12/article/2017/08/history-stem-vs-steam-education-and-rise-stream.

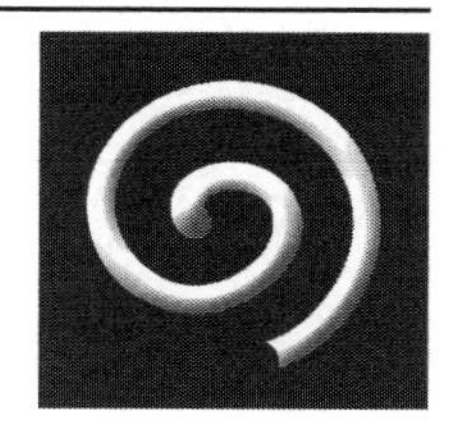

CHAPTER 2

Getting Started

IN THIS CHAPTER

- ▷ Understanding your role as a STEM programming librarian
- ▷ Getting your staff and management on board with STEM programming goals
- ▷ Enticing your community to attend STEM programs
- ▷ Including use of pop culture themes
- ▷ What kind of STEM programs you should focus on first

Understanding Your Role as a Librarian

AS SEEN IN THE PREVIOUS CHAPTER, both library and government literature alike are pointing toward the need for creative and educational places within communities where children and adults can access free programming to help develop their STEM skills. The library can be a perfect place within your area to help supplement this vital learning due to its free and flexible programming in combination with its access to partnership and information. Wondering where to go from here? Start by reviewing the following basics of your role as the librarian.

Facilitating the Learning Process

A quick but important first reminder: librarians don't need a second master's (or even an undergraduate degree) in a STEM-related field in order to provide STEM programming in their libraries. Dawn States, the teen program coordinator of Martin Library in York, Pennsylvania, wisely encourages librarians that although they may not be "superheroes or scientists," they really don't have to be "in order to continue to provide organized and consistent STEM initiatives."[1] As professional information finders, librarians are there to gather and provide resources and information for their community. They also provide patrons with a safe and supportive space that encourages learning and experimentation.

Librarians are responsible for providing *access* to these tools, machines, and information sources—they're not solely responsible for teaching a full, formal lesson content. Of course, the more informed librarians are about their individual topics, the more easily they'll be able to gather the necessary components for their STEM-focused programs. But, contrary to popular patron belief, librarians don't need to have the answer to everything—they simply need to have the research skills to help their customers *find* the answer.

Heather Love Beverley, the Children's Services assistant manager at the Cook Memorial Public Library District, reminds librarians not to be afraid to say, "I don't know." She reasons that one of the reasons STEM seems so daunting is because librarians often feel compelled to learn every single aspect of the science and technology behind a given project, in fear of not being able to answer a question that may arise in the program. It's okay to admit you don't know the answer: "I don't know, but after the program, let's look it up and find out." For kids, says Love Beverley, it can be refreshing and empowering to hear adults say that they don't know something and are looking to learn about the topic together. This dynamic "creates a wonderful, mutual learning environment that is unique for children: how often do they get the chance to explain to adults how something works?"[2]

Trina Orchard, a customer service clerk in Children's Services at the Lethbridge Public Library in Alberta, also suggests finding any hidden talents among library staff or bringing in experts from partner organizations in order to get the STEM programming ball rolling, which is particularly useful if programmers feel paralyzed with fear of not knowing enough about a topic.[3]

Even with limited STEM skill knowledge, this practical guidebook can help librarians and others prepare basic STEM skill programs with simply an enthusiasm for inspiring their communities toward discovery and learning. Librarians and library staff can stand back and let their community experiment with the given tools, information, and hands-on activities provided in these programs. It's important to let the program attendees discover their own interests and passions. Meredith Farkas reassures libraries that children, at least, "are naturally creative, so programs like this are rarely a tough sell" and that the challenge is "to develop a culture that sees this sort of tinkering and creation as a lifelong pursuit."[4] Tinkerers can also come from all age groups, of course, and so it seems a wise challenge for libraries to try and develop that lifelong pursuit in patrons of all ages.

Some library staff may be hesitant to jump into programming for STEM topics, for fear that they might get a question they don't know the answer to. But this is par for the course in library work, isn't it? Staff should work with patrons, then, to help them find the answer—perhaps it will lie in a book in the library's collection, an upcoming library program, or a locally sponsored course. Libraries should let their communities guide them as to where they would like to go with their learning. In fact, leadership author Margaret J. Wheatley notes that one of the principles to healthy community change is that organizations should "expect leaders to come from anywhere."[5] This is certainly relevant in the world of libraries and community engagement—communities are ripe with a people who hold a variety of different talents and skill sets that, by using them to help the library, could likewise be changing their communities for the better, as well.

STEM programming is also a perfectly suited opportunity to highlight the library's thematically related collections. Referring to the collection's non-fiction science, math, engineering, or technology materials, the library's databases or any other online resources when responding to STEM skill inquiries will also help encourage further at-home learning for the patron, which certainly fits well in line with the librarian's role.

Library staff might find it helpful to think of STEM programming as having a similar knowledge requirement as their ever-popular English language learning programs for newcomers. As hosts of English conversation groups, and English tutor pairings, library staff aren't usually providing patrons with trained English teachers who conduct course-based instruction on *how* to speak English. They're providing the safe space and supportive staff and volunteers to help supplement and support the practice of practical English skills. In that same vein, unless the library is providing instruction from a local partnering STEM organization or group, it's not likely to be offering trained science certificates or formal classes. They can, however, offer a supplemental learning and discovery area—a place to become a jumping-off point, where people can discover new skills, tools, and programs, or perhaps a place to further practice skills that they have learned through more formal STEM education.

In fact, as a library continues to provide more and more STEM programs, it'll likely notice that many of its community members will arrive with different, unique skill sets in the STEM fields already. This is a great opportunity. Library staff should make use of these varied skill sets by sitting back and becoming learners themselves, and take advantage of this moment of knowledge sharing so that they can use it to inspire or inform other future STEM programs. The creativity and knowledge base of young minds can be surprising—plenty of in-STEM-program snafus are often solved, not by library staff, but by the curious young minds of a budding eight-year-old future scientist.

The library is one of the last true third spaces—that public place that can be a community gathering area away from both home and work, and is also free from advertising and the pressures of spending money. Providing STEM programming can also introduce the opportunity for community members to teach skills to library staff, and it even likewise provides a gathering space where community members can teach each other. Librarians can facilitate hands-on learning and ample discussion throughout their STEM-based programs in order to watch the inspired learning and discovery grow.

Creating partner-led STEM programs is another way in which the library can help facilitate inter-community member knowledge sharing. Librarians should make contacts with any local makerspaces, universities, or STEM-based organizations that might help by providing free programming or equipment at the library. This can both help to bring new ideas, information, and patrons into the library, while also introducing regular patrons to new and further learning opportunities elsewhere in the community.

Evaluating and Improving Programs

It is librarians' role to evaluate their programs in order to ensure sustainability. Ideally, all library programs (not exclusively STEM-based events) will have been created and inspired based upon suggestions from community members with whom library staff have engaged into a trusting relationship to the point where they feel comfortable expressing what it is they need or want to see from the library. The process of communication should be continued by making sure to ask for feedback about the programs after they have been delivered. This feedback should inform any future iterations of these events, working with any positive or constructive comments to improve the next STEM program.

Libraries looking for feedback that is more formal than the casual staff-patron conversations captured during program cleanup and general info desk comments should try registering for the Public Library Association's free library survey tool, Project Outcome. Project Outcome's survey design is based on thorough library survey research. Questions focus on specific qualitative information as opposed to attendance numbers. Questions are specifically worded and controlled so that you can discover "what good" your program did. Results can also be compared across libraries.[6]

Getting Your Team on Board

Librarians will definitely want to start by prepping their staff and upper management about their intended new direction. While STEM education is a fairly common topic in library conferences today, management teams might want to hear about a few qualitative or quantitative statistics before jumping on board. Help them to understand why STEM isn't "just a fad" but is "a national priority"[7] by citing government and library literature like the articles found in the previous chapter. This should help convince senior staff about the benefits of STEM skills for the future of their community, while also reminding them why libraries are perfectly positioned to provide and promote such types of programs. Synthesizing this information with a vision for what kinds of programs might work at this particular branch or system should lend well to the buy-in from the management team.

As supervisors, librarians might also find themselves needing to motivate the staff members on their teams toward the new STEM programming ideas. Some of the more seasoned, traditional library programmers might be hesitant or outright unwilling to branch out past their traditional books-and-crafts setup. Some might even agree that it's necessary for the branch but simultaneously attempt to remove themselves as a possible planner or facilitator from STEM projects. It's important to remind staff that they're not expected to be science teachers, math students, or engineering experts themselves, but that it's about branching out and attempting to incorporate new ideas to expose their community to a variety of different and valuable skill sets.

For example, nobody needs to be a science whiz to facilitate magnet play with preschoolers, nor to follow a slime recipe from a website in a teen program. If staff are looking to start off slow, STEM library programs can simply be about exposing children and adults to the materials, ideas, and most basic of STEM skills.

Librarians can help to ease this transition period by giving their staff time to play, research, and test things out on their own. Regional or branch training days that allow staff to play and experiment with all of the new STEM supplies might go a long way in helping staff feel more comfortable with the new direction. If it's a new one-off material for a unique and specific program, try extending the normal amount of allotted planning time so that lead programmers have a bit more time to play around and make themselves comfortable with the materials.

Staff who are nervous about their own STEM comprehension levels might find that children's STEM programs are often the easiest to plan and facilitate. Remind them that a lot of this is about the discovery. If programmers don't understand every in and out of the particular process, they could try enlisting the help of the children around them to see if they can make it work together. Some of the eight-year-olds may end up understanding the project better than staff will, even after a week of prepping for it! That would be a good thing, though—as libraries are also about encouraging skill development and giving patrons a place to shine. Such an event would be an excellent qualitative story to bring to management in a report as an example of how STEM programs are helping to bring the community together in shared learning experiences.

Librarians are likely to have already encountered this who-needs-the-library-staff phenomenon if they've run a recent Minecraft program. It is almost guaranteed that if there are ten or more children registered for a library Minecraft event, they likely won't need a single staff member who knows how to do anything more than how to turn the computers on and download the game. The uber-enthusiastic children with years' worth of daily playtime experience are likely to jump to answer another child's question before staff can even think about Googling it.

Libraries looking to up the complication level of their STEM programs on topics that are truly outside the reach of their staff members can try looking for local partners who might be willing to come in and program for them. Local universities, makerspaces, and even hobby groups could be willing and excited to help their local library. More information about creating partnerships to facilitate further STEM programming can be found in chapter 9.

Other ways in which librarians help their staff buy into the STEM programming vision is by giving them the opportunity to feel real ownership over any themes, projects, and ideas. Well-known leadership author Margaret J. Wheatley says, "People support what they create,"[8] and this helps to support why the following method is so successful. Instead of dictating what new science project or gadget library staff will be working with, consider having a pitch meeting. Giving team members a broader topic (such as "preschool science," or "elementary engineering") about a month in advance of their meeting date, and asking them to research several STEM programming ideas that would fit into this theme, should allow them to feel more ownership of the project. They could be given even more autonomy with the direction of a simple, hypothetical budget for whatever STEM program or project they'd like to plan. Having staff each bring multiple project ideas to the table can stimulate a creative brainstorming session, while both allowing them to feel ownership of their future assignments and also providing the supervising librarian with the final say in his or her team's direction.

Getting the Community on Board

Once the library staff and management are on board, the next step is to grab the attention of the community. Zero cost to the customer is likely a great start, so the library is a leg up in this aspect. Since library STEM programming is also meant to supplement traditional learning in educational institutions like schools and universities, these institutions can be approached as a possible help in the way of promoting your new service.

A library's marketing team can also be an excellent resource, if available. This department will likely have the most current and creative ways for promoting new programs. If a library doesn't have the luxury of a designated marketing team, it can instead make sure to pay careful attention to creating eye-catching posters and hook-worthy social media promotions. Canva.com is a great free web resource that can be used to create unique, modern-looking posters with free, copyright-cleared images.

If libraries are really looking to create a well-loved and sustainable STEM program, they'll definitely want to start by practicing their community engagement skills. Like with any sort of library program, libraries will have the most success if they make sure to involve their community members in the entire process: from creation, through to implementation, and then feedback. Making sure not to prescribe what the library thinks the community might need can be a difficult task, and something that most libraries are still in the habit of doing in their programming today.

If a library has access to the dedicated staff time, a truly engaged community base starts with relationship building. The goal is for library staff to spend enough time with their target community in order to develop a type of trust with them, enough so that community members would feel comfortable proactively asking the librarian for whatever it is they feel the community needs. In an ideal example of community engagement, once they've asked the library for that specific need, the community member(s) would then work from there to try to involve them in the planning process, facilitation, and of course, feedback cycle. A fully engaged community is no small task, but "there is no greater power than a community discovering what it cares about."[9]

Pop Culture Twists

Another more casual way of making sure to attract communities into library STEM skill programs is through the use of pop culture themes. *Oxford Dictionaries* defines pop culture as "modern popular culture transmitted via the mass media and aimed particularly at younger people."[10] Think of those hot, current TV shows and blockbuster family films. Perhaps library staff noticed that every child who entered the children's play area in 2014 sang the entire lyrics to "Let It Go" at the top of their lungs. Did they plan a *Frozen* program in response to that? Was it pure chaos? It likely was!

Incorporating pop culture into library programs helps to draw in the non-traditional library users. The ideal goal is to hear something akin to "Mom! You have to take me to the library for that program" from a child who hasn't been there in years (or ever). Furthermore, incorporating pop culture themes into STEM programs can also help attract more than just the budding scientists or baby engineers into the programs, while attempting to grow and inspire further, new, childhood dreams of being future computer programmers or biologists.

Pop culture can be more than just TV or movies. When searching for the perfect pop culture hook, libraries can look into current social media apps—especially the content and themes of their most famous users (famous YouTubers, top Musers on Musical.ly, Instagram stars). General internet memes and current toy trends are also a good place to go for inspiration too (see: Shopkins in 2015, or fidget spinners in 2017).

If librarians are receiving additional reluctance toward pop culture programming from their more established or traditional staff, a pitch meeting setup (same format as the STEM pitch meeting above) could also work to help mine for great ideas, while inspiring staff to take ownership through their own creative suggestions. Staff should try looking beyond the internet and pay attention to what children are currently crazy about—they can talk to their own children, nieces, nephews, or other children in their families. They can also talk to any teachers they might know. It's also important not to forget to make use of the relationships that library staff are establishing with children at their branches. They should be casually engaging the children who visit them at the information desk. Perhaps staff notice that every child seems to be wearing a Bass Pro Shops hat, or flipping one of those annoying water bottles. If their relationship with the youth warrants it, they should be asking the child to tell them more.

Although traditional library users often see libraries as a place of reading, and programs centered on traditional books and literary culture, libraries are actually quite the perfect place to explore pop culture phenomena. Schools are often more regulated by their need to tread carefully and justify all educational content toward their intended curriculum. Libraries, however, are "rarely hamstrung by rigid curricula and can thus focus on what most interests children."[11] Librarians and educational professionals mused during a Pop Literacy webinar for *School Library Journal* that "the Venn diagram for what students are interested in, and topics which are school appropriate, would have little overlap."[12] If this is the case—are public libraries not perfectly positioned to step in and fill the gap? They can even maintain the educational intent by morphing pop culture topics into STEM skill programs.

What Kind of STEM Programs Should We Focus On First?

Choosing which STEM programs to implement first is really up to library programmers. They should let their inspiration lead them to this decision. If they are itching to try out the library's new Makey Makey kits, or perhaps they feel they needed to take advantage of the hottest viral trend this summer, this would likely help sway their decision. Program ideas can come from a variety of different motivations, so letting excitement lead the way is the best bet, if your budget will allow it.

Libraries can choose to start off as small as they'd like, if they feel that's necessary. If there's still a hesitance, think about starting by tweaking the crafts in a regular storytime series so it includes a more STEM-focused element, as opposed to going out and buying an entire new green screen kit.

FURTHER TIPS FOR STEM PROGRAMMING

Embrace the chaos:

STEM programming can sometimes be messy and loud. Things won't always go as planned, and experiments go awry. Beverley reminds librarians that "it happens." What's important, though, is that when it does, library staff are often the only ones to even notice. "Kids love the mess and the noise, and they don't notice when an experiment doesn't work as originally intended, or [if] program plans have shifted. If the kids are still having fun—and I guarantee that they are—it will all be okay."[13]

Have fun!

Programmers should pick STEM projects and topics that they are curious about, and find interesting or neat, suggests Beverley. If a programmer thinks something is exciting, it's likely that the children or families will, too. STEM programs are creative and engaging, and when staff take a moment to look around during the event, they'll likely see children "having a blast, trying new things, making learning connections, and exploring different ideas." Seeing all this in action, Beverley argues, is "probably the most fun and rewarding thing you can do."[14]

Make science present in your library:

Showcase it. Celebrate it. Holidays like Earth Day and Science Literacy Week, says Orchard, are interesting (and budget friendly) to turn into STEM events. The Lethbridge Public Library uses Earth Day to host a large event where library users learn about composting, plant seeds in newspaper pots, and recycle objects by making crafts. They even also bring in library partners from the local nature center and the university's science program to help provide content.[15]

Key Points

Librarians need not be experts in STEM fields in order to provide library STEM programs. They can make use of their expertise in information-seeking skills while encouraging communities to think critically and become problem solvers. They can also build relationships and partner with local community experts to provide more in-depth program topics that are above even the basic reach of the library. Building relationships with community members themselves will help the library to select popular, relevant STEM programming topics.

Get staff on board with STEM programming initiatives by providing them with plenty of training opportunities and time to experiment on their own with new projects, technology, and activities. Allow them to take ownership in this new direction by having them decide upon program themes and gadgets that interest them most.

Attract more than just your budding scientists to children's STEM programs by incorporating pop culture themes into program plans—sneaking the STEM in there for those who might not be as interested in the science or engineering portions is a common trick to exposing youth to new interests.

Embrace the chaos, have fun, and make science present in your library.

Notes

1. Dawn States, "Out of the Pickle: Promoting Food Science and STEM in Public Libraries," *Pennsylvania Libraries: Research & Practice* 3, no. 2 (2015): 108.
2. Heather Love Beverley in discussion with the author, November 2017.
3. Trina Orchard in discussion with the author, November 2017.
4. Meredith Farkas, "Making for STEM Success," *American Libraries* 46, no. 5 (2015): 27.
5. Margaret J. Wheatley, *Leadership and the New Science: Discovering Order in a Chaotic World*, 2nd ed. (San Francisco: Berrett-Koehler, 1999).
6. "Home." Project Outcome: Measuring the True Impact of Public Libraries. Accessed December 11, 2017. https://www.projectoutcome.org/home.
7. States, "Out of the Pickle," 106.
8. States, "Out of the Pickle," 106.
9. States, "Out of the Pickle," 106.
10. *Oxford Dictionaries*, s.v. "Pop Culture," accessed December 11, 2017, https://en.oxford-dictionaries.com/definition/pop_culture.
11. Farkas, "Making for STEM Success," 27.

12. "Pop Literacy," SLJ ISTE Webcast Series, *School Library Journal*, November 21, 2016, accessed December 11, 2017, http://www.slj.com/2016/11/industry-news/pop-literacy-slj-iste-webcast-series/.
13. Heather Love Beverley in discussion with the author, November 2017.
14. Heather Love Beverley in discussion with the author, November 2017.
15. Trina Orchard in discussion with the author, November 2017.

Further Reading

Singh, Sandra, Working Together Project, Issuing Body, and Canadian Electronic Library, Distributor. *Community-Led Libraries Toolkit: Starting Us All down the Path toward Developing Inclusive Public Libraries.* DesLibris. Documents Collection. Vancouver, BC: Working Together, 2008.

CHAPTER 3

Budgeting and Gathering Supplies

IN THIS CHAPTER

- ▷ Program funding options
- ▷ Grant opportunities
- ▷ Budgeting basics
- ▷ Sharing a regional collection
- ▷ No budget: common supplies inventory

LIBRARIES THAT ARE MOTIVATED to start the process of bringing STEM skills to their communities will need more than just ideas, staff support, and community enthusiasm: they'll need money. STEM programming often requires equipment and supplies, some of which staff might already have access to in their branches. Other items, however, will require a budget of funds that could be small or large, depending on a variety of factors discussed below.

Program Funding Options

Public library programming budgets come in all shapes and sizes. Programming staff could have access to next to zero dollars, or on the opposite side of the coin, perhaps thousands. This amount will often depend on the size of the branch and by extension, the size of the library system as a whole. North American public libraries are funded by a combination of different levels of government. Canadian public libraries are "primarily financed by municipal tax revenues and other local income, with provincial grants supplementing local funding," although the specifics vary from province to province.[1] Similarly,

American public library funds are primarily derived from "local government, state government, federal government" as well as other sources such as donations and monetary gifts.[2] Revenue is then divided up by departments into budget areas such as staffing, training, collections, technology, innovation, and programming.

Multi-branch library systems might have a regionally managed budget for shared items between different library locations. Sharing items is an excellent use of funds, and is a great way to obtain those shiny new gadgets that cost a lot more (see: 3D printers, virtual reality equipment, etc.). Librarians who only have access to branch-based programming budgets should check with another branch in their system (if available) and see if they'd be interested in going splits on larger purchases.

Larger library systems might also have dedicated pots of funds for things like STEM programming or emerging technologies. Librarians who have responsibility for branch-specific programming budgets will need to multitask and make sure to set aside the right amount for their intended STEM projects, making sure to leave enough left over for the rest of their programs.

If deciding where to spend a budget becomes a difficult decision, programming staff should make sure to consult with their supervisors. Supervising librarians would be wise to refer to their strategic plan: Which of these expenses falls best in line with how the library has planned to move forward, strategically? Staff might find that their library's goals and mandates already include a clause about enhancing technology or STEM skills in the community. The Berkeley Public Library in California, for example, aims in their 2015–2018 strategic plan to "bolster literacy in all its forms to bridge the achievement gap," partly by "develop[ing] a series of inter-generational STEM programs . . . in partnership with local organizations."[3] Similarly, the Toronto Public Library in Ontario believes that in order for library users to "stay competitive with today's industry and culture," they'll also need to "understand and use" such emerging technologies as "3D printers, graphic design hardware and software, audio/visual recording and editing equipment, and even virtual reality and artificial intelligence technologies," which they believe is "crucial to supporting traditional and digital literacies."[4] The Toronto Public Library has committed in their 2016–2019 strategic plan to helping their community see both "more learning opportunities for children, including . . . STEM and numeracy programming" and "new Digital Innovation Hubs and Pop Up Learning Labs."[5] If librarians notice that their own current strategic plan fails to include any even broadly applicable STEM- or technology-related goals, they should make a note about suggesting such priorities when it next comes time to provide feedback during future goal setting and strategic planning projects.

STEM programs are also often eligible for community grant funding. If libraries find themselves unable to afford all the equipment and supplies it might take to run a successful, community-driven STEM program, they should look to local, federal, and private grant opportunities that might accept applications from public libraries.

Above library operating budgets and grant funding, there is yet another way to save on a library's cost-intensive STEM programs: partnerships. Local and national programs, organizations, or educational institutions all over North America are teaming up with public libraries in order to bring their unique expertise (and costly equipment) to free, engaging STEM programs for all ages. Further information on using partnerships to help increase a library's STEM programming offers can be found in chapter 9.

Grant Opportunities

Grant funding is an exciting and extremely useful way to gather unique and costly STEM supplies and technology. Its application process can also be a serious and time-consuming task. Library management will likely need to approve any grant application processes, so once programming staff have identified a possible need for grant funding, they should then be sure to check with any necessary senior staff before launching into the application process.

In the fifth edition of *The Whole Library Handbook*, Colleen Leddy suggests to use time wisely by applying for grants that the applicant library "stand[s] a chance of getting."[6] Wendy Boylan suggests that proposal writers can do this through "some research to determine the potential funders with compatible priorities."[7] Boylan cautions that applying for grants outside the scope of your project aren't only a waste of time, it can indicate that the library did a poor job at researching the details, which "gives a negative first impression."[8] Applicants should be leaving the best impressions of their library, in case any new, more suitable grant opportunities arise at that foundation in the future.

Leddy then suggests selecting proposal opportunities that won't take "a lot of time to write."[9] She also suggests that librarians can "lobby [their] state humanities council to offer a quick grant program" if the appropriate local opportunity doesn't yet exist.[10]

While Leddy cautions libraries to use their grant writing time wisely, in his 2011 *Winning Library Grants: A Game Plan*, Herbert Landau reminds grant applicants to be "brief" and "keep it simple," since, due to the "sheer volume of applications" that are received by most foundations, proposals will "initially be read quickly."[11] He suggests using clear, simple, and positive sentences while leaving out the "emotion and hype."[12] According to Landau, proposals should be "precise" but confident: avoid using "qualifying phrases such as . . . 'hopefully,'. . . 'maybe,' or 'if possible,'" as the winning proposals are often laden with confidence.[13]

Public libraries will often meet the basic requirements to apply for local or national community grant programs that choose a successful non-profit organization and charity applicant to whom they will provide a sum of money. While some funders will request paperwork to prove that the applicant is a registered not-for-profit with the official 501(c)(3) tax exemption status paperwork, others might specifically include public libraries in their list of encouraged applications. If eligibility terms seem unclear, libraries should reach out to funders and directly inquire about their suitability. A public library that is at least noted as a governmental unit under the US 501(c)(3) Internal Revenue Code (which they often are) could still meet funders' eligibility criteria.

Examples of public library grants procured for STEM initiatives include the Cook Memorial Public Library District IEEE–Chicago Section Grant, which funded a collection of circulation science kits,[14] and the Lethbridge Public Library's Telus Community Action Team Grant, which funded $3,000 worth of technology supplies for their Mini Tech-Heads children's technology series program.[15]

Funders and grant opportunities can be found through a variety of resources such as internet searches, local organizations, and community contacts. The list below is only a small sample of community or library grants programs that could be used to write a strong STEM programming grant proposal.

Walmart Community Grant Programs:

Awards grants of $250 to $2,500 (US) or $1,000 (Canada) through Walmart stores, where each eligible non-profit organization (or recognized government entity requesting funds exclusively for public purposes, such as libraries) operates within the service area of the facility from which they are requesting funding. Areas of funding include community development, education, and environmental sustainability.[16]
US: http://giving.walmart.com/walmart-foundation/community-grant-program
Canada: https://www.walmartcanada.ca/community-giving/corporate-giving

Best Buy Community Grants:

Eligibility includes American public or non-profit community-based organizations (such as libraries) with existing local "out-of-school time program" and a proven track record of serving youth ages thirteen to eighteen. The average grant amount runs at about $5,000 (not to exceed $10,000) and is awarded for "programs [to] help teens build tech skills by utilizing cutting-edge technology" such as coding/3D printing, filmmaking and videography, Maker Faires / hack-a-thons, mobile and game app development, and robotics.[17] Best Buy Canada seems to only have school technology grants right now, so although public libraries don't look eligible, school libraries could still apply.
US: https://corporate.bestbuy.com/community-grants-page/.

Canada Post Community Foundation:

Canada Post Community Foundation grant funding is allocated to projects that will "generate maximum impact, creating lasting change for children and youth (up to the age of 21)" in several areas, one of which includes "education programming to help children reach their full potential." The grant website specifically lists "community libraries" as eligible applicants to deliver such projects. Funding from the foundation will not exceed $30,000 per grant, nor will it exceed $5,000 to unregistered organizations.[18]
https://www.canadapost.ca/web/en/pages/aboutus/communityfoundation/criteria.page

Innovation in Libraries Grant:

The Library Pipeline provides opportunities, funding, and services for libraries and library professionals, and their Innovation in Libraries Grant is $1,000, awarded monthly to innovative, library-related projects that can include both "technical and non-technical library innovations that embody the principles of diversity, inclusivity, creativity, and risk-taking."[19]
https://www.librarypipeline.org/innovation/innovation-microfunding/

STEMfinity: STEM Grants:

STEMfinity present itself as a "worldwide leader in STEM education," whose website sells STEM gadgets and equipment, offers professional development, and even hosts a section on STEM Grants. This page lists "1,000 total grant opportunities throughout the United States" that should each be applicable in some way to STEM programming. The page is divided by state, but also lists both federal and national private foundations.[20]
US: https://www.stemfinity.com/STEM-Education-Grants

Budgeting Basics

Most libraries will have a standard budgeting process in place. Systems and processes surrounding budget management can be enforced both by library management and finance departments, as well as a grant foundation for any grant-awarded revenue. If programming staff are given a sum of money with which to build their STEM-focused programs, the following tips should prove useful, whether they're regulated by a specific budgeting procedure or not.

- Spreadsheets
- Use an Excel spreadsheet to keep track of all debits from the starting budget amount, making sure to have a separate, clear line item for each individual purchase, and which specific program(s) it went to.
- Receipts
- Keep (at least) photocopies of all purchase receipts for branch documents, if originals are sent to a finance department.
- Pre-portioning
- Work ahead of time to portion out specific amounts within the given budget to go toward individual programs or larger equipment purchases. Pick a specific program focus based off feedback from patrons and staff, and stick to it. Try to avoid impulse purchases!
- Quantity estimates
- Consult past program planning sheets and attendance counts to estimate the necessary quantities of consumables for an intended program.

Planning Sheets

To create an estimated budget limit and to project in advance how much the library might need to spend on a given program, staff should ideally already be making use of program planning sheets. A document that includes the necessary equipment, supplies, staff, itinerary, and budget limit, past planning sheets can be used for future evaluation when trying to decide whether to rerun something similar, and whether the money spent was worth the outcome. Including total, final expenditures and a written evaluation area to be completed after the program is complete, these documents can help with financial decision-making, as well as the obvious planning and organizational benefits.

A thorough program planning sheet template should include the following:

- Age group
- Staffed by
- Registered?
  (attendance limit)
- Date(s)/time(s) of program
- Estimated cost
- Length of program
- Equipment needed
  (e.g., 3D printers, sound systems)
- Materials needed
  (e.g., craft supplies, food, props)

- Room setup
  (e.g., decorations, map of tables/chairs)
- Program outline
  (e.g., stories, activities, games, crafts)
- Comments/evaluation
  (e.g., including total final expenses, and notes from staff hosts and any customer comments)

Spread the Love: Sharing Regional Circulating Items

Libraries that have access to regional funds or decide to go splits on purchases of larger items with other branches in their systems will need to develop a plan for regionally circulating items, if one is not already in place. This should be kept in mind when doing the shared purchasing: make sure to buy things that are easily shared, and not so quickly consumable, unless it's a large bulk order. This will also require some extra time invested in researching and purchasing travel-safe cases for some of the more delicate items that will need to circulate between branches. Although this travel equipment might be close to the cost of the gadget itself, it will likely be less expensive than buying the item five times over, when it gets broken in transit, again and again.

Libraries will also need to decide how they want to book and keep track of the inter-branch circulating items. Shared-access calendars are a good option: set up a "STEM Equipment" (or "Children's Services," "Emerging Technologies," etc.) calendar in Microsoft Outlook or Google Calendars to keep track of when items are out. Librarians should have their staff get into the habit of checking the calendar *before* requesting the item; this will maximize efficiency and ensure that no time is wasted in sending the request form/email when it's clearly visible that, for example, someone else already has the 3D printer booked for that day.

Requests can be sent to a particular regional staff member by individual emails; however, a quicker method is submission by web form. Library staff should set up a web form either on the staff intranet or as a simple Google survey that will email the equipment request directly to the storage branch. Requested borrowing times should make sure to account for inter-branch delivery times.

Storage is another issue that will need to be solved—which branch will actually house the item when it is not in use? Who has enough space, and do they have enough staff time to be able to handle incoming email requests and delivery send-offs? Project managers should give the library delivery drivers a heads-up to ensure that vans will have the necessary space in order to transport the equipment among their regular book bins.

Quick Tip:

Program equipment submission forms should include a "send copy to requester" option, so that programmers can make sure to document that they've already completed this task on their planning to-do list. Nothing is more frustrating than rushing to send off a last-minute equipment request, only to get a response email explaining that it was already completed a few weeks ago!

If a survey or form submission process is used, libraries should think about saving any possible data from these requests—collecting statistics about what items are used most, and in what kinds of programs, for what ages, could be interesting information to have at the end of the year.

No Budget: Common Supplies Inventory

Once libraries are on board and excited to start planning and hosting STEM-filled programs at their branches, they'll need to think about gathering the necessary supplies. Before physically spending the organized budget plan from the tips listed above, staff should do a common supplies inventory to see what they already have in house.

Although STEM programming can indeed require an initial investment, Eric Drew, the Youth Services librarian of Tantallon and J. D. Shatford Public Libraries, argues that one can run a variety of programs at low cost if they only have the right, basic tools on hand, particularly because "recyclables" are really the "greatest resource for STEM programming; cardboard, box board, plastic containers and bottles, caps, and more, can easily be gathered, stored, manipulated, and ultimately tossed."[21]

Heather Love Beverley, the Children's Services assistant manager at the Cook Memorial Public Library District, provides similar advice by reminding librarians that "STEM programming doesn't have to be big and extravagant." Some of the best STEM programs, she argues, are the simplest ones: give kids straws and tape to build structures; give them newspapers to roll into paper tables, or tinfoil to make boats. Each of these simple projects "encourage exploration, creativity, and problem solving" while dealing with topics such as engineering and math—and they're also "lots of fun," to boot.[22]

The chapters that follow in this book will list a variety of different STEM programs that can be hosted with little to no purchases necessary. Even if a library has a small budget, the following common supplies are STEM useful, and can likely already be found in a branch's common craft, office, or staff supplies cupboard:

Batteries	Paint
Playdough	Marbles
Paper clips	Magnets
Corkscrew pasta	Tinfoil
Toothpicks	Vinegar
Marshmallows	Baking soda
Cornstarch	Food coloring
Pennies	Cardboard
Newspaper	Bottles
Straws	Caps

Key Points

Libraries can obtain supplies and equipment for their STEM programming initiatives from a variety of different sources, be it a branch or regional programming budget, grant funds, or by making local community partnerships.

Community grant foundations should be thoroughly researched and well suited before launching into management-approved proposal writing. Grant proposals should be written simply, with short and clear sentences, and displaying confidence.

Programming staff should make careful notation of all their expenditures by keeping receipts and marking thorough details for every line item in their budget Excel sheets. Library systems that aim to share STEM programming equipment or supplies should set up shared calendars and a survey form to handle equipment booking requests, once they find the appropriate location that has enough storage and staff time to manage the booking system.

Before heading out to buy STEM programming supplies with a newly allocated budget, libraries should do a common supplies inventory by checking their storage closets and kitchens for common items that they may likely already have in stock. Plenty of items used in the STEM activities laid out in this book are easily found in a regular craft supplies cupboard. Keep in mind that recyclables are the "greatest resource for STEM programming; cardboard, box board, plastic containers and bottles, caps, and more can easily be gathered, stored, manipulated, and ultimately tossed."

Notes

1. *Canadian Encyclopedia*, s.v. "Libraries," by Margaret Beckman, Moshie Dahms, and Lorne Bruce, accessed December 11, 2017, ttp://www.thecanadianencyclopedia.ca/en/article/libraries/.

2. Institute of Museum and Library Services, *Public Libraries in the United States Survey: Fiscal Year 2012*. December 2014. https://www.imls.gov/assets/1/AssetManager/PLS_FY2012.pdf.

3. "Planning," Berkeley Public Library, accessed December 11, 2017, https://www.berkeleypubliclibrary.org/about/planning.

4. Toronto Public Library, *Strategic Plan 2016–2019: Strategic Plans, Annual Reports & Statistics*, accessed December 11, 2017, http://www.torontopubliclibrary.ca/about-the-library/strategic-plan/2016-2019/consultation.jsp.

5. Toronto Public Library, *Strategic Plan 2016–2019*.

6. George M. Eberhart, ed., *The Whole Library Handbook 5: Current Data, Professional Advice, and Curiosa*, 5th ed. (Chicago: American Library Association, 2014), 303.

7. Wendy Boylan, "Why and When to Turn to Grant Seeking," *Public Libraries* 52, no. 6 (2013): 26.

8. Boylan, "Why and When," 27.

9. Eberhart, *Whole Library Handbook*, 303.

10. Eberhart, *Whole Library Handbook*, 303.

11. Herbert B. Landau, *Winning Library Grants: A Game Plan* (Chicago: American Library Association, 2011), 89–92.

12. Landau, *Winning Library Grants*, 92.

13. Landau, *Winning Library Grants*, 92.

14. Heather Love Beverley in discussion with the author, November 2017.

15. Trina Orchard in discussion with the author, November 2017.

16. "Community Grant Program," Walmart Foundation, accessed December 11, 2017, http://giving.walmart.com/walmart-foundation/community-grant-program.

17. "Community Grants," Best Buy, accessed November 20, 2017, https://corporate.bestbuy.com/community-grants-page/.

18. "Canada Post Community Foundation Grant Process," Canada Post, accessed December 11, 2017, https://www.canadapost.ca/web/en/pages/aboutus/communityfoundation/criteria.page.

19. “Innovation in Libraries Grant,” Library Pipeline, accessed December 11, 2017. https://www.librarypipeline.org/innovation/innovation-microfunding/.

20. “STEM Grants.” STEMfinity. Accessed December 11, 2017. https://www.stemfinity.com/STEM-Education-Grants.

21. Eric Drew in discussion with the author, December 2017.

22. Heather Love Beverley in discussion with the author, November 2017.

Further Reading

Holt, Glen E., Leslie Edmonds Holt, and ProQuest. *Crash Course in Library Budgeting and Finance*. Crash Course Series. Santa Barbara, CA: Libraries Unlimited, 2016.

Landau, Herbert B. *Winning Library Grants: A Game Plan*. Chicago: American Library Association, 2011.

CHAPTER 4

Preschool STEM Programming

There is evidence that all children love to interact with variables, such as materials and shapes; smells and other physical phenomena, such as electricity, magnetism and gravity; media such as gases and fluids; sounds, music, motion; chemical interactions, cooking and fire; and other humans, and animals, plants, words, concepts and ideas. With all these things all children love to play, experiment discover and invent and have fun.

—SIMON NICHOLSON[1]

Is STEM Programming Really Necessary for Preschoolers?

BABIES, TODDLERS, AND PRESCHOOLERS, oh my! Children ages zero to five and their parents or caregivers have long been frequent users in libraries all over the world. Lured in by the promise of free books, making a mess in someone else's play area, the early literacy skills provided in storytimes, and even socializing with other neighborhood families, families of children under the age of five can gain a lot from visiting the library. But do children this young really need to be practicing their STEM skills? Research suggests that they certainly do. Since children are naturally curious about the world around them, STEM activities can invite preschoolers to explore their world "using all their senses,"[2] helping to "capture their interest and encourage the development of early literacy skills."[3] Using everyday concepts to introduce STEM activities can "foster young children's curiosity and [lay] a foundation for science learning in K–12 settings and beyond."[4] Moomaw and Davis argue that introducing young children to STEM activities can help them focus, increase vocabulary, and collaborate with others while creating scientific relationships.[5] It is never too early to start introducing the most basic of STEM skill concepts with children, as long as it is done in a safe and chaperoned manner.

As readers of this book will see throughout the following chapters, librarians need to have neither explicit experience nor educational backgrounds in STEM fields in order to offer programs and activities that touch on these concepts. Chalufour and Worth suggest that the important part of creating STEM activities for preschoolers is to "create a rich environment" and to "engage children in inquiry explorations" by helping to focus their observations.[6] Children's STEM experiences and thinking will be deepened when library staff do this by questioning children on what is happening.[7] Stepping back, observing, and interjecting with an occasional comment or question in order to "foster problem solving" can create an environment that supports exploration for preschoolers.[8] The focus on problem solving is a key aspect to this learning environment that can and should be paired with whichever activity or craft is going on in the program that day, regardless of theme.

Preschool STEM @ the Library

Is the library an appropriate place for a young child's STEM learning, however? In her 2016 *Library Journal* article, Abby Johnson reminds librarians that library programs, where preschoolers have long since been engaging in social learning, are a "perfect fit for science interests," since young children learn best through "hands-on efforts and experimentation."[9] As a place that is not regulated by rigid curricula outlines, library staff are free to go with the flow and "adjust the learning experiences to support the children's curiosity."[10] Libraries should be ready to be adaptable to meet the needs of children: remaining flexible about child-led activity topics, even if they venture away from the intended program plan.

Preschool STEM activities are arguably the simplest to prepare and host, due to the low needs and simplistic nature. Introductory STEM programming can be "as simple as setting out materials and letting them explore," making sure to give children a chance to "predict, observe, experiment, and talk about what happened."[11] As mentioned above, asking questions is a key portion to introducing STEM concepts to preschoolers—but it's important to keep in mind that most children of this are "not yet causal reasoners" who would be able to answer "why" questions, so library staff should focus more on the "what" or "problem-posing" questions:[12]

What happens when you flick this switch?

What is your mom doing with that magnet?

What are you using to make the ball move?

Can you find a way to turn the light off?

Can you find a way to pick up the pipe cleaner?

Since preschool STEM programming is so flexible, there are a variety of options with which to start introducing it into your library programs. Librarians can invest in new kits and STEM-focused gadgets like Squishy Circuits or the Cubetto, or they can make use of whatever materials they might already have around in-branch through previous purchases or recycling, such as a variety of loose parts. Loose parts are materials "without a predetermined purpose" that can be "moved, combined, reformed, taken apart, and put back together in numerous ways."[13] The loose part possibilities are clearly limitless: sticks, rocks, buttons, foam shapes, boxes, blocks, and so forth. So too are the "possible kinds of environment determined by the discovery method and principle of loose parts."[14] The National Association for the Education of Young Children concurs, reminding educators and librarians how expanding a young child's access to "nontraditional STEM materials" such as loose parts "can serve to provide a wider range of learning opportunities."[15] Combining different types of loose parts together (sticks with blocks and boxes, etc.) will only serve to increase the creative possibilities for building and inventing new worlds.

Dialogic Reading

Jennifer Evans, the supervising librarian at the Hazeldean Branch of Ottawa Public Library (OPL), reminds librarians that "STEM skills can be incorporated in very low-tech ways."[16] Librarians and programmers at the Ottawa Public Library often use "dialogic reading" in their storytelling to make a story more engaging. A technique OPL teaches all their new storytime programmers, dialogic reading is a way to practice the scientific method by challenging the listener:

Making observations:

What is happening in this picture?

Yes, the caterpillar is eating all the food.

Constructing a hypothesis:

What do you think is going to happen next?

Testing the hypothesis and discussing the results:

You were right, the caterpillar did turn into a butterfly! I wonder how that happened?[17]

Trina Orchard, a customer service clerk in Children's Services at the Lethbridge Public Library in Alberta, also uses this method when telling oral stories by simply "having preschoolers 'predict' what they think will happen to a character: 'Why do you think that will happen?'" She later on follows up with them to see if their ideas played out the way they thought.[18] Orchard uses this technique as an excellent example as to how the "foundational aspects of STEM" can be incorporated into almost any preschool (or other aged) program by teaching the basics of "logic-based thinking, problem solving, and forming hypotheses," all of which are integral skills that libraries can easily sneak into their programs.[19]

Squishy Circuits (Science, Technology, Art, Engineering)

Plenty of library family drop-ins and preschool play programs will have an incorporated playdough playtime, which makes this first suggestion an easy way to start incorporating a little bit more science into your preschool programs. Squishy Circuits, the University of St. Thomas's creative circuitry project, takes this popular home activity and uses it to help children learn about electricity. Through the use of batteries and electronic switches such as LED lights and buzzers, Squishy Circuits make use of the conductivity of your average playdough so that children can make their hand-formed creations light up, buzz, and beep!

Squishy Circuits projects can be as complex or as simple as you need, but for preschoolers, you'll want to focus on the most basic of simple play and discovery. More complex ideas of incorporating pop culture and other technologies like the Makey Makey and Scratch coding are excellent ideas for elementary-aged programs and can be found in chapter 5, which will also tell you a variety of different ways in which to source your own Squishy Circuits kits.

With preschoolers, you'll be focusing on only the basics, so you should really only need to have the following materials:

- Playdough
- 9 V batteries
- 9 V battery clips
- A few LED lights

Children will need to separate their playdough and roll it into two balls. After an adult has helped them snap the battery clip onto the battery, they will need to eventually stick the two wires into one dough ball each, and the same goes for the LED leads. If the LED isn't lighting up, the trick is to turn it around to switch which lead goes into which dough ball. Alternatively, you need to make sure your dough balls are never touching each other.

As the programmer, you might want to walk around the table and show the children and families a demonstration of a simple circuit, but, other than that, it might be best to let the children play with the playdough and see if they can re-create it on their own. Be sure to provide them with help when needed, in the form of simple troubleshooting questions like:

"What do you think would happen if you switched the light around?"

"Oh no! Your dough balls are touching each other—I think they work best on their own; try and see what happens if you separate them."

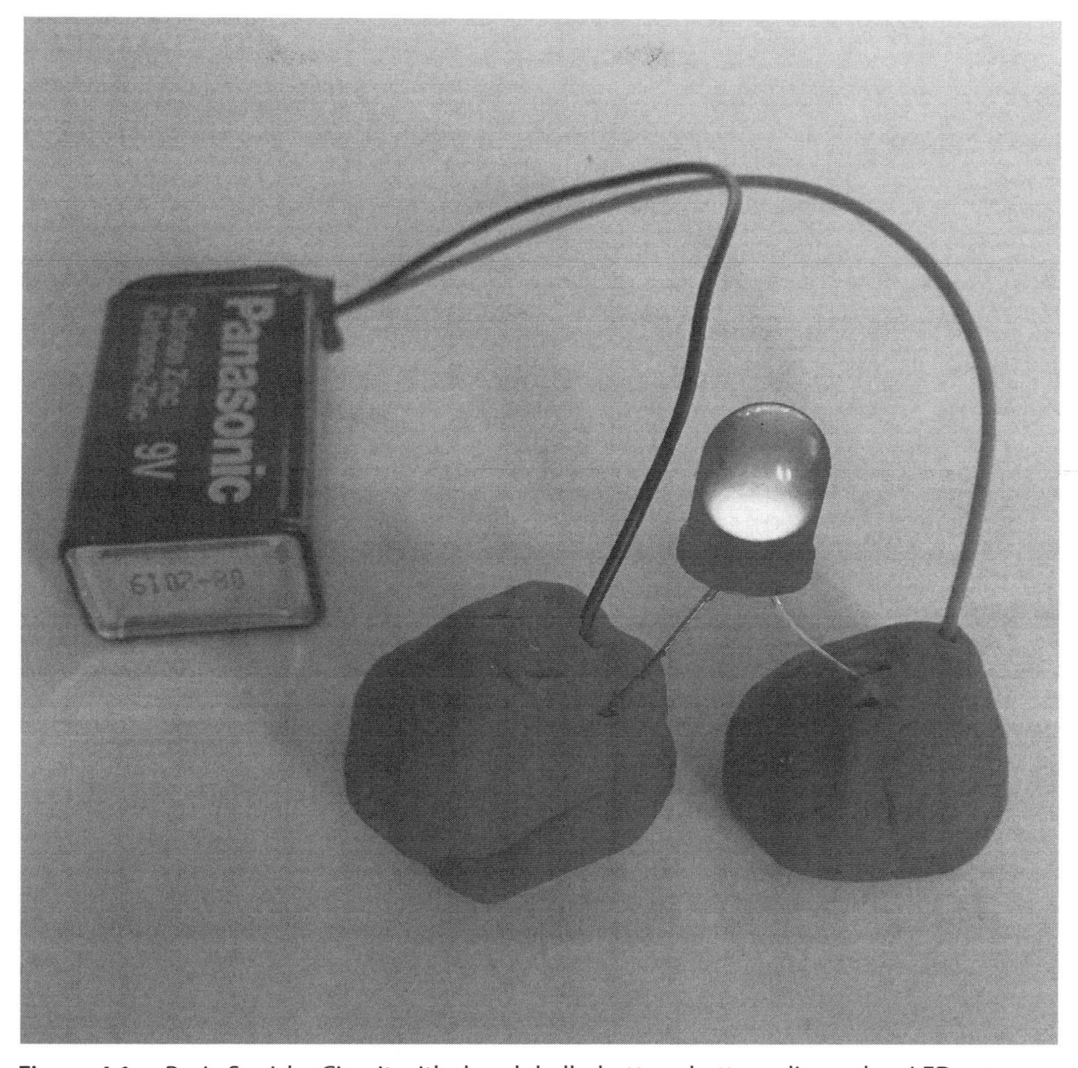

Figure 4.1. Basic Squishy Circuit with dough balls, battery, battery clip, and an LED

Once they get the hang of a simple one-light circuit, you can let them experiment by adding more LED lights or different-colored doughs, or shape different dough shapes beyond the ball. There are plenty more tips and tricks when playing with Squishy Circuits too, which can be found in the next chapter.

Magnificent Magnets (Science, Engineering, Art, Math)

Libraries can also delve further into those preschool science skills with magnet activities. Most of these activities make use of basic household and craft cupboard items, in addition to needing a good set of child-size magnets, like the Learning Resources Classroom Magnet Lab Kit, which should run you around US$43 on Amazon.com and includes seven magnetic wands, as well as horseshoes, marbles, chips, and more.

As with all preschool activities (STEM or otherwise), it's important that these are completed with adult supervision, to make sure children are not putting any of these items into their mouths.

Magnet Hunt

The magnet hunt can work much like a physical eye spy, where children can dip their magnetic horseshoes or wands into a wide, shallow bucket that is filled with either patterned paper shred or colored rice in addition to magnetic (and non-magnetic) items. Children can swish around in the bin to see what they'll retrieve. Try the following items:

Magnetic:
- Colored pipe cleaners (cut into two-inch strips)
- Paper clips
- Fridge magnets
- Screws, bolts
- Magnetic marbles
- Magnetic counting chips
- Bells
- Magformers

Non-magnetic:
- Mini erasers
- LEGOs
- Small plastic toys
- Shells
- And so forth

Plastic Bottles

Similar to the magnet hunt in a bucket, a clear plastic bottle can also be filled with small magnetic items like colored pipe cleaner bits, magnetic marbles, and paper clips. With the top screwed on, children can place their wands or horseshoes outside of the bottle to see which bits fly to the side of the plastic and which will fall off as the wand is moved around the outer edge. The bottle can also be filled with non-magnetic items, so children can try to guess which bits will stick to the magnet.

Further the experimentation by trying bottles filled with water with glitter added, or even use glass jars, and ask children if they think it will work the same!

Magnet Paintings

Magnet paintings are a creative and fun way to learn about magnets. Children and adults can take their art pieces home with them to hang on the fridge, or the library could keep them to do a display on a children's bulletin board, perhaps next to a magnet or science juvenile non-fiction display of books.

Supplies:
- Cardboard box
- Paper
- Tempera paint
- Magnetic ball bearing
- Magnetic wand or horseshoe

Instructions:

Lay a piece of paper inside the cardboard box, and squeeze a few drops of paint on top. Children can then hold the box in one hand (or have an adult hold the box for them) while they drop a magnetic ball bearing inside, and move a magnetic wand around from the outside of the bottom of the box—the wand will still attract the marble through the cardboard, and children can paint their images by dragging the wand around, pulling the marble through the paint.

Gone Fishin'

This simple activity can incorporate a variety of different themes, depending on what it is that staff choose to magnetize. Try a metal bar magnet attached to a string, which is then tied to a wooden dowel in order to look like a fishing pole. Children can then fish for any number of different things, depending on what programmers have decided to lay out. Printing off clip art pictures of fish (or letters, numbers, animals, etc.) and then backing them on construction paper and taping them to a paper clip will allow the fishing pole to pick images up out of a small blow-up kiddie pool filled with blue paper shred.

Library staff or adult caregivers can play "Go Fish" with the children, who will try to pick up the called-out item from among the visible images lying in the pool: "Can you find the red fish?" They can work on their math skills by hunting for numbers, biology skills by hunting for animals, or early literacy skills by hunting for letters. Try leaving some of the fish without paper clips too, to stimulate discussion on why some items won't attach to the rod.

Magnetic Blocks

Magnetic block play combines the best of many preschool STEM worlds—loose parts play, exposure to magnets, and basic engineering design. These magnetic squares and triangles can be used to create 3D structures like houses, pyramids, towers, or whatever else a child may imagine. They can likewise be tossed into the bucket or blow-up pool during magnet fishing and hunting games as well. Popular branded sets include Magformers, Magna-Tiles, AMOSTING, and PlayMaty, which can be found in many toy stores, school supply stores, and Amazon.

Stop the Weekly Craft Prep! Try a Mural (Art)

How many countless hours of time are spent by library staff on preparing small bits of construction paper, paper bags, and plates? This art activity is a creative way to allow children to practice their art skills while also helping to cut down on staff prep time, as well as art supply costs.

Libraries that host a term-length preschool series (nine weeks of a Tuesday morning storytime, for example) will often go through a large amount of staff or volunteer time in attempting to prep nine different weeks of preschool craft activities. Programmers can switch this out with a term-length mural project, which should only require a longer, mural-length size of paper, and some paint or coloring supplies. Children can work on their mural and collages, making sure to add something new to the piece, together as a group, each week. The collective piece of art can then be displayed in the library on a children's bulletin board, or even at the start of the next storytime term.

Screen-Free Preschool Coding (Technology)

While there are plenty of fun and unique app-based coding and robotic projects for elementary-aged children, it is a bit more difficult to find screen-free coding activities for preschoolers. Screen time can be a controversial topic with parents, and both the American Academy of Pediatrics and the Canadian Paediatric Society recommend no more than an hour a day of screen time use for children ages two to five, and ideally no screen time for children under the ages of two.[20] The following games can be fun exposure to coding and robotics for preschoolers when paired with adult accompaniment.

Littlecodr

Littlecodr is a card game that allows children to play with the basic concepts of log-in and coding "before they can even read or write."[21] Suggested for players ages four and up, this game allows children to use action cards (which have both the symbol and the word) such as "step forward," "turn left," or "turn right," to lay in a sequence of instructions; essentially, they are the "writing the code" for the adult (who plays the robot) to follow.[22]

Children can decide as a group where to send their library programmer by using the given cards to code the path. Will they send him or her to the fridge to bring out the apple juice? Perhaps they'll make the programmer walk around in circles again and again. Staff can play up on the kooky robot aspect by creating a cheap, cardboard robot helmet to put on whenever they are ready for their coded instructions. (Try making it with Makedo materials! More information on this activity can be found in chapter 8.)

Littlecodr can be purchased on Amazon.com for US$19.99, or Indigo.ca for C$24.95.

Cubetto

Cubetto is the "friendly wooden robot" that teaches children "the basics of computer programming through adventure and hands on play" while reducing "screen-time, increas[ing] engagement, and enhanc[ing] learning."[23] This coding playset comes with the wooden robot, his wooden control board that accepts the included plastic directional pieces (forward, backward, left, right), and even a themed world map play mat that children can use to for something to direct their Cubetto through.

Jenn Carson, the library director of L. P. Fisher Public Library in New Brunswick, wrote on the ALA Programming Librarian blog that this sturdy, Montessori-approved robot was a perfect solution to a screen-free children's coding activity.[24] While the Primo Toys website does include instructions for educators, Carson recommends hands-on play for library staff to learn how it operates, as it is usually kids who can quickly get the hang of it.[25]

Carson's Cubetto library program saw more than twenty people in attendance, whom she divided into small groups to draw their direction maps on paper; they would later get a chance to replicate the drawn code with pieces into the wooden control board.[26] Children can draw the arrows, use the colors of the map squares, or even write out the words, if they're able. Carson recommends getting multiple world map play mats for each group, so they have something to plan for while waiting for the single Cubetto robot to make his rounds.[27]

The Cubetto Coding Robot Playset can be purchased on the PrimoToys.com website for US$225 (shipping to US and EU only), or from Louise Kool & Galt (LouiseKool

.com) from C$329. Additional world map play mats are also available in the themes of space, cities, and deserts for US$30 from PrimoToys.com.

Ziplock Beans (Science)

Eric Drew, the Youth Services librarian for the Tantallon and J. D. Shatford Public Libraries in Nova Scotia, recommends using the ziplock bean bag activity to help preschoolers learn about plants and seeds. Children can assemble "greenhouses" and "watch the sprout grow in their window at home."[28] He mentions having used this project in a few different preschool programs, with themes like spring flowers, farming, and fairy tales. "The difference is simply in how you decorate the plastic bag: a flower pot, a barn, a giant's castle in the clouds," Drew says.[29]

Supplies:

- Bean seeds
- Ziplock bags
- Paper towels
- Water

Instructions:

1. Wet a folded paper towel (thoroughly, but not dripping wet)
2. Place the wet paper towel into the ziplock bag.
3. Place one bean seed between the wet towel and the bag and zip it closed.
4. Tape the bag to a window (in order to get access to sunlight).
5. Children can then check the bean bags each day and talk about their progress. Older children can chart the progress in a paper journal by drawing what they see each day.[30]

Block Play (Engineering)

Block play is a time-honored traditional preschool activity. Research even argues that "block building activities can address mathematical concepts relating to spatial reasoning" in preschool communities,[31] and "unit blocks need to be brought back into early childhood programs."[32]

Free play block building is a simple library program or activity in the terms of setup: clear a large space, provide the blocks, and let preschoolers and families build to their hearts' content. Large class sets of the standard wooden building blocks (unit blocks) can be expensive to procure, but will provide years and years' worth of block play opportunities. Libraries can also achieve this goal with plastic Crayola building blocks or DUPLO sets, or even with some of the more uniquely designed building blocks like those that have colored clear plastic inserts, or even floating glitter.

KEVA planks are also an alternative, lighter weight solution to add into loose parts or block play. Every maple wood piece is the same: KEVA stacking planks are "about 1/4 inch thick, 3/4 inch wide and 4 1/2 inches long."[33] More and more libraries are using KEVA planks to "instantly transform . . . into engaging, interactive learning spaces" with either "quiet unguided construction, or activities that bring stories, STEM and Art to life."[34] The KEVA Planks website suggests contacting them directly to discuss library or educator discounted purchases.

As the most basic of beginning engineering design activities, free block play can also be supplemented by providing paper and crayons so that young children can draw their design ideas before attempting to execute them.

STEM Storybooks

Preschool programs are often based on (or supplemented with) the reading aloud of stories to a group of young children. Libraries can try using the following list of picture books (both fiction and non) to start talking about casual, preschool-level STEM skills in their programs. This not only introduces such concepts to the children, but also reminds the present adults about the necessity of incorporating these skills in their daily and educational activities.

Whether you're incorporating a single book into an activity-based program, or looking for a STEM-focused theme of a book-heavy storytime, the list below should help jump-start your inspiration.

Fiction:

- Beaty, Andrea, and David Roberts. *Ada Twist, Scientist.* New York: Abrams Books for Young Readers, 2017.
- Beaty, Andrea, and David Roberts. *Iggy Peck, Architect.* Boston: National Braille, 2015.
- Beaty, Andrea, and David Roberts. *Rosie Revere, Engineer.* New York: Abrams Books for Young Readers, 2017.
- Brown, Carron, and Rachael Saunders. *The Human Body.* Tulsa, OK: Kane Miller, 2016.
- Dusen, Chris Van. *If I Built a Car.* Toronto: Penguin, 2005.
- Heder, Thyra. *Fraidyzoo.* New York: Abrams Books for Young Readers, 2013.
- Jeffers, Oliver, and Terence Stamp. *Stuck.* London: HarperCollins Children's Books, 2013.
- Micklos, John, and Clive McFarland. *One Leaf, Two Leaves, Count with Me!* New York: Nancy Paulsen, 2017.
- Offill, Jenny, and Nancy Carpenter. *11 Experiments That Failed.* New York: Random House Children's Books, 2011.
- Spires, Ashley. *The Most Magnificent Thing.* Toronto: Kids Can, 2014.
- Stevenson, Robert Louis, and Daniel Kirk. *Block City.* New York: Simon & Schuster Books for Young Readers, 2005.
- Tougas, Chris. *Mechanimals.* Custer, WA: Orca, 2007.
- Yamada, Kobi, and Mae Besom. *What Do You Do with an Idea?* Seattle, WA: Compendium, 2014.
- Yolen, Jane, and Chris Sheban. *What to Do with a Box.* Mankato, MN: Creative Editions, 2018.

Non-fiction:

- Bang, Molly, and Penny Chisholm. *Buried Sunlight: How Fossil Fuels Have Changed the Earth*. New York: Blue Sky, 2014.
- Chin, Jason. *Gravity*. New York: Scholastic, 2015.
- Glaser, Rebecca Stromstad. *Seeds*. Minneapolis, MN: Jump!, 2013.
- Hale, Christy. *Dreaming Up: A Celebration of Building*. New York: Lee & Low, 2012.
- Judge, Lita. *How Big Were Dinosaurs?* New York: Henry Holt, 2013.

STEM Storytime Series

Think about the possibilities of using STEM themes more frequently in your programs. Instead of only bringing these topics out for special occasions, you might want to try marketing a whole number of programs as a STEM-focused preschool series. This could be promoted as STEM or STEAM storytimes, where you're choosing from books like the ones listed above, and incorporating them with an associated preschool-level STEM activity each week. While most of your parents would be drawn in for the early literacy skills in general, you might then also gain access to even more families if you're promoting your series programming as preschool science education.

Heather Love Beverley, the Children's Services assistant manager at the Cook Memorial Public Library District, offers a monthly STEAM-based preschool storytime called "Picking Up STEAM" where programming staff read non-fiction books exploring a new STEAM topic each month.[35] Past themes have included gravity, snow, the human body, and plants, and after sharing stories about the topic, children and their caregivers get to try small experiments and activities based on the storytime theme.[36]

Key Points

Children are naturally curious about the world around them, and are therefore well suited to start learning basic STEM skill concepts. Library staff can step in and observe how younger children are interacting with the designated activity, making sure to create an environment that supports exploration for preschoolers by interjecting with an occasional comment or question in order to foster problem solving. Questions can be focused on the "what" instead of "why," with occasional problem solving thrown in, as well:

What happens when you flick this switch?

What is your mom doing with that magnet?

What are you using to make the ball move?

Can you find a way to turn the light off?

Can you find a way to pick up the pipe cleaner?

Preschool STEM programming needs to be flexible, and library staff will want to follow children's interests and demonstrated thought processes. Librarians can invest in new kits and STEM-focused gadgets like Squishy Circuits or the Cubetto, or they can make use of whatever materials they might already have around in-branch through previous purchases or recycling, such as a variety of loose parts.

Squishy Circuits can be used with preschoolers to get a supervised, hands-on exposure to circuitry and electricity in action. As a popular tactile for young children, the essential supply of playdough is likely to already be found in most public libraries, and helps bring in the creativity component of this circuitry activity.

Libraries should inform themselves on national pediatric-recommended child screen time usage suggestions when thinking about adding screen technology to children's programs. Screen-free coding activities like the Cubetto robot and the Littlecodr card game are fun family-friendly supplements to introduce coding to younger children.

Simple activities like magnet hunts, bean bag planters, and block play are some quick, low-prep ways to incorporate science, biology, and engineering concepts into regular preschool programs.

Libraries can try using the curated STEM-themed picture books (both fiction and non) to start talking about basic preschool-level STEM skills in their programs. These can casually worked into a regular storytime series, or, the entire storytime term's run can be fully focused on a new STEM topic each week.

Notes

1. Simon Nicholson, "The Theory of Loose Parts: An Important Principle for Design Methodology," *Studies in Design Education Craft and Technology* 4, no. 2 (1972): 6.
2. Mary Donegan-Ritter, "STEM for All Children: Preschool Teachers Supporting Engagement of Children with Special Needs in Physical Science Learning Centers," *Young Exceptional Children* 20, no. 1 (2017): 5.
3. Abby Johnson, "Preschool STEM Lab," *Library Journal* 141, no. 7 (2016): 7.
4. "NSTA Position Statement: Early Childhood Science Education," National Science Teachers Association, accessed December 10, 2017, http://www.nsta.org/about/positions/early childhood.aspx.
5. Sally Moomaw and Jaumall A. Davis, "STEM Comes to Preschool," *Young Children* 65, no. 5 (2010): 12–14.
6. Ingrid Chalufour and Karen Worth, *Building Structures with Young Children*, 1st ed. The Young Scientist (St. Paul, MN: Redleaf), 2004.
7. Chalufour and Worth, *Building Structures*.
8. Julia Stoll, Ashley Hamilton, Emilie Oxley, Angela Mitroff Eastman, and Rachael Brent, "Young Thinkers in Motion: Problem Solving and Physics in Preschool," *Young Children* 67, no. 2 (2012): 20–26.
9. Johnson, "Preschool STEM Lab," 7.
10. Donegan-Ritter, "STEM for All Children," 4.
11. Johnson, "Preschool STEM Lab," 7.
12. Johnson, "Preschool STEM Lab," 7.
13. Bree Laverdiere Ruzzi and Angela Eckhoff, "STEM Resources and Materials for Engaging Learning Experiences," *Young Children* 72, no. 1 (March 2017), accessed December 10, 2017, https://www.naeyc.org/resources/pubs/yc/mar2017/stem-materials-experiences.
14. Nicholson, "Theory of Loose Parts," 12.
15. Ruzzi and Eckhoff, "Stem Resources."
16. Jennifer Evans in discussion with the author, December 2017.
17. Jennifer Evans in discussion with the author, December 2017.

18. Trina Orchard in discussion with the author, November 2017.

19. Trina Orchard in discussion with the author, November 2017.

20. "Screen Time and Young Children: Promoting Health and Development in a Digital World," Canadian Paediatric Society, accessed December 10, 2017. https://www.cps.ca/en/documents/position/screen-time-and-young-children; Council on Communications and Media, "Media and Young Minds," *Pediatrics*, October 21, 2016, accessed December 10, 2017, http://pediatrics.aappublications.org/content/early/2016/10/19/peds.2016-2591.

21. "Home," Littlecodr, accessed December 10, 2017, http://littlecodr.com/.

22. Littlecodr, "Home."

23. "Cubetto: A Robot Teaching Kids Code & Computer Programming," Primo Toys, accessed December 10, 2017, https://www.primotoys.com/.

24. "Robot Storytime: Coding for Preschoolers," Programming Librarian, July 27, 2017, accessed December 10, 2017, http://www.programminglibrarian.org/blog/robot-storytime-coding-preschoolers.

25. "Robot Storytime."

26. "Robot Storytime."

27. "Robot Storytime."

28. Eric Drew in discussion with the author, December 2017.

29. Eric Drew in discussion with the author, December 2017.

30. Eric Drew in discussion with the author, December 2017.

31. Beth M. Casey, Nicole Andrews, Holly Schindler, Joanne E. Kersh, Alexandra Samper, and Juanita Copley, "The Development of Spatial Skills through Interventions Involving Block Building Activities," *Cognition and Instruction* 26, no. 3 (2008): 305.

32. Lynn E. Cohen and Janet Emmons, "Block Play: Spatial Language with Preschool and School-Aged Children," *Early Child Development and Care* 187 (2017): 967.

33. "Home," KEVA Planks, accessed December 10, 2017, http://www.kevaplanks.com/.

34. KEVA Planks, "Home."

35. Heather Love Beverley in discussion with the author, November 2017.

36. Heather Love Beverley in discussion with the author, November 2017.

CHAPTER 5

Elementary STEM Programming

IN THIS CHAPTER

- ▷ The never-ending possible themes for Squishy Circuits and Makey Makey programs
- ▷ How to start (or revamp) your LEGO @ the Library programs
- ▷ Incorporating STEM skills into your Free Comic Book Day events
- ▷ How to host a fidget spinner program
- ▷ How to host a squishy science lab
- ▷ How to host an Instagram camp
- ▷ Circus bridges

STEM PROGRAMMING is perfectly suited for the elementary ages range of children ages five through twelve: they're old enough to start understanding more of the basic concepts, have a higher level of problem-solving skills, and yet are still curious enough to participate in a variety of fun and engaging activities, without worrying so much about the possibility of failing or looking "uncool." The Royal Academy for Engineering suggests in their *UK STEM Education Landscape* document that the UK has a greater need for "STEM support in primary schools" due to the "increasing evidence that children's attitudes towards . . . STEM, are developed in primary school," where teachers can "nurture [this] interest in young children at this important formative stage."[1]

Jennifer Evans, the supervising librarian at the Hazeldean Branch of Ottawa Public Library, reminds librarians that STEM skills are important for children because they foster curiosity, creativity, and the abilities to take risks and to adapt to change.[2] As a public librarian, Evans of course wants children visiting her library to do well in their academic endeavors, but she also wants them "to be happy, inquisitive lifelong learners." STEM-based activities, she explains, can provide opportunities to "develop hobbies and interests which [children] may carry with them throughout their lives" even if they do not end up in STEM career fields. This will still help them to be more well rounded and resilient with a "greater sense of wellbeing."[3]

Weekends, spring break, and summer will likely see a larger influx of these school-age children into the library. Whether libraries are looking for STEM programming ideas for these peak school-age times, or planning an after-school series or even a school trip to their branch, this chapter will provide a variety of engaging STEM activities that are easily replicable. There's the limitless possibilities of the Squishy Circuit and Makey Makey combo, how to start or revamp a LEGO @ the Library program, and incorporating STEM skills into Free Comic Book Day events. There are also different ways in which to incorporate scientific observation and engineering activities into recent pop culture toy trends such as the fidget spinner, squishies, and even the DIY slime movement.

Make It Squishy: The Incredible Transforming Program Powers of the Makey Makey / Squishy Circuits Combo

Playdough has been a popular, tactile children's material for decades, but as seen in chapter 4, Squishy Circuits, the University of St. Thomas's creative circuitry project, takes this popular home activity and kicks the learning up a notch. Through the use of batteries and electronic switches such as LED lights, buzzers, and small motors, Squishy Circuits make use of the conductivity of your average playdough so that children can make their hand-formed creations light up, buzz, beep, and even twirl!

Similarly, the Makey Makey is an invention kit that allows children to create their own art, engineering, or design projects. Kids can use the included alligator clips—one end of which will be hooked up to the Makey Makey board (which kind of looks like an old-school Nintendo Entertainment System controller), while the other end can be hooked up to anything conductive—such as playdough, fruits, veggies, tinfoil, or even people! This do-it-yourself touch pad is then plugged into your computer via USB, so it can be used as the keyboard, mouse click, or directional arrows for whichever game or program you have open. A common example is the banana piano, where the bananas act in place of the piano keys. The possibilities, as you can imagine, are endless. The complexity of the project can be as simple or as complex as one desires, which makes it a great invention kit not only for children, but people of all ages.

Now, if you've ever tinkered with a Makey Makey, odds are, you've heard about Scratch. This MIT-created visual coding website is kid friendly, and chock full of Makey Makey compatible games to enhance your Squishy-Makey programs. For example, the piano used in the popular Makey Makey banana piano project is a Scratch game. Much the same as the Makey Makey itself, there are a vast variety of different coding projects to choose from. Depending upon your desired complexity level, Scratch coding can be an engaging computer science activity for children and adults alike. While this section of our chapter will focus more on the usage of pre-made games on the Scratch website, more information on teen coding volunteers for Scratch for game creation can be found in chapter 6.

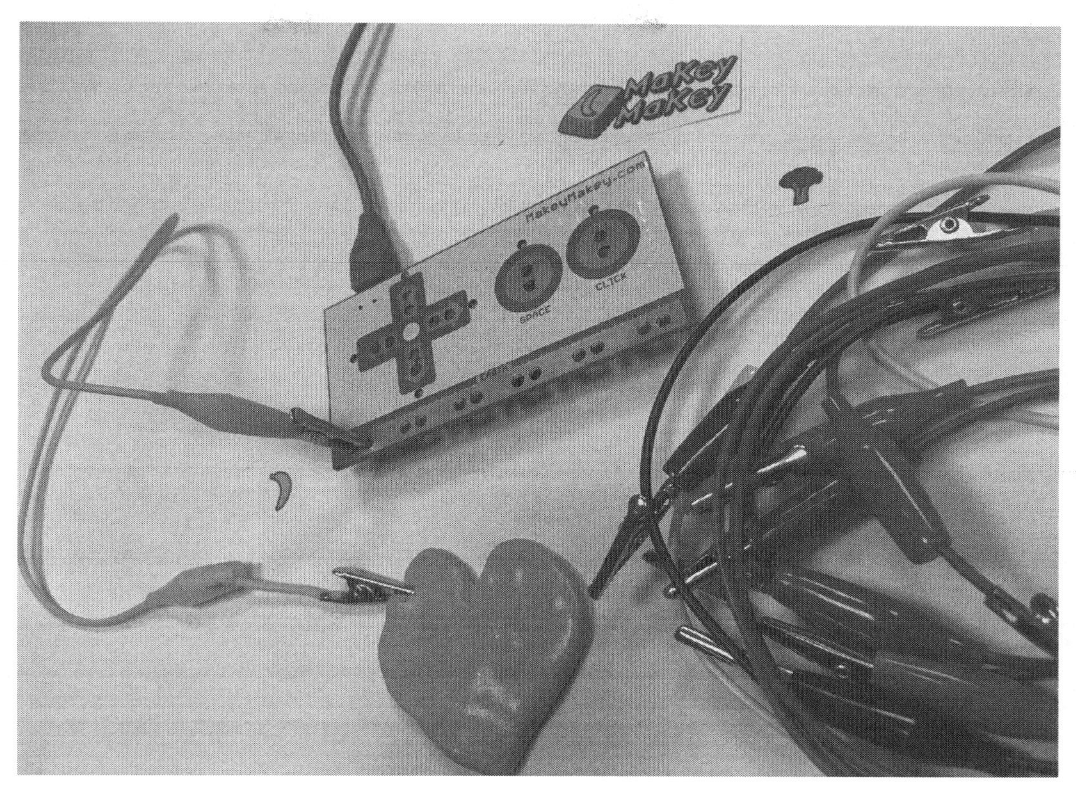

Figure 5.1. Makey Makey kit components

The popularity of Squishy Circuits and Makey Makey kits in public libraries seems to have taken off throughout 2014. Kits in hand, branches could easily hold the standard Squishy Circuits program:

"Join us to make your playdough creations light up, beep, buzz, and even twirl! Don't forget to check out our Makey Makey banana piano!"

There is certainly enough content to fill an hour-long children's program using this basic process as your inspiration. The invitation to play with playdough, and even the word "squishy," are in and of themselves likely enough to bring a few families into your programming room.

As often happens, though, things can fall out of fashion. Although the refresh rate of children's programming audiences is often high, allowing libraries to repeat the same annual programs for their new grade fours each year, there is also often a lingering buzz about the short popularity life span of children's technology. A mere year later, Squishy Circuits and Makey Makey kits might now live on the dusty top shelf of your programming closet, since "people can only stick an LED light into two lumps of playdough so many times."

So evolved the need to integrate the Squishy-Makey technology into different programs. Try Squishy Halloween—a popular annual holiday STEM program that runs in Keshen Goodman Public Library each October; the spooky Peep organ is always a hit! Beyond twisting your Squishy Circuits into holiday programs, pop culture programming is also an excellent way to casually incorporate this STEM activity in ways to invite more than just your young budding scientists to your Squishy tables.

Purchasing Items

Squishy Circuits Kits

If you're new to Squishy Circuits or Makey Makey programming, you might need to think about purchasing the supplies for a kit. There are a couple of different options, depending on your budget. The cheapest, of course, would be to find a partner like a local makerspace that might be willing to co-host the program with you and to bring all its own Squishy Circuit or Makey Makey supplies. More information on making use of local community organizations to partner up for your library STEM programs can be found in chapter 9.

Depending upon your intended frequency of use, instead of purchasing kits for your specific branch, you might want to think about asking your regional Children's Services department to purchase it for you, or going splits with other branches in your system in order to have a shared booking system for the materials and to cut down on costs.

Squishy Circuits kits can be purchased on the SquishyCircuits.com website; the standard runs about US$30 each and includes the basic components of the battery holder, a piezoelectric buzzer, a motor, an on/off switch, and a variety of different LED lights. This size kit could be used for one child, or perhaps a pair, a small group, or at a demonstration table. Because the standard kit comes without the playdough, you could then source the playdough from inside your branch (as long as it's not dried out), make your own, or buy a cheaper, smaller amount at a local retailer. It's also possible to purchase a deluxe kit from the SquishyCircuits.com website, which includes ready-made dough in addition to the basic components (and a few other things) for about $80. This website should also be your go-to source for the basic instructions on how to make your Squishy Circuits components work.

Source Your Own Squish

Alternatively, you could source your own components from an electronics distributor. If you're looking to plan for a larger program—say, a registration list of twenty people, this might be a great way to save some money. Considering that the basic kit from SquishyCircuits.com is about $30, when you can source a 9-volt battery clip and two 9-volt batteries for a total of $1.25, bulk purchases could be the way to go. Consider purchasing the following materials from an electronic supplies store like ABRA Electronics in order to build a quantity of Squishy Circuits kits (US prices and availability taken from abra-electronics.com in the summer of 2017, and could vary depending upon purchase date):

- 9-volt batteries: $1.53 each
- 9-volt battery clips: $0.23 each
- Standard 10 mm diffused LEDs (in red, green, or orange): $0.38 each
- Diffused RGB 10 mm LED common anode—package of 10: $14.95
- Large enclosed piezo element with wires: $1.45 each
- Medium-duty toggle switch on/off: $4.28 each

Unfortunately, sourcing your own parts can also be a trial and error process. Make sure your "piezo electric buzzers" are the type where the leads (the black and red wires) are long enough and exposed (so that you can stick each wire in your dough balls). Sourcing your own buzzers can be a bit tricky, but if you stick to the exposed leads, you should be good to go.

Finding your own DC motor can be a bit more complex. The original name-brand Squishy Circuits kits included small DC motors that allowed you to create a spinning ball of dough in your projects. With a limited understanding of electronics, and a lot of research on DC motors during your original kit creation, you might still fail to make use of motors. If you're unable to find what looks like an alternative retail source, and don't have the budget to purchase the full name-brand kits from SquishyCircuits.com, you might consider forging ahead without the motor portion of the activity.

Perhaps, though, all you need is a young inquiring mind. Think about purchasing a small variety of motors or different kinds of switches, and letting the curious eight-year-olds in your program see if they can figure it out. One young child at a Squishy Circuits program at Keshen Goodman Public Library offered the solution of attaching paper clips as makeshift leads to the unmoving motors—which worked! Yet another reminder that even in STEM skill programs, sometimes the children are the ones teaching library staff, as opposed to the traditional opposite. Unfortunately, this new paper-clip trick also seems hit or miss, which is why there aren't any recommended motors in my suggested purchase list above. If you're looking to include motors in your kit, your best bet would be to go to SquishyCircuits.com, which luckily, now, sells the individual components. These components might be a bit more expensive than they would at places like ABRA Electronics, but you'll at least be certain that they are compatible with the rest of your parts.

While the 10 mm diameter LED lights mentioned in our purchase list above are bigger and brighter, you can also save on cost by going down to the smaller, 5 mm diameter lights—these come in a pack of twenty-five for $4.00 at ABRA Electronics. They're just as bright!

You'll also want to avoid the "superbright" LED lights—these have shorter, stubbier lead wires, which are much less pliable. While the diffused LED lights mentioned above will occasionally encounter a broken lead from too much use, they are longer and much more easily bent so that the LED light can stretch between your two balls of dough. Most regular LED lights will survive multiple programs—where the stubby superbright LED leads often break when you first try to stretch them out.

Because the more unique switches such as the buzzers, motors, and toggle switches run a bit more money than the LED lights, you might want to think about purchasing about half as many of these for your twenty-person kits. You can make sure each child has his or her own battery, battery clip, dough portion, and handful of LEDs before having them go through the basic LED circuit building and troubleshooting and then introducing those extra switches one at a time. If you only have ten of these each, ask the children to pair up at their tables in order to share the new switches. It also provides them with a partner for troubleshooting, since handing these items out without any instruction allows them to see if they can use their problem-solving skills to make things work.

You might also want to keep in mind that the buzzers can be very loud. Some buzzers are the same pieces used in smoke detectors, and these high-pitched wails can quickly become very irritating. These can be handed out for a couple of minutes only, before collecting them back from the pairs. Alternatively, you might want to put pieces of tape over your buzzers, which can help to mute the sound.

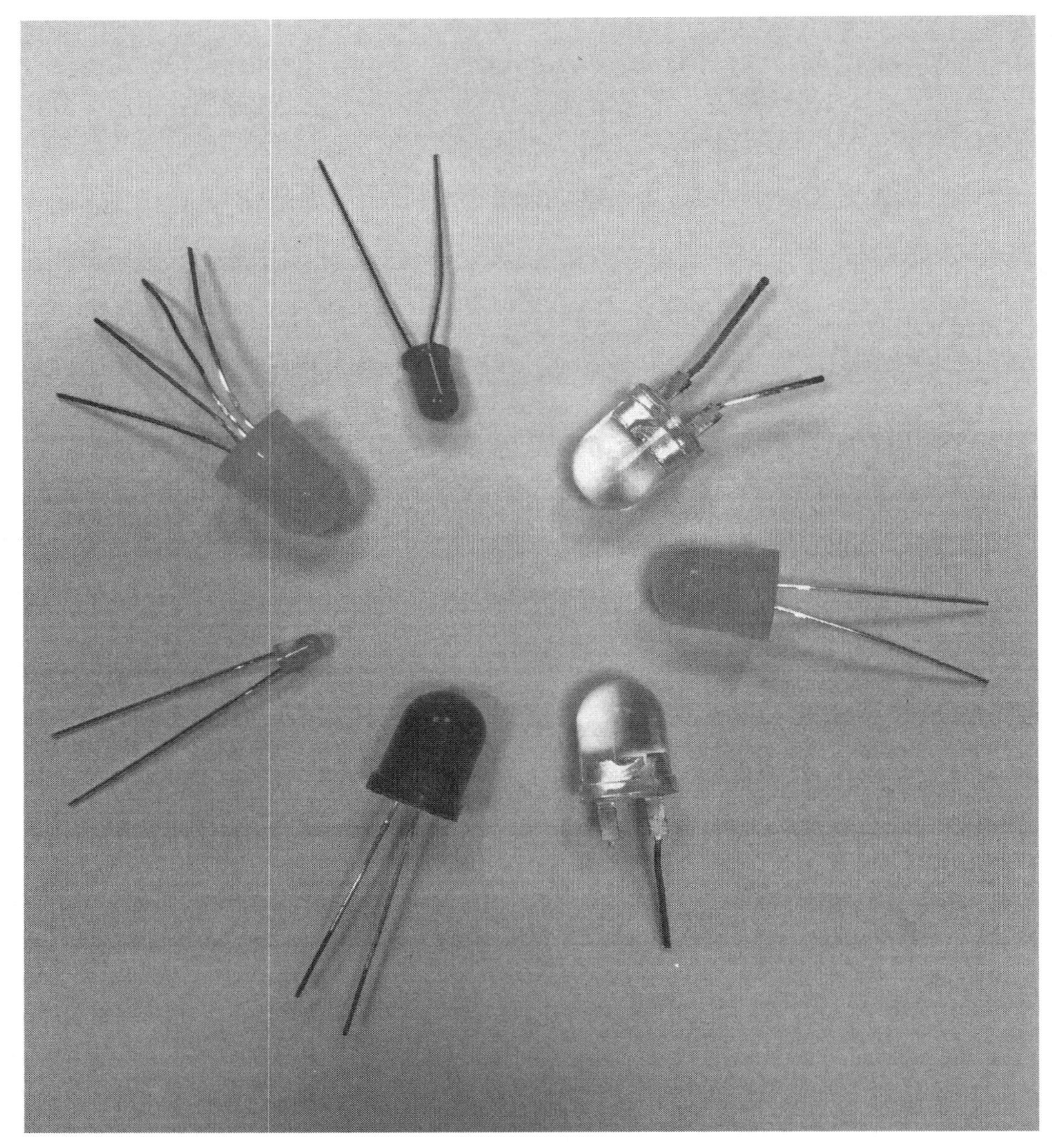

Figure 5.2. Squishy Circuit LEDS clockwise from the top: red 5 mm, stubby superbright, white 10 mm, broken stubby superbright, blue 10 mm, green 2.5 mm, RGB 10 mm ("octopus")

Looking to further cut down on costs? You could really run a Squishy Circuit activity with just the very basics—the utmost essential pieces are simply

- 9 V batteries (which you can get at the local dollar store),
- 9 V battery clips,
- a couple of standard diffused LED lights,
- and of course, the playdough.

Makey Makey Kits

Makey Makey kits are now widely available through different retailers such as Amazon, Best Buy, and Toys R Us, which will currently cost you around US$45. You could purchase a single item for your particular branch, or, you could also create a bookable regional kit for multiple branches that includes, say, five Makey Makeys each. You would really only need one Makey Makey if you were using it in a demonstration activity in your program, but of course, a couple more would allow you to break a larger attendance into small groups where they could try to create their own projects.

You'll also need access to a computer or laptop for each Makey Makey to work. You'll want to gather your conductive materials based on your activities—maybe it's playdough, tinfoil shapes, or perishable food items like fruit or marshmallows. For more information, try MakeyMakey.com for more information and ideas.

Pro tip: a box of paper clips is essential in your branch Makey Makey kits! These common stationery supplies can act as lead extenders in the alligator clips. Once you've cleaned sticky marshmallow goo out of twenty-plus alligator clips, you're going to be looking for some sort of disposable lead tip. If you're programming alone and in a crunch for time, this can be a great time-saver by tossing the sticky paper clip in the garbage when you're finished. Alternatively, if you've got teen volunteers or extra staff members helping out, you might want to save your resources, and have someone clean the alligator clips after their direct insertion into the marshmallow, banana, and so forth.

Wipe It Down, Clean It Up

As noted above, using paper clips can be a way to facilitate easier cleanup of alligator clips in the Makey Makey projects. The clean-up process in general is an important wrap-up step of both Squishy Circuits and Makey Makey programs. When packing away your materials, be sure to carefully wipe down all leads (LED prongs as well as wire casing exposures) after they have touched any dough or food items. If left uncleaned, these items can rust and eventually break off.

Minion Ba-na-na Keyboard

Keshen Goodman Public Library's Despicable Me: Minion Lab program was the first time that I was inspired to mix up my usage of Squishy Circuits, and it inspired me to continue to include holiday or pop culture themes in future Squishy and Makey activities.

The Squishy Circuits and Makey Makey tables were set up as activity stations among other *Despicable Me* party games and crafts. Our children's programmer had printed out little paper Minion suits for the Makey Makey bananas, the link for which can be found in the bibliography section at the end of this guide. While helping to dress these bananas, I grabbed the eyeball cutouts and stuck them on a couple of yellow playdough beans, and voila! My Squishy-Makey-pop-culture future flashed before my eyes.

At that point, the Makey Makey Minion banana piano was simply hooked up to the basic Scratch piano game, but future versions of this program could ideally include a Scratch piano that plays the ba-na-na song sung by the Minions in their popular movie trailers. This might not yet even exist, but you could also see chapter 6 for how to use teen coding volunteers to create your own branch of Scratch games.

Squishy Halloween (Science, Technology, Art, Engineering)

Squishy Halloween can be a popular holiday program for children ages five and up. This format is easily applicable to other holidays, such as Valentine's Day, St. Patrick's Day,

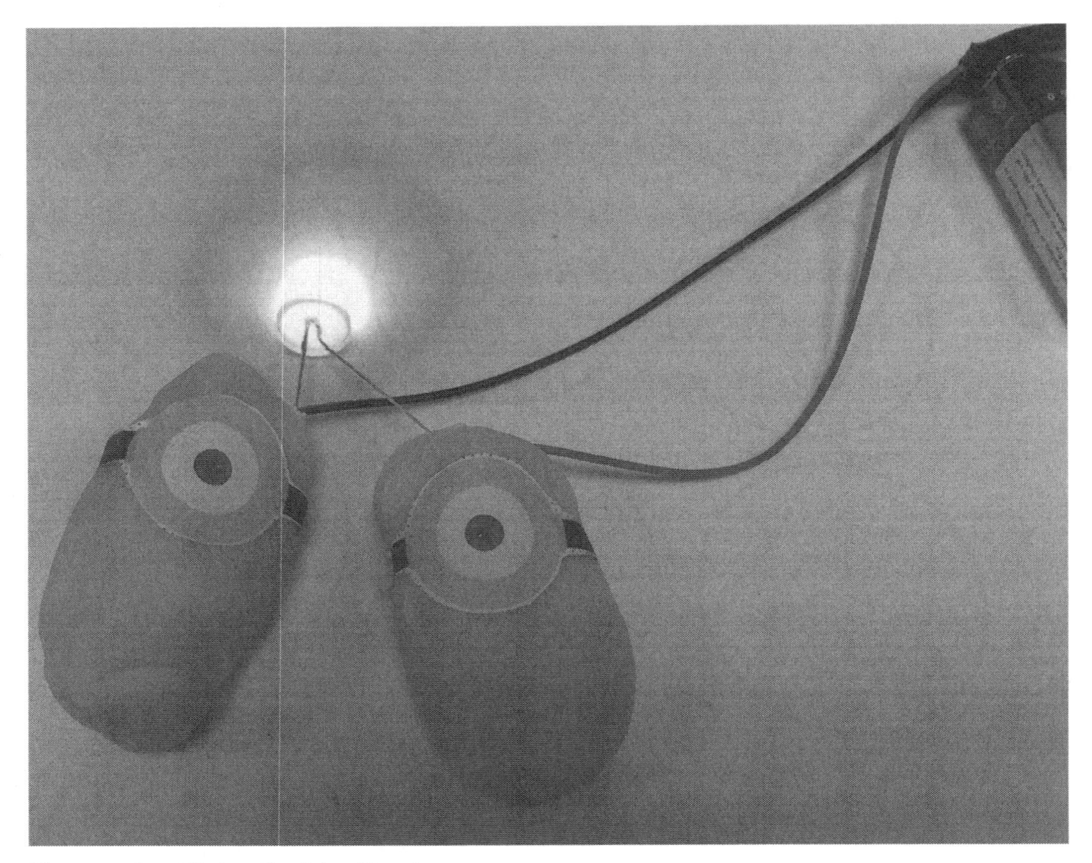

Figure 5.3. Minion Squishy Circuit

Easter/spring, and Christmas/winter holidays. It uses the current holiday excitement to draw kids and families in to practice their STEM skills while learning about circuitry and getting a hands-on look at your library's maker materials.

Spooky Peep Organ

Peeps, the sugarcoated, fun-shaped marshmallows found traditionally in the shape of chicks or bunnies, are a great way to spice up your holiday Makey Makey projects. Halloween often sees the North American release of ghosts, pumpkins, and even cats or bats. Marshmallows have the right amount of moisture to make them a nicely conductive material to use as your Makey Makey switches.

Try a spooky Peep organ: Attach ghost-shaped peeps to your Makey Makey alligator clips, and bring up a Halloween-themed piano game on Scratch. If you have access to multiple Makey Makeys, try using pumpkin or bat Peeps, with other Scratch games like a pumpkin maze or even the "Spooky, Scary Skeletons" DJ board. Peeps releases a great variety of holiday-themed marshmallows—hearts for Valentine's Day, snowmen and gingerbread men for Christmas, as well as eggs, bunnies, and chicks in all colors of the rainbow for spring. They even have ads for Independence Day–colored Peeps in the US!

It's always amusing when one or two children inevitably ask to eat the remaining peeps still attached to the Makey Makeys during program cleanup time. You can gently remind them that they've been mauled by many other hands, but if you have some left over in the untouched package, and their accompanying adult has pre-approved the con-

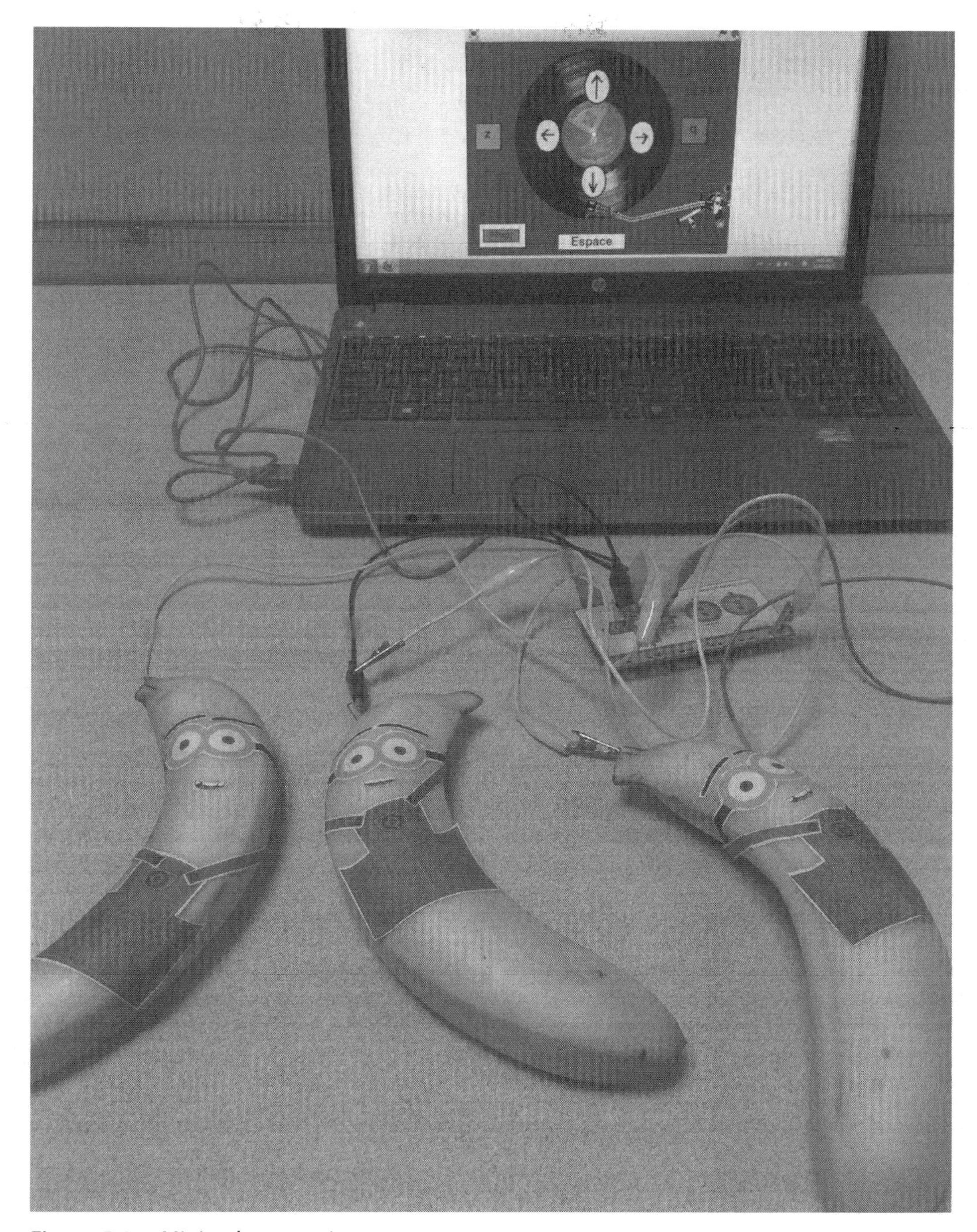

Figure 5.4. Minion banana piano

sumption, you might be okay to go ahead and hand them out if you have enough. You might want to remind them that marshmallows do include gelatin in the ingredients list, though, since this isn't something that everyone is comfortable consuming.

Don't forget—a regular marshmallow will do just fine too. If you don't have access to your perfect character Peep, you could always try decorating a plain white marshmallow. Spoiler alert: this works for Stormtroopers at the Squishy Star Wars program!

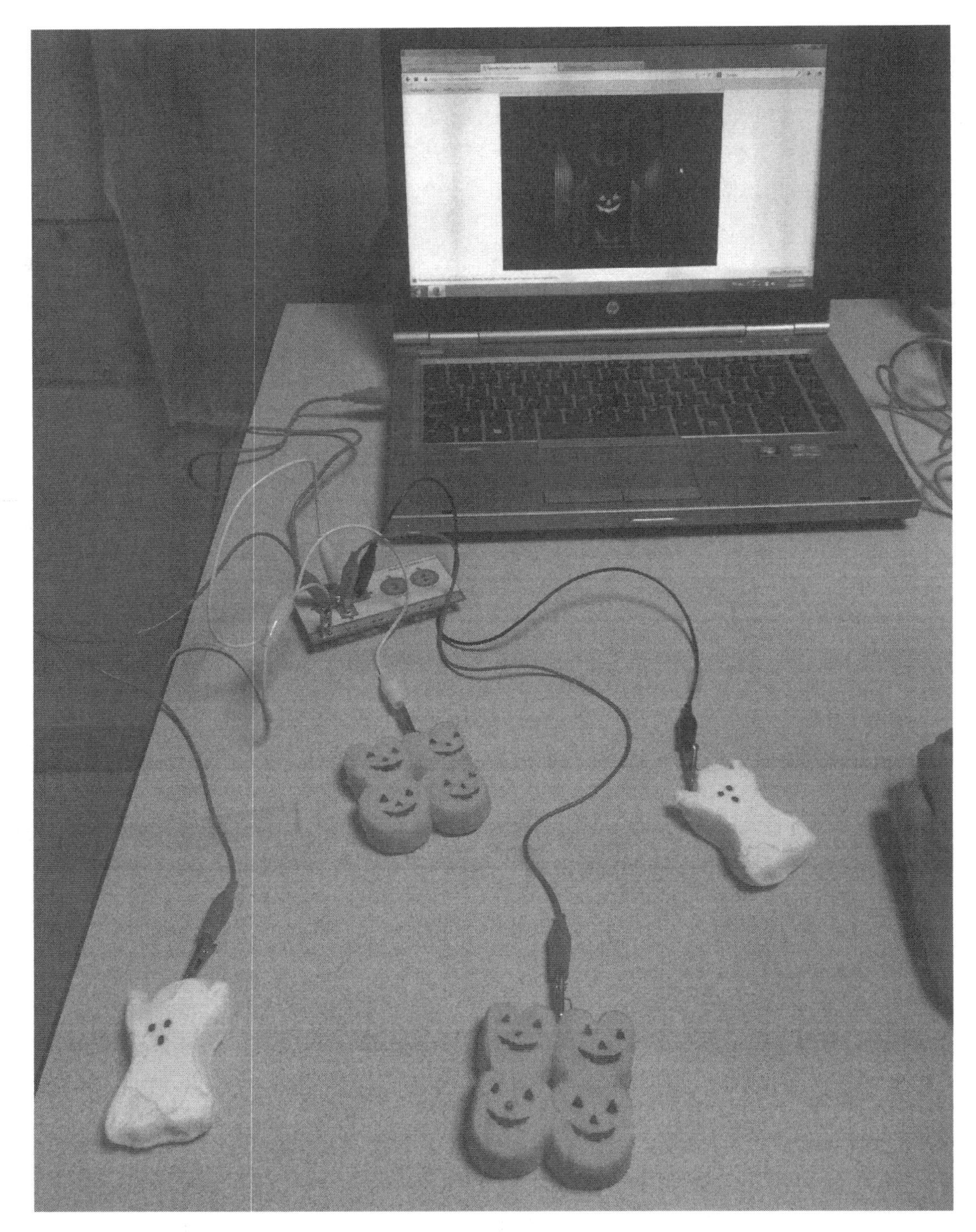

Figure 5.5. Makey Makey spooky Peep organ

Other holiday-themed Makey Makey materials can include tinfoil or playdough—try making classic holiday shapes out of these conductive materials, and pick your favorite holiday Scratch game. These can be prepped ahead of time by staff or teen volunteers, or you could incorporate their creation into your program layout, and see what the kids come up with!

Don't forget to cross-check how many, or what kind, of controls the Scratch game requires though—you don't want to plan on using the Pac-Man-esque pumpkin maze if you've only prepped three tinfoil witch heads, when you'd likely need four (one for each direction key).

Scary Storytelling

After your basic how-to-make-a-circuit lesson using two dough balls and all the possible switches, it's then fun to ask the kids to create a story scene. Try providing thematic play-dough color options—in the early fall, you can often find name-brand Play-Doh party packs that include mini tubs of a variety of Halloween colors such as orange, white, black, and green. Meant for trick-or-treaters, these mini portion tubs are the perfect size for individual circuit story creation. Don't forget to encourage your young storytellers not to mix the colors, though, and you should be set to keep the tubs and use them again for a couple of years. Some retailers also have Valentine's Day Play-Doh sets too that come in mini tubs of white, red, and various shades of pink.

Looking for a bit of extra social media promo? Don't forget to take pictures of all the scenes made by the young creators in your Squishy programs. As you circulate to snap the pictures of their Halloween-themed circuits, ask them to tell you what's going on in their project:

"This gravestone is lit by a white light because it's the ghost of the spider in front of it! Ooo-ooo-oooh!"

This is a great use of creativity and storytelling skills. Some children may even incorporate their toggle switches, motors, or buzzers to really tell an in-depth story.

Figure 5.6. Squishy Halloween Circuit

Stormtrooper Piano

Squishy Star Wars is another pop culture variation on the traditional Squishy-Makey program setup. Storytelling variations may include many LED lights acting as lightsabers. For those die-hard trivia buffs, you might want to have LED lights available in the authentic lightsaber colors—you might be teased mercilessly if you allow Yoda to wield a red lightsaber, but perhaps your storytelling skills can pull you out of the blunder.

The Stormtrooper keyboard works quite similarly to the basic Makey Makey banana piano or the spooky Peep organ, but with one exciting difference: if you use the "Star Wars Day 2014" Scratch game listed in the notes section below,[4] when you touch your Stormtrooper-decorated marshmallows in correct sequence, you can play the Imperial March. To facilitate easy learning of this game, think about laying each marshmallow/key on a colored circle, and tacking the "sheet music" on the table beside your laptop.

Similarly, tinfoil lightsabers can also act as thematic Makey Makey switches for your alligator clips, attached to one of the many more Star Wars games available on Scratch.

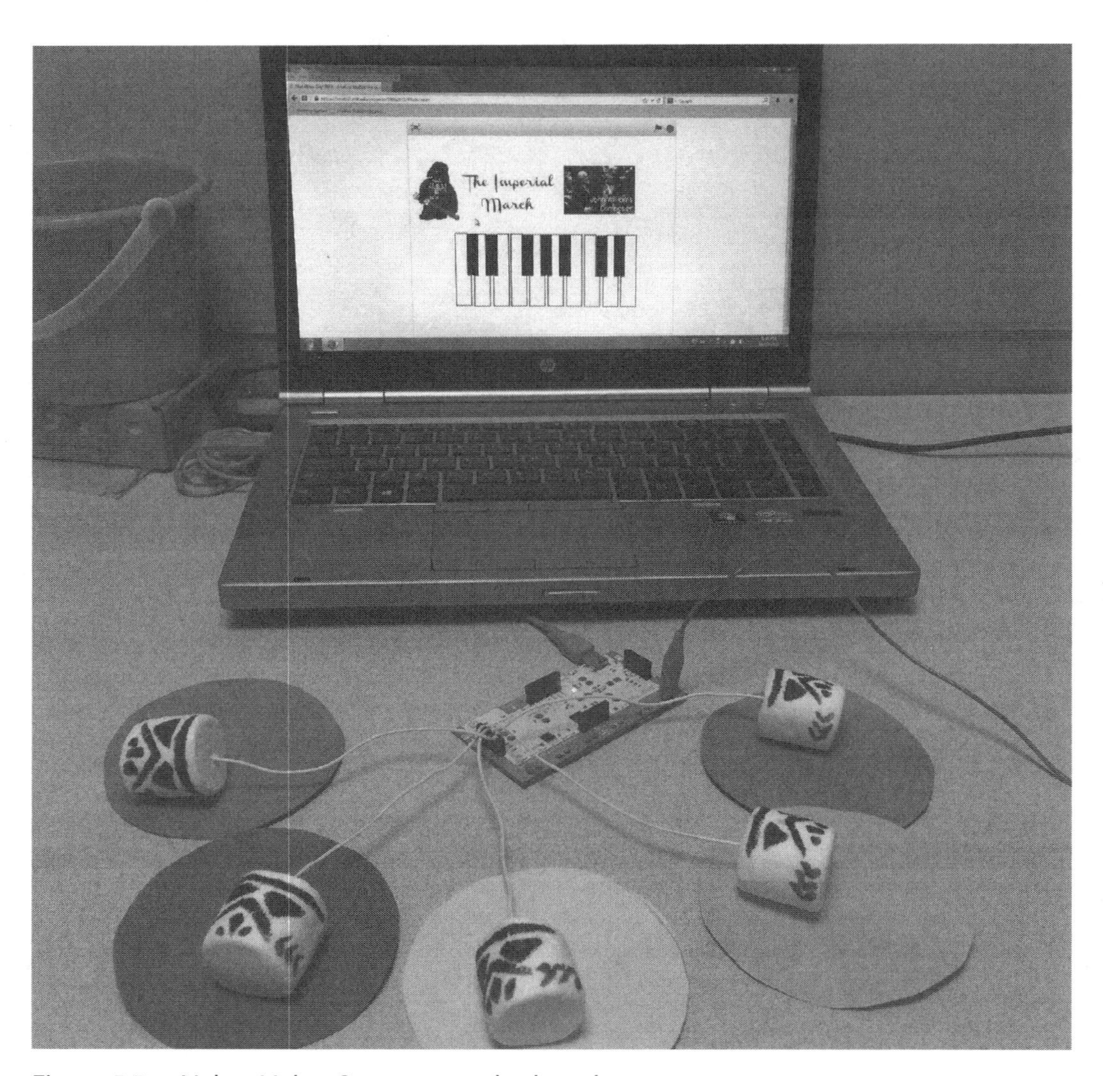

Figure 5.7. Makey Makey Stormtrooper keyboard

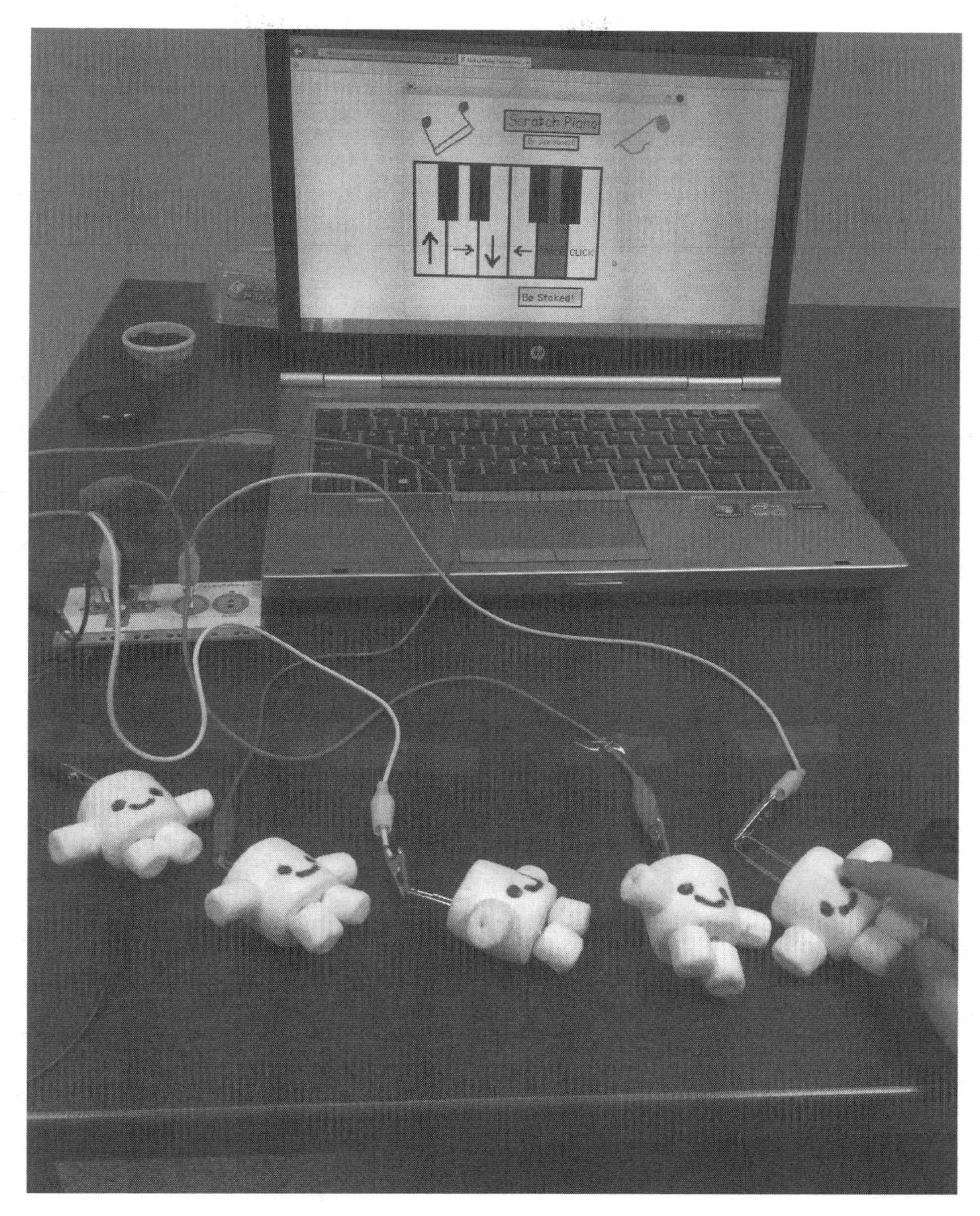

Figure 5.8. Makey Makey Adipose keyboard

Dr. Who Science Lab

Drawing upon the formats noted in the programs above, the Dr. Who Science Lab follows the same ideas. Expect to see a few TARDIS dough stories, or maybe someone will be creative enough to sculpt a weeping playdough angel circuit. Although many libraries host Dr. Who–themed programs for teens, you might want to think about opening them up to younger elementary children too; younger Dr. Who fans have been known to attend the all-ages and age-five-and-up programs at Keshen Goodman Public Library.

Makey Makey projects in this program make use of the easy marshmallow for an Adipose keyboard. Programmers will need mini marshmallows, toothpicks, and markers to construct their adipose, which can also be a fun activity for attendees.

Tinfoil shapes can be made in a variety of different Dr. Who icons, such as the fez, a bow tie, a weeping angel, a TARDIS, or a Dalek.

Squishy and Makey Tips and Tricks

Squishy Circuits

The Octopus / The Magic Light

You may have noticed the included diffused RGB 10 mm LED common anode light pack in the original purchase list, a few pages back. I like to refer to the color-changing RGB LED light as an "octopus." Which, to be fair, isn't a great use of scientific classification, since there are actually only four leads (legs), as opposed to eight. They are great discovery tool and troubleshooting tool when using teaching the basic light circuits in your Squishy programs. Hand an "octopus" or "magic light" out to each child, or pair, and ask them to tell you what color it is. Children will notice that many lights will differ from each other, since it depends on how you separate your leads—two versus two, one versus three, and three versus one will all get you different colors.

Fading Lights and Wire Strippers

You might also want to have a pair of wire strippers included in your Squishy Circuits programming bin. Occasionally you may notice that your LED lights aren't lighting up as bright as they usually do. This can be for one of a few different reasons—depending on the amount of power used in the full circuit, sometimes the toggle switches will dim your LED lights instead of completely turning them off. Lights can also start to dim if you have too many lights drawing power from one single battery. Sometimes, though, an LED light will look dimmer than usual, even when you only have one single LED switch attached to the circuit. Here is where you should check your battery clip leads. Through frequent dough insertion, the exposed wire tip popping out of the red and black wire casings will sometimes break off. If your battery clip leads have nothing protruding from the wire casings, you'll need to strip some of the casing back in order to expose a bit of the bare wire again. Please note! Make sure your battery clip is detached from the battery before you do this, though, to avoid possible sparks.

Insulating Dough: Is It Worth It?

When doing further research on the basic how-to process on the Squishy Circuits website, you'll notice that they mention the possibility of using non-conductive dough, to be used as an insulating layer to avoid short-circuiting single creation circuits. This can really be considered an upgraded activity to your basic Squishy Circuits program, since the insulating dough requires a special prepared recipe—or the obtaining of a tub of it directly from their website. While the insulating dough certainly ups your creative possibilities, by using the ideas mentioned in this chapter, you should have plenty of content for your programs without having to obtain this unique product.

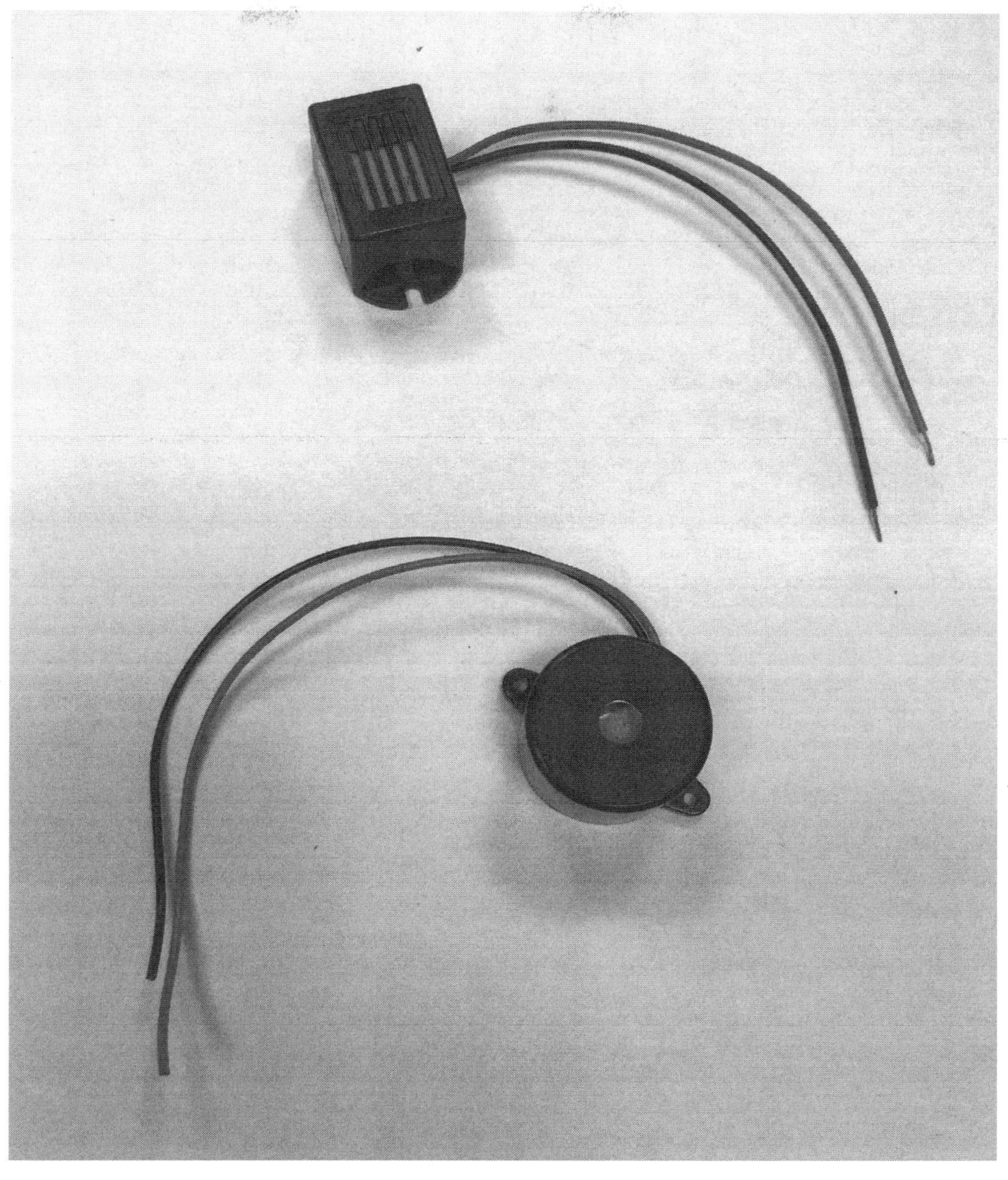

Figure 5.9. From top to bottom: piezo buzzer with exposed leads, and another piezo buzzer with broken lead wires

Makey Makey

Choosing Conductive Materials

As mentioned earlier in this chapter, the options for conductive materials to use in your Makey Makey projects are certainly abundant!

- Playdough
- Marshmallows
- Most veggies, fruits, or foods that aren't too dry

- Metal objects such as paper clips, coins, metal bows
- Tinfoil
- Graphite from pencils
- Even people (see below for the "high five"!)

To further engage scientific inquiry, try letting the children in your program discover what is conductive and what isn't! Provide a variety of conductive and nonconductive materials, and let them discover what types of items work, and have them think about why that is.

High Five!

The Makey Makey high five is always a hit. Instead of attaching your alligator clip to a marshmallow, coin, or tinfoil shape, have one person hold on to the metal portion of the alligator clip. Another person holds on to the ground wire, as is always necessary to make a Makey Makey circuit. When these two people high-five (using the hands that aren't already holding wires), the switch will engage! This even works if the first person puts his or her hand directly on the conductive material itself (so, if you already have the banana piano set up, the first person's hand is on a banana). Pairs can then try high-fiving out the beat to their favorite tunes on the marshmallow keyboard, which often results in giggles and squeals of delight.

Tape Those Wires Down

Depending upon the number of switches you're using in your Makey Makey project, you might end up with a bird's nest full of wires. Keyboard games might be especially tangled with the need for a new wire for each note, in addition to your ground wire. Consider taping these down to your table once you have each conductive switch placed in its ideal location. This also allows kids to more clearly identify what switch to touch, and when.

Alternative LEGO

Having been popular for many years now, LEGO @ the Library programs were one of the first and possibly most obvious examples of STEM-based activities being run in public libraries. Understandably, there are several research papers reporting on the studied "effectiveness of engineering design to improve science learning by using Lego."[5] Li et al. explain in their 2016 *Journal of Educational Technology & Society* article how game-based learning can "encourage students to acquire knowledge" and "offer a rich context that allows [them] to reinforce and consolidate their knowledge through practice."[6] As a set of toys based on design technique, they note that "Lego bricks . . . are in line with the cognitive characteristics of students and provide a good game-based learning tool for engineering education."[7] A quick and simple program that requires little to no planning or preparation after initial implementation, LEGO @ the Library (or whatever it may be locally titled), for many libraries, consists of rolling out large bins of LEGOs into their programming rooms, and then simply inviting children and families in to play, create, and coincidently, practice their engineering skills.

Building Your Collection

Before offering ways to mix up your regular LEGO pit programs by making them even more STEM skill stimulating, let's make sure to cover the basics. If your library has yet to try its own LEGO program, you might even benefit by simply starting to implement the basic plan discussed in the section above. But if you're looking to start or increase your LEGO collection, consider the following tips:

If you've got a budget to work with, LEGOs can likely be sourced from any of your local toy stores. If you have a finance department within your library, consider checking with it first to see if there is a particular supplier with which it might already have access to purchasing discounts. To build up a base, going for the larger sets of generic one-thousand-plus pieces is a good idea. You can supplement with specific themed sets, and even a set of building plates and sets of minifigures (LEGO people).

You might also receive community donations—lots of families like to give back to the library after their kids have grown up through your children's programs. Families might offer toys or LEGO collections that their children no longer care to play with—if it's acceptable within your library's policy, you could accept these LEGO donations in order to start or supplement your pre-established LEGO collection.

If you're finding it difficult to find the funds or donations to create your own branch LEGO set, consider a regional, bookable kit that could circulate to different branches within your library system whenever you plan a program. This might help pool together the funds to purchase it, or give you access to a different regional budget.

DUPLO

Don't forget to add some DUPLO blocks into your LEGO collection, so that preschoolers can take part in programs, too. Make sure to separate these out from the regular LEGO blocks when creating your storage system and program room setup—many tots at the DUPLO age should avoid handling those tiny LEGO pieces. Of course, preschoolers will likely be accompanied by their supervising adults, but it's best not to leave anything to chance. Think about setting out your DUPLO blocks on a soft and squishy blanket with maybe a few soft toys in the corner, away from the LEGO play proper, to encourage a younger play area.

Storage

If you're amassing a large amount of LEGOs, you'll need to think about how you want to store the collection. Rubbermaid bins will work—or whatever sort of bin your library uses in deliveries might, too. Make sure to use multiple bins to ensure they don't become too heavy to lift. If you've got extra accessible delivery bins lying around, you might not even have to spend any money on this part of the collection.

If you're creating a smaller collection, and have the budget, you could look for the adorable name-brand LEGO storage accessories like the giant hollow plastic bricks, or the zip-up brick pouches. Another option for small to medium collection storage is the LEGO storage mats, like the Lay-N-Go Large Activity Mat & Toy Organizer, which is a "5 foot diameter patent pending activity mat that converts into an easily transportable shoulder satchel, allowing for quick and effortless clean-up of small toy pieces. . . . Once playtime is over, the drawstring is pulled and the activity mat is converted back into a completely sealed, soft storage bag."[8] These can be purchased from Amazon, ThinkGeek .com, and even Pinterest has plenty of similar homemade versions or DIY patterns to make your own.

Separating Your LEGO Minifigures

Minifigures have a tendency of getting lost in the shuffle, and what's a super awesome rocket ship without Benny the Spaceman to fly it? In order to avoid the inevitable "Where are all the LEGO men?" question from every child that enters the room, it's best to house your minifigures in a separate container within your LEGO kit. Try doling them out from your collection one at a time to each child, or, if you really need to dump them all out onto the floor at once, make sure you have the children and families play "minifigure hunt" about ten minutes before cleanup time, so that everyone can help mine them out again to go in their special box. This will save you time in your cleanup process, while also adding a bit of fervor and fun to the program.

Speaking of dumping things out—consider how much LEGO product you have, and whether or not you want to set your program up with only a portion, or all of it out on the floor. If you're using the bin storage noted above, you might want to wait and see if you've got enough attendees to warrant dumping every piece of LEGO out onto your mats. If you've only got a couple of kids in the room, it likely doesn't make sense to dump five full Rubbermaid bins out on the floor. You might be better suited to let the kids pour things out as they see fit, in an attempt to cut down on cleanup time. Alternatively, you could again use them to help you tidy up near the end of the program by making a game out of it, or, if you've got your drawstring LEGO mats, you can just scoop it up and tighten the string!

Pump Up the STEM (Science, Technology, Art, Engineering, Math)

While LEGO pit programs can certainly help to promote and practice engineering skills, there are a number of ways to take your LEGO programs even further by incorporating a few extra activities to get the maximum STEM skill promotion out of this common library playtime. Considering the following:

Stop-Motion

Exciting for both children and adults alike, the free LEGO Movie Maker app allows people of all ages to make simple stop-motion movies using LEGOs or any other small toys that might strike your fancy. A great way to practice your technology skills, this project will require the use of a library iPad (or multiple, depending on how many simultaneous projects you want to stimulate). Kids can add and delete scenes, change the look with filters, or even add background soundtracks before emailing their completed videos to their families or uploading them to a library YouTube account.

The kicker in this project, is, of course, the iPad access, but you might be able to use any that are available for loans to the public in your branch, or perhaps suggest your library purchase a branch or regional programming iPad if you don't already have access to one otherwise.

Board Game Math

You can also incorporate some casual math skills with the Pinterest-popular LEGO tower Building Block Fun board game (link in the notes at the end of this chapter).[9] Children can roll a die, which lands them on a square that will ask them to add or subtract a certain number of pieces to their LEGO tower. The person who has the tallest tower at the end wins!

Lego Batman Chain Reactions

If you haven't already invested in a copy of the LEGO Chain Reactions kit (US$17 on Amazon), you definitely should! A collection of simple and complex machines using LEGO, cardstock ramps, tubing, and marbles, kids can create their own Rube Goldberg machines. Rube Goldberg, also an adjective meaning "accomplishing by complex means what seemingly could be done simply,"[10] by a series of domino effects, is both a popular assignment in first-year undergraduate engineering programs, as well as a fun and trendy activity for kids like those who play with the GoldieBlox invention kits. Remember "Mousetrap"? Where a ball falls on a thing, which pops another thing into the air, landing on something else, setting that off . . . with a bunch of chain reactions? You can use this kit to help kids make their own similar machine with your LEGO collections. Although the book only comes with one set of each cardstock piece, you could grab some further cardstock from your craft supplies closet and use them as a template to duplicate these pieces for group play.

And who doesn't love Batman? To add a pop culture twist to this STEM program, consider using your LEGO Batman minifigures into the mix and telling kids they're building machines to help LEGO Batman rescue Unikitty, or to help solve the latest crime with Wyldstyle.

Build the Library!

Challenge your budding engineers to build the library out of your LEGO collection. Have them work together in a group to re-create your branch or another local landmark. You can ask them to create their own blueprints, decide on the intended size, and brainstorm as to what pieces might work best for specific structures. You can later display their creation at your information desk or book display case!

LEGO Challenges

Trina Orchard, a customer service clerk in Children's Services at the Lethbridge Public Library in Alberta, has the perfect solution to kids who roll their eyes at tired LEGO programs, claiming they have "plenty of LEGOs at home": provide them with a specific challenge! Orchard suggests some of the following:

Incorporate specific challenges into your LEGO pit programs for an opportunity for kids to practice their scientific observation skills. Teams or individuals can also work to create their own LEGO balloon cars before racing them down a ramp. Encourage discussion on what they're seeing: Why do you think this car was faster? Why did that tower fall over so quickly? This gets them casually thinking about weight, aerodynamics, structure stability, and so forth. Once they think they've mastered the science, have them rebuild and retest.

Who can build the tallest tower in 10 minutes? 20 minutes?

Who can build the strongest bridge?

I've set two tables 1 foot apart. Build me a bridge to connect them.

How many geometric shapes can you create using Lego?

Tying a "zip-line" out of yarn or string to the wall then challenging participants to make an object to go down without falling off or stopping.[11]

Ottawa Public Library provides an ongoing passive LEGO challenge at one of its branches with a "retrofitted book drop box that now functions as a five-sided LEGO building platform," which allows children to think about not only building up, but building out, says Candice Blackwood, the Teen Services librarian at the Nepean Centrepointe Branch.[12]

DUPLO Printing

Go full STEAM ahead and incorporate those art skills! DUPLO blocks make great stampers—kids can flip them upside down, dip them on an ink pad or in some paint, and see what sort of beautiful pieces they can create on your paper stock! Will they create a creature, a nature scene, or maybe even a blueprint for a building they can build right afterward in the pit? Washable inks and paints are a must-have with children's programs, and as a bonus, you can clean your blocks and pop them back into the regular collection after you're finished with the masterpieces. You might even let the kids find their own favorite block from the pit to use for their artwork! You can also try incorporating any holidays or current library themes into this artwork by making LEGO print greeting cards.

LEGO Han Solo's Carbonite Cube

LEGO Star Wars fans will love this fun science activity. Originating on fun-a-day.com, a blog about child learning activities, this play on the baking-soda-and-vinegar experiment has kids rescuing LEGO Han Solo (or whichever minifigs you have access to) from blocks of "carbonite." Mixing three parts baking soda to one part water gives you the "carbonite" mixture to fill half of an ice cube tray before placing in the minifigs, and covering the rest of the tray/toys with the leftover mixture.[13] A few hours in the freezer will solidify the baking soda minifig cubes, so you can then pop them out for children to rescue their LEGO friends by covering them in vinegar. Try using pipettes for vinegar application to give kids another hands-on experience with lab tools.

LEGO Mindstorms

LEGO Education provides "solutions for teaching and hands-on learning" and aims to inspire a child's interest in STEM by targeting students in preschool, elementary, and middle school.[14] Solutions are based on the "LEGO system for playful learning combined with curriculum-relevant material and digital resources," which include educational

LEGO sets, curriculum and lesson plans, and more.[15] Schools and libraries all over the world have been using LEGO robotics in K–8 settings for an "authentic and kinesthetic way to improve children's problem-solving skills, reinforcing science applications and concepts, while building upon informal learning activities often done at home."[16] One of LEGO Education's most popular kits includes the LEGO Mindstorms EV3 robotics kit, which lets students "design and build programmable robots using motors, sensors, gears, wheels and axles, and other technical components."[17] Li et al. confirm that these robotics "build spatial visualization skills as students manipulate LEGO pieces to build the robot."[18] Other mathematics skills are also included, such as the "proportional reasoning as students calculate wheel rotation and approximate the distance the robot will travel once it is programmed."[19]

Although LEGO Education targets its product sales toward schools and teachers, anyone in the US can purchase from the site. Libraries outside of the US can still purchase LEGO Education equipment through an authorized local distributor—like Spectrum-Nasco.ca in Canada, or PhillipHarris.co.uk in the UK. Individual core sets will cost around US$400, but a small amount will still work well if attendees are grouped together in teams, and if the library program is kept to a small, registered number. Even one solo kit can be used with small focus groups or as a demonstration at a larger STEM-focused event.

Fidget Spinners, Squishy Toys, and Instagram Camp

Early 2017 saw the internet, and elementary-age students' world at large, taken over by the fidget spinner. As discussed in the second chapter of this book, pop culture fads can be a great way to draw in non-traditional library users to your library programs, STEM themed or otherwise. Although these items were originally marketed as a way to help relieve anxiety or to increase focus, they quickly became the go-to toy that every child had to have. They reached the height of mass popularity with fidget spinner demonstration and haul videos cropping up all over YouTube and Instagram, and the resulting early days of the 2017 trend saw retailers repeatedly selling out of their fidget spinner stock. If you worked with children in any capacity in 2017—public libraries or otherwise, it's likely that you heard several retailers remark how almost every student in their class had one (or how they were later banned by some teachers because they were too distracting in the classroom). Such widespread popularity is the perfect program topic to present to elementary-age students during your annual Summer Reading Club school visits—which inevitably, in 2017, was sure to lead to an entire classroom filled with cheers. While they took advantage of mainstream popular culture by trying to engage youth in general library programming, fidget spinners will also provide a great opportunity for STEM skill learning for some time to come, even a year later when your corner gas station is trying to pawn its overstock off on you for two bucks apiece. Kids practice engineering skills when creating their own, learn about physics with inertia, and can be encouraged to use scientific observation to consider why some spinners spin longer than others.

A similar yet somewhat less popular internet phenomenon of 2017 was the collection and assessment of squishy toys. These soft, foamy toys are often made to look like food items such as cake slices, bread loaves, or donuts. Countless videos have cropped up on YouTube and Instagram where kids and adults alike will show their squishy "hauls" or collections, or even assess the quality of different brands. Although squishy observation is likely to fall out of usefulness to programming quicker than the fidget spinner will, consider using this as an example of how to use future trendy pop culture items as inspiration for children's library programs incorporating scientific observation.

Fidget Spinner Program (Science, Technology, Art, Engineering)

In the early days of fidget mania, a DIY fidget spinner program at the library was, first and foremost, a way for kids to get their own without paying the $30 price point, or having to source a $5 version from the internet. While they're now widely and cheaply available at every local corner store, the DIY fidget spinner activity still provides for a lot of fun, creativity, and practicing of STEM skills.

Make Your Own

First things first—you'll want to remind your child attendees that the quality of their handmade fidget spinner will most likely be lesser than the manufactured versions. Try asking them why they think that is—does it have anything to do with the materials used? How so?

You can find a plethora of DIY fidget spinner videos on the internet, but there are three main types, which I've listed here in order of price point from low to high:

Cardboard Spinners

You'll need the following easily obtainable items:

- Cardboard
- Hot glue and glue gun
- Toothpicks
- Cardstock / construction paper / stickers / paint for decorations
- Pennies

Fortunately, most of these items will usually be found in your library craft supplies, or can be collected as donated recycling items from your home or other library staff. Check out Red Ted Art's "Easy Fidget Spinner WITHOUT Bearings TEMPLATE" on YouTube for instructions on how to construct these simple fidget spinners.[20] Check out the links below the video for a free template, too.

If you have access to teen volunteers, you might want to think about asking them to drop by for this program—the cutting of the sharp toothpicks and using of hot glue requires adult or older supervision for younger children, but encouraging parents to stay in the room can work too if you've got a particularly large crowd.

LEGO Spinners

There are plenty of Pinterest posts and YouTube DIY videos on how to make your own fidget spinners out of LEGO pieces. As you can imagine, this option would be more costly than using recycled bits and craft items from your supplies cupboard. Instead of using your budget to buy individual LEGO pieces for every child to take a spinner home, you could

Figure 5.10. Cardboard fidget spinner

alternatively use your now-established programming LEGO collection (from the useful information above) to mine for the necessary pieces, which kids can return to you at the end of the program. You could even build this into your LEGO program proper!

Check out IncredibleScience's video for step-by-step instructions on making a LEGO fidget spinner.[21]

3D Printouts

You can also try printing one of the many fidget spinner designs from Thingiverse.com[22] if you have access to a 3D printer, which would of course also require your desired printer filament, along with store-purchased bearings, and the time needed to print each spinner piece.

If you're unable to spend the couple of dollars for every set of bearings needed, you could also try Thingiverse user kroyster's "Bearing-to-HexNut Adapter" design that allows you to use hex nuts instead—which usually cost about thirty cents at your local hardware store.[23]

The time and commitment level of 3D printer fidget spinner projects likely lend better to smaller, older children / teen programs, makerspace projects, or perhaps class demo and instructions, as opposed to programs where you're aiming to provide large quantities of takeaways to attendees.

Safety First

With increased fidget spinner exposure and hype, June 2017 also saw the rise of newspaper articles citing the choking hazard of fidget spinners, in both brand-name and knockoff versions that had parts that "could choke children under three if they broke off."[24] While any preschooler at a library program is obviously there with a supervising adult, it seems important to make a quick note at the start of your program about the importance of never, ever putting creations or toys in your mouth, for any reason. Many children and families will have likely heard the news story about the ten-year-old girl from Texas who choked on a bearing when she put the fidget spinner in her mouth to clean it off, an article that circulated like wildfire on social media in late spring 2017.[25]

When introducing the topic and projects, you'll likely also end up discussing the fidget spinner's original intended purposes of managing anxiety and stress and helping with focus. Many families with children on the autism spectrum or children with ADHD have reported their therapeutic benefits, but it might also be wise to take that moment to encourage children in the room to try and talk to an adult they trust, like a parent, teacher, or counselor, if they're having stressful or anxious feelings too.

Further Activities

Beyond using their engineering skills to construct their own spinners, there a couple of other activities children can partake in during a fidget spinner program. Try a spin-off challenge: kids can bring in their store-bought fidget spinners to see whose spins the longest. Engage them in a discussion of scientific observation and ask them to hypothesize:

Why does one spin longer than the others?
Is there a difference between metal bearings versus plastic?
What about the spinner body materials?
Shape of the arms?
Strength of the person spinning it?
Do both sides work best?
How do the store-bought spinners compare to the DIY versions?
Look at the spin-off through a smartphone camera—what happens? Why?

For extra fun, have kids work together in groups to see how many spinners they can stack and spin in a tower. Watch as they learn or hypothesize which spinners should go on top or bottom according to weight and size. You can also hold a trick talent show, where kids can show off their skills in balancing fidget spinners on the tips of their fingers, tops of their hats, and even noses.

Squishy Science Lab (Science, Math)

For this program, you'll need to buy a variety of different squishies, which can be found in a variety of different places, such as Amazon, SillySquishies.com, or even the brick-and-mortar Showcase stores in Canada. You can buy a variety of different designs from a particular brand (breads, pandas, cakes), or you might decide to buy all of the different dessert or cake squishies you can find.

The idea here is for children to decide, as a group, upon how they wish to measure the squishies in order to assign one as the winner. See what they come up with on their own, but think about suggesting the following assessments if they haven't come up with the ideas themselves:

Figure 5.11. Fidget spinner spin-off

- Softness (time to rise)
- Price comparison (Save this info to provide when requested)
- Portability (length/width)
- How realistic? (Assess paint job, how likely you are to confuse with real food, etc.)
- Assess packaging (Open criteria: How wasteful? How cute? Reusable?)
- Accessibility (Where did it come from: local store, or shipped from the internet—in two days, or two weeks?)

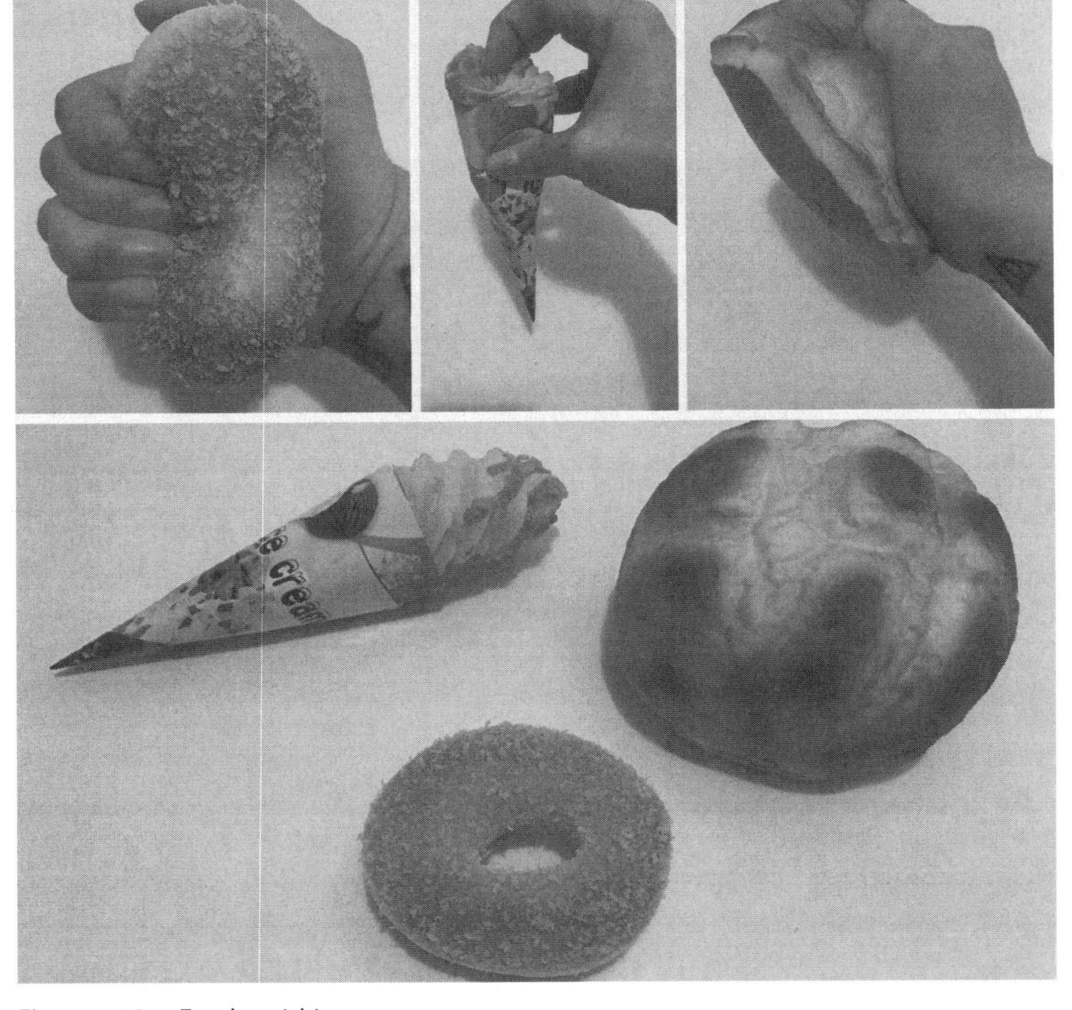

Figure 5.12. Food squishies

You'll need to provide paper, pencils, and some basic measurement tools such as rulers, stopwatches, calculators, and so forth. You might need to have a discussion on weight of the criteria—are all assessment categories weighted equally? Or do aesthetics matter more than accessibility?

Instagram Camp (Science, Technology, Art, Engineering)

Both squishies and fidget spinners were all over social media in 2017. Children and teens flocked to YouTube and Instagram to experience these internet phenomena, including another mega internet trend that will be further explored in chapter 6—slime! While teens took to slime social media like crazy in 2017, the process of making slime will also likely be very appealing and applicable for your ages eight and older crowd too.

Using the program ideas for the three trends noted above (or other future pop culture fads or internet challenges), try creating an Instagram or other social media platform camp (YouTube, etc.) depending on what the kids in your community seem into.

Gathering your library iPads (singular, or multiple, if you have them available), invite children to come in and perform all three trendy STEM activities in one day- or afternoon-long camp. You'll want to start the day off with talking about internet safety, and some best practice tips when using the internet and social media. Then, have kids film the process, demos, and assessments of each of the squishy, slime, and fidget spinner projects and observations, using the provided iPads.

For safety and privacy purposes, you should decide in advance whether you will allow children's faces to be on film, where the completed videos will be uploaded, and what your media consent form might look like. Regardless of whether you're using visible faces, a media consent form is a wise idea when having children create any social media content at your library.

While this type of program allows children to practice their technology skills and learn about social media safety practices, it can also provide them with access and the outlet for content sharing that might not otherwise be available to them. Children can come with the log-ins to their own social media accounts (if they have them), or, for those who don't, think about uploading the videos to a special library- or program-made social media account: "Townville Library Instagram Camp" or "Townville Library," or similar. If your library has a communications or marketing team, you might want to make sure that this falls within their policies of acceptable social media creation. If it doesn't, perhaps they can help you out by uploading a few key videos to the official library social media accounts instead. Children can decide what sorts of hashtags to use on their posts, and since the accounts are intended to be public, they can take the information home to later observe view counts and comments (which, since public, should ideally be monitored by library staff in order to ensure deletion of any inappropriate messages). Both the opportunity for inappropriate comments and watching view counts could also promote further discussion about social media safety—do view counts really matter, or is it about the creation process and having fun? Why is it important not to release personal information over the internet, and to stay anonymous? And so on.

Circus Bridges (Engineering, Math)

Heather Love Beverley provides a recent example of a successful school-age STEM program from the Cook Memorial Public Library District, called "Circus Bridges." Based on the book *Twenty-One Elephants and Still Standing* by April Jones Prince, and inspired by a blog post from *Playground Parkbench*, this program for children in grades 1–2 focused primarily on engineering and math concepts.

Programmers began by reading the book and talking about how much elephants weighed, and calculated how many tons the Brooklyn Bridge would have held when twenty-one elephants traveled across it. The group then watched a short video that explained how bridges worked and the various shapes that bridges can take, followed up with a brief discussion on bridge building. After that, children worked in groups of three and four to create bridges out of Popsicle sticks and cups; the challenge was that they needed to be constructed to be able to hold all twenty-one toy animals.

Additional challenges were also given, such as building double-decker bridges to hold the animals or making segments of a bridge that held three animals or five animals at a time. During the last ten minutes of the program, children also designed paper mosaic bridges as a craft. Children clearly demonstrated having a good time, particularly when they each eagerly showed their parents their various bridges at the end of the program.[26]

Key Points

Squishy Circuits and Makey Makeys provide for almost limitless reincorporation into programs again and again without the risk of getting stale, as long as libraries make sure to keep changing their themes to include popular culture or holidays.

LEGO @ the Library programs are a classic, time-honored children's event that helps provide the basics of early hands-on engineering design skills, but even if these are falling out of fashion, libraries can still use a variety of different ways to shakes things up and add more STEM skills, such as stop-motion, block art printing, and LEGO challenges.

Free Comic Book Day @ the Library can not only highlight a branch's graphic novel collection while bringing new users into the library, the library can also use this annual celebration to incorporate STEM skills programming through cosplay creations and contests and green screen photo booth technology.

Libraries can look to social media and popular fad toys and trends to develop high-interest STEM programs; examples of these for 2017 were fidget spinners, squishies, and Instagram.

Notes

1. Royal Academy of Engineering, *The UK STEM Education Landscape*, May 2016, accessed December 10, 2017, https://www.raeng.org.uk/publications/reports/uk-stem-education-landscape.
2. Jennifer Evans in discussion with the author, December 2017.
3. Jennifer Evans in discussion with the author, December 2017.
4. "Star Wars Day 2014—MaKey MaKey Version," lucybarrow, accessed December 1, 2017, https://scratch.mit.edu/projects/19662631.
5. Yanyan Li, Zhinan Huang, Menglu Jiang, and Chang Ting-Wen, "The Effect on Pupils' Science Performance and Problem-Solving Ability through Lego: An Engineering Design-Based Modeling Approach," *Journal of Educational Technology & Society* 19, no. 3 (2016): 143.
6. Li et al., "Effect on Pupils' Science Performance," 143.
7. Li et al., "Effect on Pupils' Science Performance," 143.
8. "Building Block Fun," Teach with Laughter, February 7, 2014, accessed December 1, 2017, http://teachwithlaughter.blogspot.ca/2014/02/building-block-fun.html.
9. "Lay-N-Go—Activity Mat and Storage Bag," The Green Head, December 23, 2014, accessed December 11, 2017, https://www.thegreenhead.com/2012/04/lay-n-go-activity-mat-storage-bag.php.
10. *Merriam-Webster*, s.v. "Rube Goldberg," accessed December 11, 2017, https://www.merriam-webster.com/dictionary/Rube%20Goldberg.
11. Trina Orchard in discussion with the author, November 2017.
12. Candice Blackwood in discussion with the author, November 2017.
13. "This Is Such an Awesome Star Wars LEGO Science Idea!" Fun-A-Day! April 26, 2017, accessed December 11, 2017, https://fun-a-day.com/star-wars-lego-science/.
14. "LEGO Education," LEGO Education, accessed December 11, 2017, https://education.lego.com/en-us.
15. "LEGO Education."

16. Tanja Karp and Patricia Maloney, "Exciting Young Students in Grades K–8 about STEM through an Afterschool Robotics Challenge," *American Journal of Engineering Education* 4, no. 1 (2013): 54.

17. David C. Moores, "We're All About Educational Supplies," SPECTRUM Nasco, accessed December 11, 2017, https://spectrum-nasco.ca/catalogpc.htm?Category=ES—LEGO EDUCATION.

18. Li et al., "Effect on Pupils' Science Performance," 156.

19. Michael Grubbs, "Robotics Intrigue Middle School Students and Build STEM Skills," *Technology and Engineering Teacher* 72, no. 6 (2013): 12.

20. Red Ted Art, "Easy Fidget Spinner WITHOUT Bearings TEMPLATE—How to Make a Tri Fidget Spinner DIY," YouTube video, 14:18, May 7, 2017, accessed December 11, 2017, https://www.youtube.com/watch?v=0Lthvm6yOvY.

21. IncredibleScience, "7 DIY LEGO Hand Spinner Fidget Toys! How to Make Spinners!" YouTube video, 10:34, April 17, 2017, accessed December 11, 2017, https://www.youtube.com/watch?v=OhJL8dtcLhk.

22. "Fidget: A Collection by glitchpudding," Thingiverse, last updated August 29, 2017, accessed December 11, 2017, https://www.thingiverse.com/glitchpudding/collections/fidget/page:1.

23. "Bearing-to-HexNut Adapter by kroyster," Thingiverse, January 17, 2017, accessed December 11, 2017, https://www.thingiverse.com/thing:2044157.

24. Diana Hembree, "Fidget Spinner Choking Hazard Alarms Parents, but Fire Hazards Top Recall List," *Forbes*, July 21, 2017, accessed December 11, 2017, https://www.forbes.com/sites/dianahembree/2017/06/01/fidget-spinner-choking-hazard-alarms-parents-but-fire-and-shock-risks-top-this-months-recall-list/#5a1e48a317c7.

25. Sarah Schreiber, "Mom Warns Parents after Her Daughter Reportedly Choked on a Fidget Spinner," *Good Housekeeping*, June 22, 2017, accessed December 11, 2017, http://www.goodhousekeeping.com/life/parenting/news/a44244/mom-warns-fidget-spinner-choking-hazard/.

26. Heather Love Beverley in discussion with the author, November 2017.

CHAPTER 6

Teen STEM Programming

IN THIS CHAPTER

- ▷ Button making
- ▷ Slime programs
- ▷ Musical.ly programs
- ▷ Food technology programs
- ▷ Anime Clubs and STEM programs
- ▷ Harry Potter LED wands
- ▷ Using STEM skills through youth volunteer engagement

ACCORDING TO THE Young Adult Library Services Association (YALSA), libraries are "uniquely positioned to support teen acquisition of STEM related skills" due to their nature as hubs for information, community resources, education, and programming.[1] Dawn States, teen programming coordinator from Martin Library in York, Pennsylvania, agrees, arguing that it is important to incorporate STEM subjects into library programs while also making them appealing for young adults who are "entering a highly STEM-driven workforce" with a "future that will be largely STEM based, even if they do not enter into a directly STEM-related field."[2] These statements certainly reflect the statistics and research shown in the first chapter of this book, which explained the growing necessity for skilled applicants in the large number of future STEM-based career openings. Shannon Peterson, the Youth Services manager for Kitsap Regional Library, explained in a 2016 YALSA interview that due to the drastic change in the career and information landscape over the past ten years, "teens inherently need the 21st century skill sets that a STEM education can provide" by learning to "collaborate, to adapt, to constantly use critical thinking skills, to problem solve, [and] to be able to translate information across content areas."[3] Peterson recommends being "intentional" about the ways in which libraries support these skills, making sure to "leverage community networks and expertise, while allowing "the opportunity for teens to have voice in the content and process."[4]

As the population between children and adults, teens are that perfect middle ground for a variety of STEM programming options; libraries can scale their teen STEM programs as casual or as in depth as they'd like. There might be teens who are interested in learning how to code through a structured, formal course provided by a local partner at a branch, or, library staff might simply slide some technology skills into a program that otherwise seems to have been created purely for entertainment value.

There will also likely be a wide variety of interests and levels of dedication within any given teen community. This is a perfect reminder for libraries to make sure they're making relationships with these youth. Having an open line of trust and communication with the teen community will allow youth to feel comfortable enough to tell library staff what it is they want or need from any STEM program. Creating program rosters based upon this feedback will help to ensure that the libraries, programs, events, and series will be well received and sustainable.

Candice Blackwood, the Teen Services librarian at the Nepean Centrepointe Branch of Ottawa Public Library, recommends adding STEM elements into existing programs that already have an audience, if libraries are having trouble getting teens to attend STEM-based programs.[5]

Button Making (Technology, Art)

The button maker is a quick and easy machine that can likely be found in many a library makerspace. Teens can learn to use this quick and simple technology as an additional activity in a themed program. They can design and make their own buttons based on Star Wars, *Riverdale*, Dr. Who, *Hamilton*, or whatever they're into!

EQUIPMENT AND SUPPLIES

Tecre 125 (1¼") round button making machine ($250, Tecre.com):

While this might sound expensive, this little machine really is quite adaptable. It can be used in programs for all ages, themes, and levels of skill. Consider purchasing one regionally and loaning in between branches to save money!

The machine might look a little confusing when it first arrives, but it won't take long to learn the ins and outs. Try watching the official how-to video on YouTube before you start. If you put the button pieces in upside down on the wrong die, it can jam the machine, which requires physical dismantling in order to fix it (and even then, if this isn't done by a professional, you can mess up the tension of the machine, causing a frustrating number of defective buttons).

1¼" Button Pieces (Price Varies by Quantity):

The Tecre.com website sells the 1¼" round button complete set at 1,000 pinback pieces for $48. But, if you're looking for a smaller quantity, you can also get a 100-count pinback.

Everything for Pinback Buttons:

If you're looking to save a few dollars, these are $23 over at PeoplePowerPress.net, and come in 100-count pieces.

Everything for Lock Pin Buttons:

For $16 these lock pin and pinback have the same function—but the difference is that the lock pin version, which is cheaper, has you inserting the sharp pin on your own (as opposed to pinback, where the sharp pin is already attached to the back piece).

Both sites sell other kits to use with your 1¼" button machine—magnets, zipper pulls, and even hair ties! Having a variety of project options could increase the learning of your button-making activity—have teens watch the how-to videos and make one of each different project based on their own designs.

(Optional) Model 1629, 1¼" Round Graphic Punch ($159):

This circle punch is a professional piece of equipment that allows manufacturers to quickly and accurately cut out their 1¼" circle images in large quantities. If you've got some extra money to spend and would like to give your community another tool for them to experiment with, this could be a fun addition. Regular scissors, which are obviously already kicking around your branch, however, will also do just fine if you don't want to shell out that kind of money.

Selecting Images

For images, you'll want to start with a 1¼" circle template (easily found online). All you need to do is paste it into Microsoft Publisher and insert a circle shape on top of each of the templated button outlines. You'll then want to fill the circle with your chosen digital image. Make sure the picture stretches just past the dotted line—this is where the paper wraps around the back of the button. If you don't, and the image shifts even in the slightest, you'll have an ugly dotted line or white space on the side of your button. Ideally you won't see anything past the dotted line, but it's nice to have a buffer just in case.

As with any image that you're using, make sure that you have the copyright for it. If you have access to a library marketing and communications department, you can ask them to create an image for you, or you can find something through the Creative Commons search on Flickr, Pixabay, or Google Images.

Teen Art

You can also amp up the creativity in this project by having the teens design their own buttons—through either digital image creation using your library computers and software (or whatever they might bring in from home), or by hand, directly onto a printed button blank. This project too, just like the screen printing activity in chapter 8, can provide teens with an opportunity to create and showcase their art through the use of library tools and technology. You might even inspire a few teens to create their own local business! Mini buttons are all the rage in vendor rooms at local comic and science fiction conventions. Teaching them this new skill could motivate them to go out and obtain their own machines.

Instagram Slime Shoots (Science, Technology)

The year 2017 wasn't only the year of the fidget spinner—it was also the year of SLIME! Kids, teens, and the internet at large were inundated with slime recipes, pictures, and especially videos, all capturing this oddly satisfying squishy goo. YouTubers like Karina Garcia (the internet "slime queen") saw their rise to fame because of the slime movement—in late 2017 her YouTube channel had more than 6.7 million subscribers to her videos on slime recipes, reviews, and challenges. She even authored a popular DIY slime book (more on that below).

The #SLIME hashtag on social media continues to expand its result lists, even today—late 2017 saw Instagram retrieving more than 5.5 million resulting pictures and videos. Be careful when setting out to do this kind of program research, though—you might find yourself stuck in an internet slime hole—watching squishy, stretchy, swirling goo being pulled, poked, and pressed for hours on end. It's weirdly hypnotic! But luckily, it also provides great inspiration for some creative, fun, and on-trend chemistry programs.

Homemade slime recipes have been around for some time—babysitting courses in the late 1990s used to teach teens how to make gak or oobleck (with cornstarch, water, and food coloring) in order to entertain younger children. While slime is often thought of as a creative, fun activity, Brian Rohrig also reminded educators in 2004 that it can "provide a platform for learning many important chemical principles."[6] Rohrig's "The Science of Slime" article for *Chem Matters* is a great read if you're looking to highlight the more explicitly educational elements of slime science—it touches on viscosity, polymers, and Newtonian fluids—in layman's terms that could be easily adapted even by library staff who are without a science background.

Borax

Slime programs might indeed come with controversy, however. Traditionally, the quickest and surest way to make slime involves the use of borax—a common household cleaning product. Slime, gak, and flubber recipes have called upon this product for decades, but in July 2016, Health Canada released an information update advising "Canadians to avoid using boric acid for arts and crafts projects, such as homemade slime, or modelling clay" due to the "potential to cause developmental and reproductive health effects."[7]

In March 2017, *Good Housekeeping* online released an article titled "Parents Everywhere Are Worried about DIY Slime after Multiple Kids Are Burned," but it cited varying opinions on the safety of borax usage in DIY slime. An NYU pediatrician was quoted as recommending children and families to stay away from the substance altogether, given that touching borax multiple times "can cause burns."[8] The chair of the American Academy of Pediatrics' Council on Injury, Violence and Poison Prevention has a differing view: he claims borax is only a "mild irritant" that is "generally safe," and he has even used it for slime with his own children.[9]

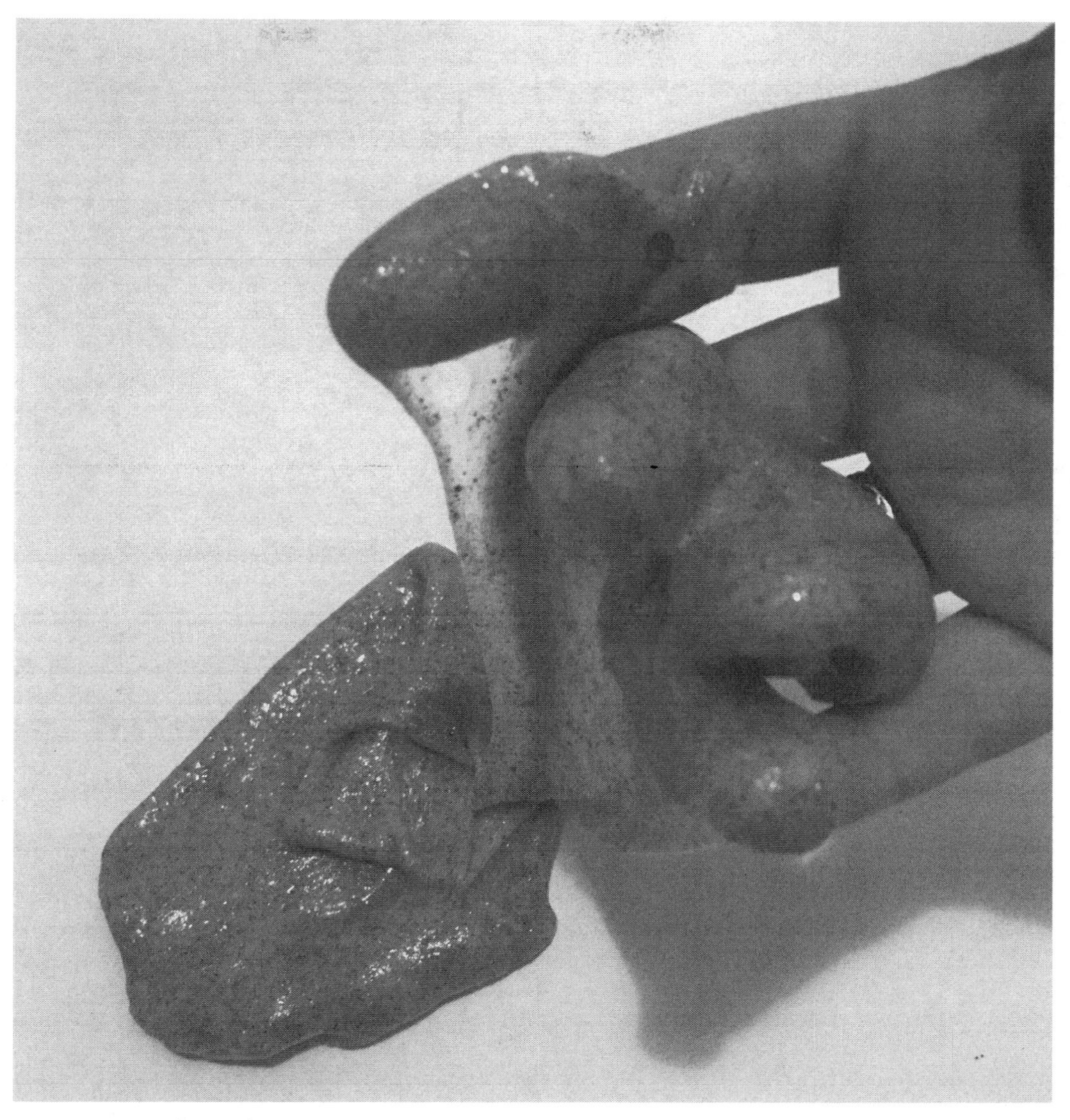

Figure 6.1. Glitter slime

Whether your library has subsequently implemented policies demanding the removal of borax or boric acid in your programs or branches, you should still be able to find a suitable slime recipe in the variety of sources below. The recent controversy surrounding borax use has certainly cultivated a large borax-free slime recipe craze on the internet—but it's important to do your research. Plenty of borax alternatives often still have a high content of boric acid—prime examples include liquid starch and laundry detergent, for example.

Even if you're avoiding borax, or ingredients containing high levels of boric acid in your slime programs, the topic can still motivate some interesting and educational conversation to have with the children, teens, and family attendees:

- Why does borax work best?
- Why isn't it safe?
- Why do these other activators work too; what is the active ingredient?
- What are some proper safety techniques?
- What are some safe alternatives?

Figure 6.2. It's slime time!

You will find the standard borax-inclusive DIY slime recipe below. If you choose to go this route, make sure to check that you're not breaking library policy by using the ingredient, and prepare yourself to have a serious discussion with all attendees about the following safety precautions (which should be applicable in program, but also at any future at-home activities). Most of these safety measures are also generally applicable to any slime recipe.

Slime Safety

Like with most chemistry experiments, adult supervision is recommended. Remind teens to check with their parent or guardian to make sure the adult is okay with their use of borax or boric acid. Advise younger children to make sure the adult is present during the slime-making process. Slime is not an appropriate activity for children under the age of three.

If you're using borax in your library slime program—be prepared with info sheets for adults and families, including all ingredients to be used in the program in addition to the safety tips below. These sheets would also be handy to have at your information desk during the program promotional period—you're likely to get questions from adults about whether borax will be used in your upcoming program.

- Never, ever, put slime in your mouth.
- Don't eat *while* making the slime, either.
- Borax powder should be handled by an adult, and properly diluted in the specified amount of water.
- Wear protective gloves when making and handling slime made with borax.
- Borax solution should not be made in the kitchen or near any food preparation areas.
- Make sure to wash hands thoroughly before and after playing with any slime.
- If you're planning on keeping your slime, make sure to store it in an airtight container, in a cool environment (for a couple of weeks, at most). If the slime starts to smell, change color, or grow mold, dispose of it immediately.
- Make sure to disinfect any containers, surfaces, or tools after they are used with slime.

Standard Borax Slime

Ingredients:

- School glue (clear or white, depending upon your desired opacity)
- Water
- Food coloring
- Borax powder
- Extras: glitters, sequins, and so forth

Instructions:

1. Mix 4 ounces glue with 4 ounces warm water in a bowl.
2. Add in a couple of drops of desired food coloring.
3. Make the borax solution by adding 1 teaspoon borax powder to ½ cup water.
4. Slowly pour the borax solution into your glue mixture.
5. Stir until it all comes together—you may have some leftover borax solution in the bottom of the bowl.
6. It may look stringy, or overly gooey at this point, but this is where you need to knead it together with your hands for a few minutes.
7. You can now start to add in any of your extras—glitters, sequins, etc.—and start to play!

Pro Slime Tip: Don't sweat the measurements of ingredients! Slime making is often hit or miss, but that's a lot of the fun. It's a great use of scientific observation skills to talk about why each slime turns out differently, according to which ingredient you may have tweaked.

Elmer's Glue Slime

The following is currently the most widely used safer alternative slime recipe, and can be found on the Elmer's glue website. Elmer's promotes newly developed slime recipes that are "safe to make at home" because they contain common household ingredients such as baking soda as well as contact lens solution—which contains "only trace amounts of boric acid . . . can be purchased over the counter and is regulated by the FDA."[10]

Ingredients:

- Elmer's glue (clear, glitter, or white, depending upon your desired effect)
- Baking soda
- Food coloring
- Contact lens solution
- Extras: glitters, sequins, and so forth

Figure 6.3. Slime supplies with borax

Figure 6.4. Slime supplies: borax-free

Instructions:

1. Mix 4 ounces glue with ½ tablespoon baking soda in a bowl. Stir thoroughly.
2. Add in a couple of drops of desired food coloring.
3. Add 1 tablespoon contact lens solution into your glue mixture.
4. Stir until it all comes together.
5. It may look overly gooey at this point, but this is where you need to knead it together with your hands for a few minutes.
6. If it's still sticky after this, add an additional ¼ tablespoon contact lens solution.
7. You can now start to add in any of your extras—glitters, sequins, etc.—and start to play!

Pro Slime Tip: Buy your glue in bulk! Elmer's glue sells by the gallon!

Pre-made Slime

If you've got a smaller, registered group (or perhaps, a larger budget) you can also go for the option of pre-made slime bottles, which can be purchased in most party-favor aisles of places like the Dollar Store (about $3 for six) or Party City ($10 for twelve)—that is, when they're not sold out. Although you lose the hands-on chemistry portion of the activity, you could still watch slime videos and discuss different slime recipes and safety techniques, in addition to adding the slime fixin's to a couple of bottles of pre-made slime, and also making the videos discussed in the program plan below.

> Pro Slime Tip: Finding pre-made slime online: Make sure to use a variety of different search terms—putty, goop, gak, flubber, goo, and so forth. Party City was seemingly sold out of slime until we used the word "putty" in the search field—an in-store inspection confirmed it was indeed up to "slime" standards, and ripe for the inclusion of glitter, confetti, and Styrofoam balls!

Oobleck

While teens will quickly remind you that oobleck and slime are very different things, this runny goo still provides the opportunity for satisfying play, and can be heaped with color, glitter, and/or crunchy bits. As a non-Newtonian liquid, it can still provide a hands-on learning experience for children, as it acts like a solid as well as a liquid depending upon its manual manipulation.

Oobleck is a safer, easier recipe than any of the slime or slime alternatives, but be warned—it's a fair bit messier! Oobleck looks like a liquid—but when pressure is applied to the substance (with the squish of a hand, let's say) it feels like a solid. The recipe is simple:

Ingredients:

- Cornstarch
- Water
- Food coloring
- Extras: glitters, sequins, and so forth

Instructions:

1. In a bowl, mix two parts cornstarch to one part water.
2. Add in a couple of drops desired food coloring.
3. Stir until it all comes together.
4. You can now start to add in any of your extras—glitters, sequins, etc.—and start to play!

> Pro Slime Tip: Have ziplock bags ready so the oobleck can be taken home. If it's squeezed from the outside of the bag, you can still crumple it into a ball, let go, and see it ooze back into a liquid. This should also help avoid a future mess in their own homes—although, let's be honest. Getting messy is often the best part, right?

Slime Fixin's

While slime is both a great opportunity to talk about chemistry and a mesmerizing tactile project, it also provides some great opportunity as a creative outlet through customization.

Kids and teens can dress up their slime with a variety of different ingredients. When stocking up on the items below, don't forget to think about shape and color stories that might help to bring out any holiday or pop culture themes in your potential slime programs.

- Food coloring
- Shaving cream (for fluffy slime)
- Glitter (both chunky and micro)
- Pearl pigments
- Styrofoam balls (for crunchy slime)
- Glass beads (for fishbowl slime)
- Essential oils (for scented slime—double-check your library's scent policy first)
- Orbeez
- Mini erasers
- Confetti (plastic, not paper)
- Sequins

Slime Program Planning

Registration

If slime continues to be as on trend as it was in 2017, you'll definitely want to make sure to have a registration list for this program. This will also be a wise choice given that you're using consumable products. Having a maximum number of attendees will allow you to

Figure 6.5. DIY slime bar with all the fixin's!

more accurately estimate the necessary quantity of each ingredient so that you don't run out. Having a registration process should also allow you to field any questions about the ingredients—and to assure any concerned parents or guardians, whether it be a borax-free program, or one with strict safety procedures.

Portion Cups

If your registration count is likely to be high, you'll want access to plenty of disposable cups. Bulk purchases of portion cups, paper ramekins, or condiment cups (one to two ounces) work well for on-site mixing, but if you're hoping to allow your attendees to take their slime home, plastic portion cups (one to two ounces) with matching tops are your best bet, since you can use them both for the mixing process as well as the transport home. You can usually find both plastic and paper portion cups in places like Party City, Costco, or Sam's Club. Don't forget that the plastic lids are often sold separately!

If you don't have access to plastic portion cups (with tops), you could also make paper Dixie cups work for the mixing portion, and have attendees transport the slime back home in a sealable ziplock bag.

Slime Portions

Two-ounce portions are an ideal approximate size if you're expecting quite a large program (say, fifty-plus attendees). However, if you have a larger budget, or if you're expecting a smaller group of attendees, you could up your portion size or, to enhance creativity, allow each person to make a couple of different portions, each with different fixin's.

DIY Slime Bar: With All the Fixin's!

Given that #SLIME is so popular on social media, your attendees might want to talk about their own slime experiences—if you bring out a laptop and projector, teens can suggest their favorite kinds of slime (fluffy, crunchy, glitter, butter, etc.), or even their favorite

Figure 6.6. Portion cups laid out for a Halloween slime program

slime videos. Fall deep into the Instagram slime hole yourself, and have a few popular videos ready to play for inspiration prior to your slime-making activity.

Each table in your room can be set up with pre-portioned ingredients, enough for your attendance count (don't forget about tablecloths or recycled newspaper barriers—the cleanup process can be quite a chore!). After your slime video viewing and a discussion on safety procedures, teens can then get to work on creating their own slime concoctions by incorporating different items from your fixin's bar (a table set up with all your glitter, food coloring, Styrofoam balls, and any other bits and bobs you think they might want to add in). Try incorporating your slime science learning bits as casual questions or interesting factoids as you walk around the room, observing the slime-making process. This will make the program feel as least school-like as possible.

What's in a Name?

Depending upon your available ingredients, teens can choose to make a variety of different slime recipes or looks, and along with that comes the process of naming the slime! Plenty of slime Instagram accounts will have weekly contests where they ask their followers to name their newly created slime. Perhaps your blue slime with fishbowl stones and greenish gold glitter will end up as a "mermaid's dream"! Once everyone has created their slime, give interested attendees a chance to present their slime name and its inspiration. It's great fun!

Insta-slime

Social media documentation will allow you to incorporate technology skills into your slime programs. Bring out your iPad(s) and have teens film close-up clips from both the DIY slime-making process as well as their final gooey products. Once the slime is ready, there are a variety of fun things you can film—for example, the sound it makes when you poke it repeatedly, or the way it stretches and swirls like a soft serve ice cream cone. You can try cutting it with scissors, or smushing it into cookie cutters. Other popular activities include the slime smoothie and slime pressing.

For the slime smoothie, creators simply film an empty clear bin as it is filled with multiple samples of different kinds of slimes, and the resulting mixing process and outcome. This could lend well to a large group library program—if everyone makes two different slimes (one to take home, and one to add to the smoothie), you could get a great variety of smoothie ingredients! Smoothie of course is just a fun name for a giant concoction—no one intends to ingest anything in this activity!

Slime pressing requires some sort of mesh wire—like a cheap badminton racquet or potato masher, which is pressed down into a flat, wide pile of slime. When the racquet is pulled upward, the slime sticks to the mesh, stretching it out into fascinatingly long, square columns. If you then slowly bring the racquet down to the pile again, a large quantity of air bubbles form, which you can then film as you squish them with your hand, making a satisfying crunchy popping sound. Have teens use a variety of different pressing tools to see which works best—do different mesh shapes make different sounds? Have them hypothesize where the crunchy sound comes from.

Once you have a variety of different pictures and video clips, there are a variety of things that you can do with them. Teens can log into their own social media account to post the content from there. If you're incorporating personal social media into the program this way, you might want to think of a collective hashtag that everyone uses—like #LibrarySlime or #YourBranchNameSlime, for example.

If you have access to library social media accounts, you could also post a select few videos on there—be sure to get any necessary required media consent forms, or keep any faces/voices out of the clips. This should be easy, though, as you'll see when doing some slime video research—most shots are very close-up, showing only hands and the slime itself, with isolated audio to really hear those gooey slime sounds.

If you've got a bit more time on your hands, you might even be able to have teens use the iMovie app to make one larger video, incorporating clips of multiple different slimes, allowing them to practice their video editing skills.

Pro Slime Tip: Not an expert at slime making? Don't worry! STEM programs are about experimentation and the learning process—try different quantities and mixings with your teens and work together to see what works best for the perfect slime. If they're slime fanatics, they'll probably come in with more knowledge than you, anyhow—sit back and let *them* teach *you*.

Slime Collection

Library staff have long used their programs as an additional way to promote their collection by incorporating a display of books that are topical to an event's theme. Checking out one of these displayed materials is also an opportunity for teens and families to continue their learning and experimentation from home after the event. Below is a quick list that you might find useful for your own slime program research, or even just as a popular, trendy addition to your juvenile or YA non-fiction collection.

- DK. *The Slime Book*. New York: DK, 2017.
- Garcia, Karina. *Karina Garcia's DIY Slime*. New York: Sizzle, 2017.
- Jagan, Alyssa. *Ultimate Slime*. Beverly, MA: Quarry, 2017.
- Shores, Lori. *How to Make Slime*. Mankato, MN: Capstone, 2011.
- Wright, Natalie. *Slime 101: How to Make Stretchy, Fluffy, Glittery & Colorful Slime!* Mineola, NY: Dover, 2017.
- Zhang, Selina. *Slime Workshop: 20 Borax-Free Recipes for DIY Slime*. New York: Lark Books, 2017.

Musical.ly Challenges (Technology)

Musical.ly describes itself as an "entertainment social network for creating, sharing, and discovering short videos."[11] This popular social media app allows its two-hundred-million-plus users to create and share fifteen-second videos of lip-syncing, dances, comedy, and internet meme challenges.[12] Alex Zhu, the cofounder and co-CEO of Musical.ly, says the app "enables anyone to be a content creator," and its interactivity and saturation in entertainment and pop culture has this video app blowing up with young teens and older elementary children.[13] It should be noted that official terms of use state that Musical.ly is "intended for users age 13 and over," though, so Musical.ly programs in the library should be targeted for teen populations.[14]

Since it involves a social media app, a library Musical.ly program could be promoted to remind teens to bring their own devices and Musical.ly accounts with them to the program, if they have them. However, libraries that have access to an iPad or iPad kits would benefit from using them in the program as well. As suggested in the Instagram slime shoots above, it's a good idea to create a collective hashtag so everyone can tag the videos on their personal accounts to one access point, such as #YourBranchNameMusicallyChallenge, for example. They should also tag videos with any other special challenge hashtags they might be using.

If the library has access to branch or regional social media accounts, teens who show up without their own Musical.ly log-ins could post a select few videos on there, but be sure to get any necessary required parental media consent forms if there are any faces/voices in videos.

Musical.ly has plenty of fun video editing features that allow teens to film, for example, in slow-mo or epically fast. Users can create a transition effect by lifting their thumb off the Record button to change the scenery before recording again from the next video frame, creating interesting and unusual jump cuts. Searching through the #TransitionChallenge on Musical.ly will demonstrate some of the most amazing video editing skills of young teens who will black out, flip, and spin their camera angles. Transition filmings can be somewhat tedious with multiple attempts at recording, but this only equals more practice at editing skill for the young creators.

Musical.ly is most well known for its lip-syncing videos. Users can search for their favorite songs in the Search > Sounds tab. Selecting the intended song brings users to a page where they can hear the sound clip, or even see the most popular or recent videos from other users who filmed to the same song. This same page also has a large Post Video button at the top—clicking this takes users to the recording screen where they can start selecting their film speed and any desired "lenses" (which are similar, although less in quantity, to the Snapchat filters; fall 2017 Musical.ly allowed users to turn into puppies, fawns, scholars, and even shark-bite-hat wearers).

Musical.ly will be a good introductory conversation to searching techniques too. Library staff can provide assistance in helping teens to find their favorite songs or challenges. Will they search by the artist, Muser (Musical.ly user account), or the song/skit title? These criteria can be entered into the search bar to find the selected audio page that offered the Post Video link noted above, but there's another, more immediate way to create videos when inspiration strikes. In each video, there will be a small circular button at the bottom right corner, with a dot (it looks like a spinning record). Clicking this button will take users to the recording screen to start filming their own video clips over the same audio track as the video they were watching. This also generates an "inspired by @username" tag on the video.

Library Program Outline

A library Musical.ly Challenge program is extremely customizable due to the variety of different challenges and trending memes that will be hot on the app during any given season. Since it's a social media program, staff will want to start with a discussion about internet safety. Remind teens about the dos and don'ts about social media use and about making sure to avoid providing any personal information on public profiles and checking with their responsible adults to make sure they're okay with their usage of the app. Staff should also take this moment to remind teens to be selective with their audio choices—

some songs and comedy clips might include inappropriate language, which should not be used during the program.

A projector cart can be set up in the programming room so that teens can watch a few example videos—have a few prepared for the program, but allow teens to suggest some of their favorite Musers or challenges to watch together as a group. Keep in mind that there is no desktop version of Musical.ly, so projected videos will either need to come from an adapter that hooks a smartphone into the projector, or perhaps from YouTube Musical .ly clip compilations, if it's something that was popular enough to have been documented that way.

Next, staff can have teens start to compose some of the following challenges suggested below. Break apart for video creation, and then gather as a group to watch the completed videos and praise the teens on their skills. Stand back and watch as some of the youth experts teach each other how to produce some of the trickier transitions and filming techniques.

Musical.ly Challenge Activities

Remix Comedy

Comedy is another popular area of Musical.ly, with short joke clips and comedy skits generating thousands of remixes using the "inspired by @username" feature. Check the top trending comedy skits for an appropriate video and have each teen re-create the audio clip with their own visuals. Great examples include the #CoinciDANCE, #IsThat-MyVoice, and a librarian fave, #BeautyIsNothingWithoutBrains, which goes like so:

> *Voice A:* Hello, I'd like to order french fries, a burger, and a milk shake.
> *Voice B:* This is a library!
> *Voice A:* (whispering) I'd like to order french fries, a burger, and milk shake.

Check out some of the more popular comedy Musers like @rebeccazamolo, @ash_lay, and @enouchtrue for some great examples.

#MagicPen Challenge

The page for this challenge asks, "If you had a magic pen, what would you draw?" Video clips show a close-up shot of a hand drawing an object—the hand will then bop the completed picture with a fist or the magic wave of a hand, and a real-life version of the object magically appears (through a transition jump cut). Videos are simply set to a favorite song in the background.

Selfie Lip-Syncing Challenge

Teens can pick their favorite songs and lip-sync to them. Famous Musers have developed a method of impressive techniques for the one-hand selfie dancing (as the other hand is holding the phone in selfie mode to film) including hand swipes, half-hand heart shapes, and hand and camera twirls. Check out some of the more popular lip-syncing Musers like @babyariel (the Musical.ly queen), @missjaydenb, @annieleblanc, and @lisandlena for some great examples.

Dance Challenges

Viral dance crazes have been around for decades—think "Thriller," the macarena, and so forth. Musical.ly has loads of dance videos capturing them all. Pick a more recent viral dance trend like #JuJuOnThatBeat, #WhipNaeNae, or the super amazing #ShuffleDance, and ask teens to create videos of their performances.

Duets

Musical.ly has an interactive duet feature that can be accessed by tapping on the three dots in the bottom right corner. This allows creators to split screen record themselves doing the same challenge or song as the selected original Muser (there's also an option to flick back and forth from original to remix every few seconds). Teens in the program could duet with each other, or everyone can try duetting off the same video.

Trending Challenges

Take a look on the Trending section of the main search page for the most current and popular viral challenges, or have teens suggest their favorites. You never know what will become viral, and plenty of Musical.ly memes have been pretty random. For example, summer 2017 saw the trending of the #WatermelonDressSong, and the audio clip that went, "Watermelon dress / watermelon dress / This, is, my watermelon dress." Musers made dress shapes out of construction paper (or actual watermelon flesh) and would hold them close to the camera, at an angle where it would look like the person dancing in the background was wearing it as clothes. Some Musers even inserted a collection of watermelon emojis in a dress shape on top of the video during the editing process.

EXTRA TIPS!

Have teens work in teams. Some challenges like #MagicPen and #MannequinChallenge are particularly difficult to film without a tripod or just alone in general. Teens who aren't comfortable showing themselves on camera don't need to—some challenges like the #MagicPen require only hands. Others, like anything with a comedy or song track, could be done with a toy or stuffed animal moving along to the sounds. Some teens might feel comfortable enough showing themselves on camera once they have an over-the-top lens on them—for example, one of them makes them look like a bug-eyed piglet!

Food Tech

Technology found in the kitchen can be another great gateway into further STEM learning. Taking accurate measurements of ingredients is a transferable skill required for the science lab, converting measurements practices math equations, and there are plenty of new tools and machines with which to study kitchen technology. Learning about healthy ingredients and nutrition touches on biology, and presenting beautifully designed plates and creative food designs can even bring out a teen's artistic side.

Dawn States, the teen programming coordinator at the Martin Library in York, Pennsylvania, reminds librarians that food science programs can address two needs: feeding hungry teens and teaching science concurrently.[15] As a form of "recreational education," these food technology programs can underscore for teens that "learning can and should be entertaining."[16] Try the following food technology programs below to capture a teen's hungry interest with STEM-related learning.

The PancakeBot (Technology, Art, Math)

There are plenty of "pancake art challenge" videos all over YouTube these days—skilled artists use a combination of pancake batters in squeeze bottles to draw various designs by first laying down the outline of their image, and then filling the empty spaces in with more batter. The staggering of the layers creates a gradient effect to show the drawn lines of one's intended image—Pokeballs, unicorns, Yoda's head, you name it! Understandably, there are also plenty of #PancakeChallengeFails, where creators are unable to master the batter consistency, drawing technique, or staggered layer cook times, and end up with burnt images or messy, undefined blobs.

There is, however, an excellent solution to these struggles: the PancakeBot, the world's "first food printer capable of printing pancakes by automatically dispensing batter directly onto a griddle."[17] Users can choose one of the many downloadable designs from the PancakeBot community website, or even design their own through the provided free software. Designs are then loaded onto the PancakeBot via SD card.[18] This unique machine lets "kids and adults express their creativity through food while exploring technology."[19] It can be purchased from the product's website for US$300, and will ship to both the US and Canada.

Teen programs with the PancakeBot could include a laptop lab set up with the free PancakeBot design software. Teens can design their own pancake image to load to the memory card (which, keep in mind, if your laptops don't have that particular SD card slot, you might need a memory card reader). The design process is quite simple—teens can freehand draw their images, or there's even an option to layer a pre-made image underneath the design screen so that creators can trace over the image with the different gradients of batter.

As with any consumable product, if you're expecting a large crowd of attendees, you may want to have a registration for this program, so that you make sure to have enough laptops/batter for everyone to get a turn. The pancake designs themselves only take a few minutes to print, although it certainly can depend on the size/complexity of the design.

Teens can then follow the recipe for making the pancake batter—ideally using the provided recipe from the PancakeBot literature itself, as the batter needs to be a bit runnier than usual. This is where the finicky part of this project comes in. It can take some tweaking and finessing to get the batter at the perfect consistency so that it's not over-running and blurring the image, nor is it so thick that it's pixelating the image because it won't spread enough.

Beyond getting the right batter consistency through using the PancakeBot-provided recipe, the pressure setting for the air tube will also be important. The runnier the batter, the less pressure you'll need for the air tube to push the batter through, but you can adjust this pressure gauge as the batter starts to drip.

Figure 6.7. The PancakeBot prints a Legend of Zelda pancake

Take care not to tip the batter bottle upside down—if batter gets in the air tube, it will be quite a chore to clean it out afterward without ruining the tube or having things become unsanitary if not properly cleaned. While cleaning the entire rig after setup can also be quite the chore, the griddle itself does attach from the robot arm so that it can be washed like any other griddle would.

DIY Unicorn Smoothies (Science, Technology, Math)

Starbucks' Unicorn Frappuccino took the internet world by storm in April 2017. Making use of the growing unicorn hype, the Starbucks website explains that the Unicorn Frappuccino was made with "a sweet dusting of pink powder, blended into a crème Frappuccino with mango syrup and layered with a pleasantly sour blue drizzle."[20] It was then "finished with vanilla whipped cream and a sprinkle of sweet pink and sour blue powder topping."[21] This limited edition drink, which was on the menu for only a few short days, created an internet phenomenon. After its release, DIY versions started cropping up all over the internet so that people could re-create this pink-and-blue magic drink.

Similarly, teens at the library can also use kitchen equipment and a variety of healthy ingredients to try to make their own unicorn smoothies. Speaking about unicorn smoothies—be careful about actually calling them "Frappuccinos" in any of your promotions, as it's a copyrighted term that belongs to Starbucks. Those who know about the fad will understand what you're going for without having to say this word explicitly.

Having access to the proper equipment will be essential, such as blenders, mixers, measuring cups and spoons, as well as consumables like the ingredients, clear plastic cups,

Figure 6.8. DIY unicorn smoothies

and spoons/straws. When purchasing fruit, try the bulk frozen packs, as they will often be cheaper, and are still blendable in the kitchen equipment.

Library staff can have a quick discussion about what the Starbucks original was made with, while then giving healthier options that should make a visually similar yet healthier smoothie. Go for things like yogurt blended with fresh red berries and mangoes for the pink base. The blue drizzle might be a bit trickier—there is a process of making natural blue food dye with red cabbage and baking soda, but if this process is too finicky, you might need to go for blue food coloring in your yogurt instead (try a squeeze bottle to make the wavy line inside the clear cup). For the whipped cream topping, try whipping coconut milk and vanilla extract for a sugar-free whip cream.

October 2017 also saw the limited-time release of Starbucks' Zombie Frappuccino, with a green apple crème base, pink whip cream, and reddish, bloody-looking caramel drizzle. Libraries could also have teens experiment with a variety of different ingredients to try to make a healthier version of this one too, and even morph the program into a Unicorns vs. Zombies: Smoothie Edition!

Anime Clubs and STEM

Library Anime Clubs are popular with teens who are enthusiasts of trendy Japanese animation (anime) and their graphic novel counterparts, manga. Groups that meet to discuss their favorite anime and manga, and screen episodes from sites with public performance licenses for registered library Anime Clubs like Funimation.com or Crunchyroll.com, will also enjoy the incorporation of anime-themed activities and games, which can also incorporate STEM skill projects.

Anime Scratch Games (Technology)

Chapter 5 discussed how adaptable the Squishy Circuits and Makey Makey kits are into holidays and pop-culture-themed programming. You can make use of this adaptability in Anime Club by finding homemade Scratch Makey Makey games, based on some of the favorite shows the teens in your club might currently be watching. Plenty of anime enthusiasts are quite into Pokémon as a video game too, so it's a safe bet that they're up for experimenting with a few new video games in the program.

Interested in teaching teens how to make their own games through Scratch? More information on assigning these projects to teen coding volunteers can be found later in this chapter.

Materials:

- Laptops (based upon your branch availability and predicted attendance)
- Makey Makey kits (one per available laptop)
- Playdough
- Tinfoil
- Fruit, or any other conductive materials

Give yourself some extra setup time for this program, because it can take a lot of time to connect each individual wire onto each Makey Makey. If you have teen volunteers, you might want to have them around for this setup, as it is quite tedious!

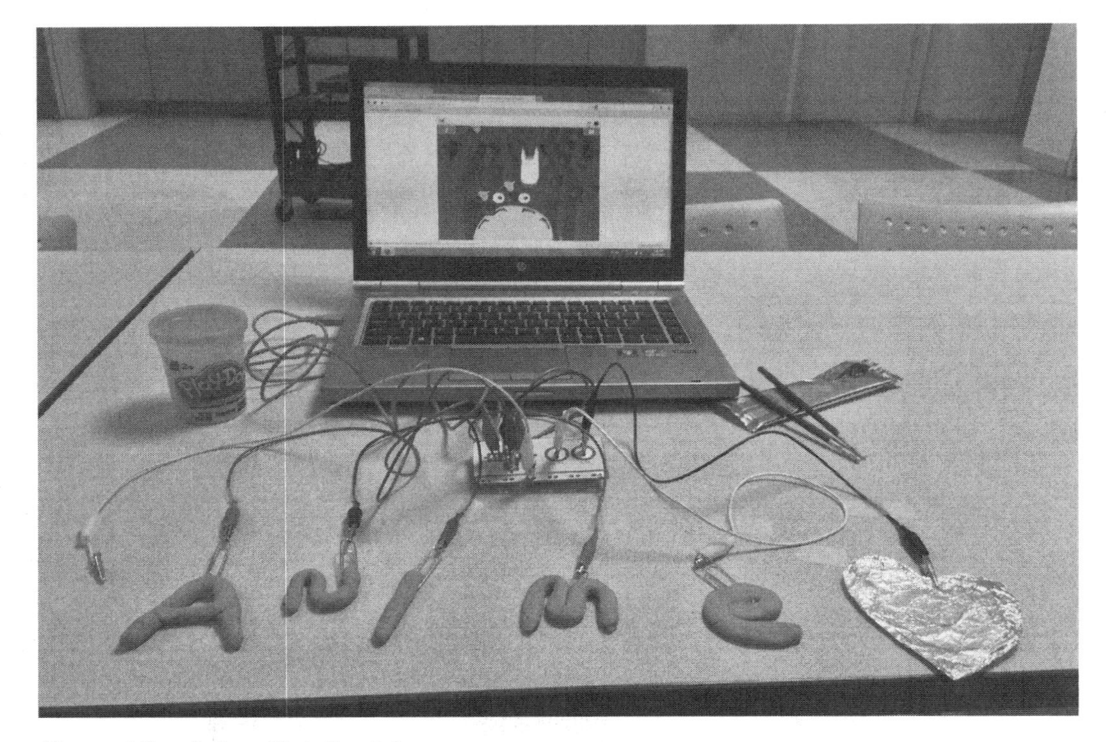

Figure 6.9. Anime Club Scratch games

Set up each Makey Makey onto a laptop, according to instructions included in the product packaging. You can choose a variety of different conductive materials to act as your switches. Try making playdough shapes (perhaps a Pokeball, or the Wings of Freedom from Attack on Titan) or kawaii tinfoil shapes. The more prep or volunteer time you have, the cuter and more unique your tinfoil shapes could be.

Open the Scratch website on each laptop, and navigate to some of your pre-chosen favorite anime-themed games that are also compatible with the Makey Makey, or check out the recommended options below:

PUBLICALLY AVAILABLE ANIME SCRATCH GAMES (SUITABLE FOR USE WITH THE MAKEY MAKEY)

(My Neighbor) Totoro Bounce:

Great, adorable graphics from this classic anime film. It's easy to use with the Makey Makey (uses Left and Right only). You might occasionally fall off Totoro's head and get caught in the side hole, but the music and kawaii-ness makes up for it. https://scratch.mit.edu/projects/46331122/

Attack on Titan—Parkour with Eren:

This is sure to be a winner in your Anime Club Scratch Games program! Attack on Titan has become a new timeless classic anime that many teens will be familiar with. It's also sure to solicit a few laughs as Eren's head bobbles around and jumps off the maze walls. It's quite hilarious! It also has the bonus inclusion of that recognizable theme song too. The Makey Makey controls (Left, Right, and Up) take a bit to get used to—the jumping motion is a combination of pressing Up and Left or Right at the same time while touching a wall, but once you get the hang of it, it's super fun!

https://scratch.mit.edu/projects/19735664/

Naruto Maze:

Pretty simple to work with the Makey Makey (uses Left, Right, Up, and Down). Good, recognizable graphics, and cool background music.

https://scratch.mit.edu/projects/51848738/

Don't Forget These Useful Tips

Choosing Scratch Projects

If you're looking to branch out and find further anime-themed Scratch games, keep in mind that not all the projects on the Scratch site are made with the Makey Makey in mind. Try searching for your anime theme word in combination with the term "Makey," but if that doesn't bring up anything interesting, just make sure that your selected game/project works with a combination of the Up, Down, Left, Right, or Space buttons. Some projects require moving your mouse around and clicking on things. While you can use the Makey Makey to "click," you can't really use it to navigate the mouse itself.

Full Screen Size

Don't forget to press the Full Screen button so you can really see all the details in the chosen games. This is the blue square in the top left corner.

Green Screen Cosplay (Technology, Art, Engineering)

Many anime fans have long been avid cosplayers. Teens love to be able to re-create their favorite characters from their most loved shows or manga, and plenty would be excited at the chance to test out their newest cosplay before their next entry into the local comic-con cosplay contest.

Try hosting a Green Screen Cosplay Night for your Anime Club! Invite teens to show up in cosplay (handmade, closet, or whatever they'd like to wear) and have your green screen kit ready for a pop-up anime photo booth. You can even have teens pre-create and submit their digital or hand-drawn backgrounds that they think might best suit their character.

Cosplay can be as casual or as complicated as the creator desires—there are plenty of engineering techniques that are employed by cosplayers in the creation of their costumes. Encourage teens to tell the group about their costume-making process, and ask them to highlight what tools they might have used to get their pieces to where they are now. More information on cosplay programming in libraries can be found in Ellyssa Kroski's 2015 *Cosplay in Libraries: How to Embrace Costume Play in Your Library*, which is a great addition to professional collections supporting programming departments looking for more information on cosplay and its associated maker activities.

More details on the supplies and plans of green screen programming can be found in the "Green Screen" section of chapter 8: "STEM Programs for All Ages and Families."

The Price Is Right: Fandom Haul (Math)

Here's an idea to sneakily get your teens practicing their math skills! Be forewarned that you might get a few complaints about the obvious math component in this activity, but ideally all the shiny, fandom swag pictures will distract them enough to have fun with it.

Based on the popular *The Price Is Right* game show, this game involves scouring through the Amazon.com website to find a bunch of anime-related merchandise—think: figures, costumes, jewelry, art pieces, manga sets, DVDs, and so forth. Organize items into "showcases" based upon a theme—perhaps you're taking three different Studio Ghibli items, or four different pieces of Pokémon merchandise. Screencap the pictures of the items (making sure to edit out the price) onto a slide in a PowerPoint presentation, making sure to cite your links somewhere.

Participants can work as individuals or in teams, but for each showcase that pops up on your screen, they should be guessing how much money the entire package or "showcase" might cost. The person closest to the approximate Amazon (or whichever site you've taken your prices/pictures from) retail value wins that round! Small prizes for the winner of the most rounds will go a long way too—perhaps a box of Pocky, or some pre-made anime buttons with your button maker.

While teens are obviously already learning heavier concepts than addition at this point, this activity requires them to estimate prices based upon their fandom knowledge, and then quickly add their totals together in their heads.

Harry Potter LED Wands (Science and Technology)

Candice Blackwood, the Teen Services librarian at the Nepean Centrepointe Branch of Ottawa Public Library, suggests making these LED wands with teens for Harry Potter, Halloween, or other magical-themed programs. While this program is intended for teens, it could also work for older elementary students; but if this is the intended age group, programmers should make sure to have enough teen volunteers on hand to help with the glue gun, to dole out paint, and to help with building the circuit around the wand.[22]

Supplies:

- LED lights
- Long, straight twigs or chopsticks
- Conductive tape or wire
- Coin batteries
- Glue gun and hot glue (for larger programs, multiple glue guns are even better)
- Beads or other items for texture

- Acrylic paint (the good stuff, not the flaky, tempera stuff)
- Paintbrushes
- Napkins
- Water cups
- Scissors

Instructions:

1. Explain how to make the wand light up by making a circuit.
2. Have participants test their batteries by inserting a coin battery between the prongs of the LED light—let them know about positive/negative sides of the battery and LED.
3. Next, participants can use their coin battery, LED, and conductive tape to create a path along the stick/chopstick. The goal is to have the LED at the top of the wand and the battery somewhere near the bottom so that it is hidden when the wand is being held.
   A. Wand making can become more complicated by challenging participants to make a switch with their conductive items so that the wand is not lit up all the time. Maybe a tab that closes the circuit when the user squeezes the wand?
   B. Challenge participants to create a wand where the battery can be replaced! Cell batteries will last awhile, but of course they're an exhaustible source of power and eventually will stop powering the LED.
4. Once the circuit is finished (and works!), it's time to decorate! Blackwood suggests having photos of famous wands around: if one desires to create the Elder Wand, one can—but beware, having photos of wands can sometimes stifle creativity.
5. Start with the glue guns and cover the stick so that it has some texture. Think of tree bark, swirls, and ridges.
6. Add more elements of texture in certain spots before the glue dries. You can add beads and/or little rolls or balls of tinfoil (don't let this interfere with the circuit, though)—maybe even some literal tree bark!
7. Finally—paint it up! Add a layer of black as a base and then go over that dry coat of black with brown. The black base adds of bit of depth and helps make the textured elements pop with the brown paint. Magic has no limits, though, so go ahead and let young wizards use whatever color they want.

Not only do program attendees get to leave the library with a super cool wand, but they've also leave with a spark of electricity—wondering what else they could make, and how they could take this new knowledge further.[23]

Youth Volunteer Engagement

While some teens might come to your library looking for a place to hang out, socialize, and participate in entertaining activities and programs, others might arrive looking for help with their resumes, study skills, and volunteer hours (nay, some might want it all!).

Given that STEM skill activities can be approached from a variety of different skill levels and project lengths, keep in mind that you shouldn't need to forgo the more time-intensive projects just because they don't fit into your one-off hour-long planning slot. Think about incorporating STEM skill projects into volunteer opportunities for your teens. This can be motivating to set aside a weekly series time slot for larger STEM projects. Teens will not only walk away with new STEM skill knowledge, but volunteer hours and completed projects and references for their resumes as well. As library volunteers, they will ideally be creating finished projects for use within your library too.

Teen Coding Volunteers

Plenty of libraries have been offering a "Learn to Code with Scratch" program, particularly since the boom in the makerspace movement after 2013. Scratch, the free visual coding website, was created to "help young people learn to think creatively, reason systematically, and work collaboratively" by creating their own animations, games, and interactive stories.[24]

While the basics of Scratch coding can indeed be introduced in a one-off hour-long library program, the language has almost limitless possibilities for customized games and animations for people of all ages. And as it was mentioned in program suggestions for both children and teens throughout this book, it is handy to have a good arsenal of Makey Makey–compatible games for library staff looking to incorporate these causal skills into STEM and pop culture programming. Teen coding volunteers can purport to spend a series of time—perhaps, one night a week over the eight weeks of summer—to learn different Scratch coding techniques, before developing their own pop-culture-based Makey Makey–compatible games, for future use in library programs.

Of course, you'll need access to a computer lab or set of laptops, depending on the number of volunteers you take on. Having pre-planned your STEM or pop culture programs for the next calendar year in advance will help determine what game assignments you want to give to your teen volunteers. Perhaps they will be passionate enough about something else, though, and provide you with inspiration for a different game and thereby program theme!

Scratch Collection

It is not the purpose of this section to re-create an entire Scratch coding tutorial in this chapter. The best, and easiest, place to start to make yourself familiar with this content is through the "Getting Started with Scratch Guide" on the MIT Scratch website, which comes both in PDF and online video tutorial format.

You can also check out the following materials to further support your learning—or simply add them to your collection to help your teen volunteers (and further community) deepen their learning. Try putting some on display during your volunteer nights, if you're not using them in the program proper!

- Breen, Derek. *Scratch for Kids for Dummies*. Hoboken, NJ: Wiley, 2015.
- McManus, Sean. *How to Code in 10 Easy Lessons*. Lake Forest, CA: Walter Foster Jr., 2015.
- *Super Scratch Programming Adventure! Learn to Program by Making Cool Games*. San Francisco: No Starch, 2014.
- Woodcock, Jon. *Coding Games in Scratch*. New York: DK, 2016.

Fine Art Volunteers

Teen fine art volunteers can provide a creative, artistic outlet for those budding artists in your community. Fine art volunteers can meet once a month, or once a week, for a term, creating art pieces assigned by library staff. Pieces can be used for bulletin board or poster frame displays, in house posters, or program room decoration.

Teens get to hone their art skills and practice project independence, time management, and taking directions, all the while benefiting from using library-provided art supplies for items they can later add to their future art school portfolios (offer to take a picture of the piece if it's still in use, or to return it to them once it's no longer needed). Make sure to remind them to sign and date their work, as they should be recognized for the skills. Like with other volunteer opportunities, teens can also gain volunteer hours for any IB programs, resume additions, or potential references from their library staff supervisors.

You could even have an art show at the end of the term—invite other library staff, volunteers, and their family and friends to see a collection of all the pieces made that term. Serve refreshments and small snacks and make sure to praise each volunteer's unique skill set.

Key Points

As go-to places for information, programs, and community resources, libraries are a perfectly suited place to "support teen acquisition of STEM related skills."[25] As the generation that is about to launch itself into the STEM-skill-laden workforce, teens are a vital and important community with whom libraries should be building relationships in order to provide relevant and entertaining programs and services that will help aid these young adults in their future careers.

Button making is a quick and simple addition of an easy technology that allows teens to be creative and artistic with their image designs. It also requires them to follow specific processes laid out for the machine's usage.

Slime making, while having been around in youth science activities for many years, has experienced a massive resurgence in pop culture with its trending social media explosions on platforms like YouTube and Instagram. While the use of borax as a slime activator has received some recent controversy surrounding safety concerns with skin contact, there are alternative, "kid-safe" recipes that instead use a combination of contact solution and baking soda. Slime hysteria has created a wide variety of ways to be creative in slime design, such as crunchy slime, fluffy slime, glitter slime, or even fishbowl slime.

Musical.ly programs can make use of another pop culture entertainment phenomenon while taking advantage of viral internet trends, memes, and challenges, and most importantly, allowing teens to practice their video editing, production, and even performance skills.

Food technology programs provide a solution to two important needs: feeding hungry teens while keeping their interest during STEM skill acquisition. Following exact instructions, converting measurements, and learning how to use any food-based technology or equipment can all help teens to practice their STEM skills, be it with a magical unicorn-colored smoothie, or their own uniquely designed pancake.

Anime Clubs provide an entertaining base with which to attract teens into programs, and can easily incorporate anime-themed STEM activities like Makey Makey games, green screen cosplay photo booths, or *The Price Is Right* fandom hauls, all of which sneak STEM skill learning into otherwise entertainment-focused programs.

For young adults who are looking for a bit more from the library (such as volunteer hours, more explicitly acquired skills to add to a resume, etc.), STEM-based projects can be more formally instructed to registered teen volunteers, who then create projects for the library's benefit, such as Makey Makey programs or children's bulletin board displays. This allows teens to collect the necessary STEM or art skills and volunteer experience, while also allowing them to give back to the library.

Notes

1. Young Adult Library Services Association (YALSA). *Issue Brief #3: Libraries Help Teens Build STEM Skills.* http://www.ala.org/yalsa/sites/ala.org.yalsa/files/content/IssueBrief_STEM.pdf.

2. Dawn States, "Out of the Pickle: Promoting Food Science and STEM in Public Libraries," *Pennsylvania Libraries: Research & Practice* 3, no. 2 (2015): 106.

3. "Make, Do, Share: Sustainable STEM Leadership in a Box; An Interview with Shannon Peterson," *Young Adult Library Services* 14, no. 3 (2016): 14.

4. "Make, Do, Share," 14.

5. Candice Blackwood in discussion with the author, November 2017.

6. Brian Rohrig, "The Science of Slime," *Chem Matters*, December 2004, 13–16, https://www.acs.org/content/dam/acsorg/education/resources/highschool/chemmatters/articlesbytopic/solidsliquidsgases/chemmatters-dec2004-slime.pdf.

7. "Information Update—Health Canada Advises Canadians to Avoid Homemade Craft and Pesticide Recipes Using Boric Acid." Recalls and Safety Alerts, Government of Canada, accessed December 10, 2017, http://www.healthycanadians.gc.ca/recall-alert-rappel-avis/hc-sc/2016/59514a-eng.php.

8. Caroline Picard, "Parents Everywhere Are Worried about DIY Slime after Multiple Kids Are Burned," *Good Housekeeping*, April 4, 2017, accessed December 10, 2017, http://www.goodhousekeeping.com/life/parenting/news/a43500/slime-safety/.

9. Picard, "Parents Everywhere Are Worried."

10. "Elmer's Slime," Parent Craft Projects, Elmer's, accessed December 11, 2017, http://elmers.com/slime.

11. "For Parents," Musical.ly, November 15, 2017, accessed December 10, 2017, https://support.musical.ly/knowledge-base/for-parents.

12. "Musical.ly Acquired by Chinese Startup for $800 Million," *Billboard*, November 10, 2017, accessed December 10, 2017, https://www.billboard.com/biz/articles/news/legal-and-management/8031196/musically-acquired-by-chinese-startup-for-800-million#print.

13. "Bytedance and Musical.ly Announce Agreement to Merge," *PR Newswire*, accessed December 10, 2017, https://en.prnasia.com/releases/apac/Bytedance_and_Musical_ly_Announce_Agreement_to_Merge-193715.shtml.

14. "For Parents."

15. States, "Out of the Pickle," 103.

16. States, "Out of the Pickle," 103.

17. "Print Your Pancakes," PancakeBot, accessed December 10, 2017, http://www.pancakebot.com/tutorials.

18. "Print Your Pancakes."

19. "PancakeBot 2.0," StoreBound, accessed December 10, 2017, http://www.storebound.com/storebound/pancakebot-products/pancakebot-2-0.

20. "Starbucks New Color and Flavor Changing Unicorn Frappuccino," Starbucks Newsroom, June 12, 2017, accessed December 10, 2017, https://news.starbucks.com/news/starbucks-unicorn-frappuccino.

21. "Starbucks New Color."

22. Candice Blackwood in discussion with the author, November 2017.

23. Candice Blackwood in discussion with the author, November 2017.

24. "Scratch—Imagine, Program, Share," Scratch, accessed December 11, 2017, https://scratch.mit.edu/.

25. *Issue Brief #3*.

Further Reading

Joiner, Sara K., and Geri Swanzy. *Teen Services Today: A Practical Guide for Librarians*. Lanham, MD: Rowman & Littlefield, 2016.

Kroski, Ellyssa. *Cosplay in Libraries: How to Embrace Costume Play in Your Library*. Lanham, MD: Rowman & Littlefield, 2015.

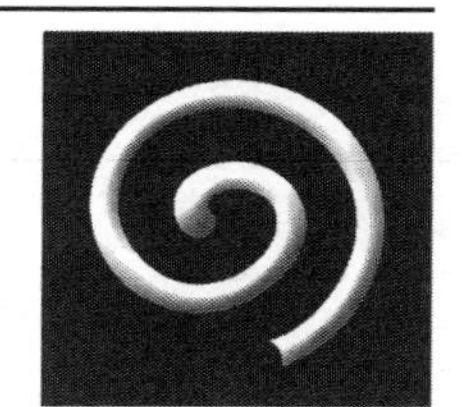

CHAPTER 7

Adult STEM Programming

IN THIS CHAPTER

- ▷ Adults need STEM skills too!
- ▷ Public computer training
- ▷ Dating app courses
- ▷ LEGO speed dating
- ▷ Fake news workshops: information literacy
- ▷ Appy hours and digital petting zoos
- ▷ Screen print holiday cards

Adults Need STEM Skills Too!

THE PREVIOUS CHAPTERS have provided a wealth of STEM programming ideas aimed at children and teens, but children and families aren't the only ones who need STEM skill supplements. Libraries can offer a wide range of adult STEM programs too. These educational areas are indeed important for community members of all ages. While some may counter that adults can gain their STEM knowledge from simply reading the texts in a library's collection, research confidently shows that students of any age "gain a much deeper understanding of science when they actively grapple with questions than when they passively listen to answers."[1] Hands-on experimentation is therefore essential when learning or updating STEM skill knowledge—in fact, evidence has been "accumulating for decades" that people who actively engage with learning material will end up "retaining it for much longer than they would have otherwise, and they will be better able to apply their knowledge broadly."[2]

Candice Blackwood, librarian at the Nepean Centrepointe Branch of Ottawa Public Library, reflects that libraries have always done more for literacy than simply to "provide access to books"—they've been teaching literacy skills for all ages since they started delivering programs. "So why stop there?" Blackwood argues that libraries need to provide more than simple access to technology and other STEM resources: they need to instruct in the realm of digital literacy, which can provide customers, young and old, with the skills they need to problem solve, think critically about the technology they're interacting with, and navigate the "smart" world they live in. Providing instruction along with the access can empower our communities.[3]

Public Computer Training (Technology)

Libraries have long been known for providing public computer and internet access to their communities. Indeed, "virtually every public library in the United States provides public access to internet computers," and this is now often seen by both the public as well as libraries themselves as the "central to the mission of the public library."[4] Most importantly, however, libraries are making use of this wide access to technology in order to teach their communities the necessary technology skills needed to become technically literate. Bo Kinney cautions librarians, however, about making the mistake of thinking that "libraries are relevant only because they provide computer and internet access."[5] These technology-laden spaces are most importantly by extension "imbued with [the] greater power to help individuals and communities precisely because [these tools] are provided in a public library."[6]

Training courses such as computer basics, Microsoft Excel, Twitter, Facebook, e-readers, and many other topics help public libraries look beyond the provision of simple access to provide necessary technology skills to their communities in order to address the digital divide that exists between technology users who own and have the operating knowledge of new computers and technology gadgets, and those who don't. Although "four-in-ten seniors now own smartphones, more than double the share that did so in 2013," the digital divide is still alive and well, and it also exists in communities beyond simply seniors.[7] Kinney argued in his 2010 *Public Library Quarterly* article that there was still much for libraries to do to "improve their training role," which still holds true today, more than seven years later. Public libraries will still continue to benefit from providing "better training for staff, more time for staff to help computer users, and more outreach to library patrons about the training possibilities available."[8] With the constant introductions of new computer technologies such as apps, gadgets, and new social media, this need is unlikely to die down anytime soon. Public libraries can continue to rest assured that providing supplemental technology training, based upon the needs of their specific community, will be a necessary task in their futures.

Dating App Courses (Technology)

A 2016 Pew Research Center survey found that "15% of American adults have used online dating sites or mobile dating apps."[9] While usage by the usually technology-savvy eighteen- to twenty-four-year-old age group has "increased nearly threefold since 2013," the statistics for users ages fifty-five to sixty-four has also recently doubled.[10] How many more adults might be interested in using online dating, only to avoid signing up for fear of not knowing how to navigate the sites?

Public libraries can consider offering dating site technology courses. While library staff should remind community members that they aren't experts in matchmaking or relationships, they can certainly teach someone how to sign up for an account on Plenty of Fish, Match.com, eHarmony, or whatever other popular dating site that staff have had time to teach themselves. Course content can include account creation, uploading profile pics, filling out a profile, internet safety tips, and privacy best practices.

LEGO Speed Dating (Engineering)

LEGO @ the Library is, as mentioned in chapter 5, a popular free block play program found on many a public library's children's programming roster. Adults often also love playing with these retro building blocks, as it can bring about a sense of nostalgia and let one's inner geek flag fly free.

Since the library likely already has access to a large LEGO collection, programmers can think about incorporating these into adult programming as well. Adult LEGO programs practice engineering design skills—perhaps a local university's Engineering Society will want to host a social night at the library to play with the branch's large LEGO collection. Adults are capable of creating larger, more complicated structures, which can be used to turn into a contest—perhaps the most unique contraption, or even a speed race to see who can complete a specific design plan the quickest.

Speaking of speed . . . if 15 percent of all American adults are using online dating options,[11] perhaps there are some who might enjoy a more personal way of meeting potential new partners at a library LEGO speed dating event. Organized much like any other speed dating event, potential suitors are split into two groups, while one group stays seated at their tables, and the other group rotates to visit each table for a set amount of time. Meeting a potential partner for the first time can often be awkward, and having something tactile like a LEGO project will give participants something to do with their hands, and a reason to collaborate together as they work to build the small LEGO set at each table. Once all table visits and LEGO projects have been completed, participants can leave their ideal matches and contact info with the library host, who will let them know if there are any mutual matches in order to exchange contact information.

If libraries feel uncomfortable with the notion of involving themselves in the romantic pursuits of patrons, they could alternatively opt for a similar program aimed at finding friends: "Speed friending" works much the same, but is simply a way for people to get to know each other and find new friends, without any romantic connotations attached.

Fake News Workshops: Information Literacy (Technology)

Summer 2017 saw Pew Research Center and Elon University's Imagining the Internet Center conducting surveys with "technologists, scholars, practitioners, strategic thinkers and others" about the future crisis surrounding "the future of truth and misinformation online."[12] Respondents were clear about the need to improve the information environment, noting a specific "need for massive efforts to imbue the public with much better information literacy skills," which will require an "education effort that reaches out to those of all ages, everywhere."[13] Libraries are well suited for this challenge due to their longtime focus on both information literacy as well as community educational efforts for all ages. Journalist and previous library administrator Marcus Banks notes a similar need in his late 2016 *American Libraries Magazine* article when he suggests that librarians can play a "vital role in helping everyone, of any age, become critical and reflective news consumers."[14] In fact, as early as February 2017, libraries all across North America were "stepping up to help patrons gain the information literacy skills they need" by providing information literacy programs centering on "how to spot fake news."[15] Public libraries can provide their own workshops on evaluating information sources by reading through the variety of examples found in the Programming Librarian article found in the "Further Reading" section below. As a controversial topic, which is also a part of mainstream media and popular culture, these programs are sure to be well attended. In fact, a Pew Research Center study that was conducted just after the 2016 US presidential election found that 64 percent of adults "believe fake news stories cause a great deal of confusion" and 23 percent even admitted that they had "shared fabricated political stories themselves—sometimes by mistake and sometimes intentionally."[16]

Appy Hours and Digital Petting Zoos (Technology, Engineering)

Catchy names might be mostly for marketing purposes or the amusement of library programming staff, but these technology-related programs should still provide useful content for public libraries and their communities. Program planners should consider having a weekly "appy hour," where library staff are on hand, out on the floor, ready to respond to any technology troubleshooting. Library staff and users will grow to know the specific, recurring time slot if it is kept consistent.

Some libraries keep their appy hours drop-in technology advice to mobile devices specifically, while others treat the passive program like a general, technology-related information desk, answering whatever technology-related questions roll in.

Digital petting zoos are created in a similar drop-in format, where library staff will often have a large array of new and unique technology gadgets out on display for library users. Common items include the 3D printer, Makey Makey kits, Chromebooks and iPads, e-readers, Dash and Dot robots, littleBits, and any other new technology that the library might have access to.

While digital petting zoos would certainly welcome library users of all ages, this does provide adults in the community with a more tailored reason to check out some of the more unique robotics and coding items that are all too often relegated only to youth programming. Programming or IT staff should be on hand to explain how each item works, allowing users to wander in, ask questions, and get a hands-on feel for whatever strikes their fancy. If libraries notice that one particular item in the petting zoo drew the most interest, they should consider offering or creating a specific program tailored around that equipment, as the community has expressed an interest in that knowledge.

Screen Print Holiday Cards (Technology, Art)

Chapter 8 explains all the details of screen printing for T-shirts, pillows, and other fabrics, but with one small twist this information can be suited for holiday card print making. Using the information and supplies found in the following chapter's screen printing section, library staff can also create cardstock print making programs by using acrylic speedball ink pots (as opposed to the suggested fabric versions) and switching out pieces of fabric for pieces of cardstock.

Printed pieces of cardstock can be framed and hung on the wall as art, or they can be folded and used as a hand-printed holiday card. Participants looking to add an extra little sparkle to their print can even add a layer of fine glitter while the ink is still wet to give it a quick bedazzling.

Key Points

People of all ages retain more learning benefits when they are able to practice with tools in a hands-on environment, allowing themselves to think creatively and come up with answers to a problem on their own. Gone should be the days where one sits back and simply listens to a slew of knowledge. Interactivity is key in lifelong learning.

Public computer training continues to remain a widespread community need for public libraries. As technology continues to advance, simply providing access will not suffice: library staff will need to receive proper training or make the appropriate partnerships so that they can in turn teach their communities how to use this technology and software themselves.

Libraries' computer instruction course rosters can be lightened up by the addition of some dating site classes. Library staff, while avoiding any image of relationship or matchmaking experts, can help adult patrons to create and complete online dating profiles while also teaching them some best practices when it comes to online internet safety and privacy.

Adults can enjoy library LEGO programs too! LEGO speed dating can be a good way for adults to practice that hands-on engineering design experience, while also bringing back feelings of nostalgia and giving them something to collaborate on with potential future partners, helping to bring some further comfort into what can be an awkward situation.

Fake news continues to be a common, concerning buzzword in the media, and public libraries are perfectly suited to create educational efforts to teach their communities how to properly evaluate internet information sources, so as to create more informed news consumers.

Appy hours and digital petting zoos, while catchy in name, are also a great way to have library staff out on the floor and ready to provide community members with casual or more in-depth knowledge of any new or personal technology that strikes the customer's fancy.

Screen print holiday cards use acrylic ink and cardstock to make a small twist on the fabric screen printing instructions found in chapter 8. Cardstock prints can be framed and used to hang on a wall, or folded and sent as a hand-printed card.

Notes

1. M. Waldrop, "The Science of Teaching Science," *Nature* 523, no. 7560 (2015): 274.
2. Waldrop, "Science of Teaching Science," 273.
3. Candice Blackwood in discussion with the author, November 2017.

4. Bo Kinney, "The Internet, Public Libraries, and the Digital Divide," *Public Library Quarterly* 29, no. 2 (2010): 105.

5. Kinney, "Internet, Public Libraries," 151.

6. Kinney, "Internet, Public Libraries," 151.

7. Monica Anderson and Andrew Perrin, "Technology Use among Seniors," Pew Research Center: Internet, Science & Tech, May 17, 2017, accessed December 10, 2017, http://www.pewinternet.org/2017/05/17/technology-use-among-seniors/.

8. Kinney, "Internet, Public Libraries," 148.

9. Aaron Smith, "15% of American Adults Have Used Online Dating Sites or Mobile Dating Apps," Pew Research Center: Internet, Science & Tech, February 11, 2016, accessed December 10, 2017, http://www.pewinternet.org/2016/02/11/15-percent-of-american-adults-have-used-online-dating-sites-or-mobile-dating-apps/.

10. Smith, "15% of American Adults."

11. Smith, "15% of American Adults."

12. Janna Anderson and Lee Rainie, "The Future of Truth and Misinformation Online," Pew Research Center: Internet, Science & Tech, October 19, 2017, accessed December 10, 2017, http://www.pewinternet.org/2017/10/19/the-future-of-truth-and-misinformation-online/.

13. Anderson and Rainie, "Future of Truth and Misinformation."

14. Marcus Banks, "Fighting Fake News." *American Libraries Magazine*, December 27, 2016, accessed December 10, 2017, https://americanlibrariesmagazine.org/2016/12/27/fighting-fake-news/.

15. "Fake News: A Library Resource Round-Up," Programming Librarian, October 20, 2017, accessed December 10, 2017, http://www.programminglibrarian.org/articles/fake-news-library-round.

16. Anderson and Rainie, "Future of Truth and Misinformation."

Further Reading

Programming Librarian. "Fake News: A Library Resource Round-Up." October 20, 2017. Accessed December 10, 2017. http://www.programminglibrarian.org/articles/fake-news-library-round.

CHAPTER 8

STEM Programs for All Ages and Families

IN THIS CHAPTER

- ▷ Free Comic Book Day and STEM
- ▷ Green screen programs
- ▷ Screen printing programs
- ▷ Escape rooms
- ▷ Virtual reality
- ▷ Makedo construction

AS SEEN THROUGH the preceding programming chapters, STEM programs can come in all shapes and sizes, for all age ranges. Plenty of families visit the library together as a family unit, looking for an activity where they can share experiences together through learning and having fun. All-ages programs welcome parents and adults to join their children and even teens to participate in scalable activities meant for all age ranges.

Heather Love Beverley, the Children's Services assistant manager at the Cook Memorial Public Library District, explains that her library's quarterly "Family Maker" and "Family Science" events are programs designed for "parents and children to attend together" where the library provides participants with instructions and materials for "various projects and experiments."[1] Instruction packets contain information on "the scientific aspects of the projects" as well as discussion questions for families to talk about as they "work together on the tasks" that are "chosen and designed to be something that families can do together."[2]

All-ages programming also helps to encourage attendance from all those who are curious—the eleven-year-old who feels perhaps just too young to venture into the teen programming room, or a single adult who is interested in the preschool program concept, but feels awkward walking into the room without any toddlers.

Encouraging shared adult participation can transform plenty of age-specific programs into all-ages events. Let's look at a couple of engaging examples of ways to incorporate STEM activities into all-ages programming, below.

Free Comic Book Day (Technology, Art, Engineering)

Free Comic Book Day is an exciting annual event celebrated on the first Saturday in May that sees many comic shops and libraries handing out free comics to its attendees. Depending on the location, participants can go home with one to a handful of this year's Free Comic Book Day comics. Many participants show up in superhero or anime cosplay, and hop from shop to shop around the city trying to get as many free comics as possible! Comic shops will have purchased limited-edition Free Comic Book Day comics, which are created and released each year for this event only (collector's items!) and they hand them out for free.

Having a Free Comic Book Day event brings people into the library—you might see some new faces who drop by to pick up that extra issue of this year's Rocket Raccoon just because the library is on the local Free Comic Book Day events map. What an exciting event to welcome them into your branch for the first time! Likewise, it highlights the library's graphic novel collection—of course, you'll want to tell any library newcomers that you circulate comics and graphic novels for free, and you might even grab some branch regulars who weren't aware that the library even had such resources too.

It also gives library programming staff an opportunity to work with community partners—partnering with local comic shops and convention coordinators not only allows you to gain access to their customers, but also fosters a relationship the library might be able to draw upon in the future, perhaps for possible prize donations or panel hostings at an upcoming Library Mini Comic Convention. And of course, it provides libraries with a great, fun theme for incorporating STEM programs!

The Power of Partnership

Before organizing the STEM programming portion, to really make the most of Free Comic Book Day, libraries will need to secure a partner. This will usually come in the form of a comic shop in your catchment area, but if you really want to step up your Free Comic Book Day game, you could even think about approaching your local comic convention coordinators.

Although Free Comic Book Day is mainly an event to "showcase and promote local comic book shops,"[3] teachers and librarians are encouraged to find cross-promotion partners through local comic shops on the Comic Shop Locator Service. This service allows libraries to type in their zip or postal code to see a list of nearby comic shops anywhere in North America. From this list you're looking for a shop with the "School & Library Partner" stamp. Diamond Bookshelf's Comic Shop Partner Page describes shops willing to affix this stamp to their listing as being open to helping "libraries and schools promote comics and graphic novels," whether that's through programming, purchasing discounts, presentations, or the like.

Using the contact information found on this listing, libraries can call or email their chosen shop and ask for some support. There are a couple of different ways the shop can offer help. Libraries can approach the shop (via email to the manager) asking whether it would be willing to purchase some of this year's Free Comic Book Day comics for you if the library is able to provide the shop with the funds (only comic shops have access to this purchasing power). Be prepared to have a budgeted amount of money set aside for this possibility.

The comic shop might, however, offer to subsidize this cost for the library. There is usually an area on each Free Comic Book Day comic to place a stamp or sticker advertising your comic shop or library. If a shop is able to buy the comics for you, it will usually place its own stamp/sticker in the advertisement area.

For libraries who are unable to secure a donation by their partnering shop, keep in mind that the prices vary by comic. There are both Gold and Silver comics seen on the annual listing. Gold-sponsored books are often less expensive because they're produced by some of the larger publishers. Regardless, the price lists for the annual Free Comic Book Day comics usually range from about $0.25 to $0.45 a comic. You can create your budget based upon your expected attendance needs, and how many you're looking to give out per customer (one is fine!).

When selecting which comics you'd like to order from the annual roster, make sure you check the age ratings. If you're hosting an all-ages event, try to go for an even range of adult, YA, and kids' comics.

Although the free comics will be the main motivator bringing people to your Free Comic Book Day events, this is yet another great opportunity to incorporate some STEM skill learning once you have a captive audience.

Cosplay Contest (Engineering, Technology, Art)

Offering a cosplay contest provides an opportunity for the library's local community to show off their handmade costumes using a variety of different maker techniques. The contest can have special winners for handmade as well as pre-purchased costumes, in addition to the overall grand prize winners. Divisions by age groups are useful as well—the costume creation skills of an elementary student could often pale in comparison to those of an adult. Common age-group divisions include preschool, elementary, teen, and adult.

Prizes don't necessarily need to cost any money—libraries could use their button makers to make some superhero-themed buttons from some comic and manga discards in order to provide button sets as prizes. The supplies and equipment can even be brought out so that staff can teach participants how to make their own buttons out of comic discards.

Other low-cost prizes can include superhero stickers and coloring books as prize packs for the younger participants. Libraries could also try to secure some prizes from any of their partnering comic shops. Funko Pop! figures are always a great hit, and come in a variety of comic-themed and superhero designs.

Costume judging can be done by the audience or staff members, depending on staff availability. Libraries should also think about approaching any local professional cosplayers or any local science fiction convention for helping to judge and host a costume contest. Professional cosplayers will be well versed in ways in which to judge the contest, but if it's left up to more inexperienced staff judges, they can give numbered marks based on things like demonstrated handmade-costume-making skills, or even just sheer enthusiasm of the costume presentation.

Superhero Costume Construction (Engineering, Art)

Libraries can also provide a station where children can construct their own superhero costumes for Free Comic Book Day. Hold this activity sometime prior to the cosplay contest so that children can later enter their creations into the contest. Adults can help their younger children with some of the more complicated portions of these creations. Costume creation can include things like:

- Blue bag superhero cape:
  Provide a blank template for children to draw their own superhero symbol. Have a few sample creations posted for examples (a large letter for one's first name, or a particular animal, or a favorite shape). They can then cut out the symbol and tape it to the back of a blue recycling bag cape (which can be one side of the original bag, laced with string around the top).
- Wrist cuffs:
  Cardboard toilet paper rolls can be pre-cut in half, lengthwise. Children can paint and decorate these with stickers and fun foam shapes before fitting them onto their wrists.
- Masks:
  Superhero mask templates on cardstock or foam craft sheets (with pre-cut eye-holes) can be cut out and decorated with feathers, glitter, sequins, foam shapes, or paint, and tied around the face.

Build and Smash Superhero Walls

Once young children are finished their superhero costumes, they can move on to a fun building activity with build and smash superhero walls. Cover one side of a dozen medium-sized cardboard boxes with a colored print out of a brick wall. Children can then build tall or wide structures with the brick boxes.

Box structures can be placed at the end of a foam-mat path, just before a blanket-covered table. Children can run down the path, smash through the boxes, and climb underneath to "rescue" and return a stuffed animal back to the starting point. Try timing this process with a stopwatch (try this with a laptop, so that everyone can see the counting), and list times in order of quickest superhero rescue, in order for kids to practice numeracy skills.

Green Screen

Free Comic Book Day is also an excellent celebration to bring out a green screen! Cosplayers and other attendees will love taking pictures in front of a sci-fi-related background, or polka-dotted comic book pages. This surprisingly simple technology will also show families how they can easily re-create this project in their own homes, with a few simple supplies. Don't forget to get a group picture of all your cosplay costume contest contestants in the photo booth too!

There are multiple ways to build a library green screen kit. The simplest is to purchase a pre-made kit that includes a pop-out backdrop with an adjustable stand, such as a collapsible chroma-key blue/green background, which can be found on Amazon starting at around US$80. Collapsible, pop-out versions of this screen will increase its ability to travel from branch to branch if it is meant to be an item to regionally share. Libraries should keep in mind that the 5' × 7' size, however, won't capture any feet in the pictures, as it doesn't roll out onto the ground. That being said, a cheaper alternative option is using a green (or blue) plastic tablecloth from a local dollar store or Party City, or even a large solid, green (or blue) piece of fabric. Both of these options will allow for photo booth attendees to stand over the green area, making sure to capture from their head to toe in the image. The tricky part about these options, however, is the possibility of wrinkles, which can distort the image. Fabric should work better than a plastic colored tablecloth, if staff are prepared to iron it before each use.

Once libraries have secured their green or blue backdrop, they'll need the appropriate chroma-key, green screen software. The Do Ink app for iOS devices is an excellent, easy-to-use choice. The iTunes App Store sells Do Ink: Green Screen for only $3.99. Having this pre-installed on an iPad (or multiple) for use in the program will allow library staff to teach children and families how the green screen process works. They can give quick and simple explanations about the green screen effect and how it combines "images from two sources into a single image," where the software then stacks these in layers, one in front of the other, so that "portions of the foreground image [become] transparent, allowing the corresponding parts of the background image to show through" by finding "a specific color (like green, for example!) in the foreground image and then erasing any portions of the image that contain that color."[4]

When hosting projects with screen printing and button making, libraries should make sure they're using only background images that they have the copyright for. Options include scanning images that children or teens draw by hand for their own backgrounds, or creating them digitally via computer software. Simple comic book backgrounds can be made with black or white polka-dot patterns in front of a solid-color background, easily created in Microsoft Publisher.

Libraries can also ask their communication and marketing departments to create an image for them, or they could search for creative commons licensed images on places like Google and Flickr.

The green screen can work as a stand-alone program, with a whole kit of iPads, and even multiple chroma-key backdrops, if they're available. Families can group into a couple of teams and create a green screen movie from start to finish—they can start by mapping out their scenes, then take care of designing the background, and dress up in costume. Encourage attendees to bring their own, or the library could have a variety of dress-up clothes available for them from the children's play area, or maybe through staff donations. If there's a small budget available, small props can be purchased at a local dollar store, or staff could even have teen volunteers create paper or cardboard props on sticks (try painting the sticks green to create a floating item!).

Groups would then act in and film their scenes in front of the green screen, and take care of the editing within the Do Ink app. Library staff could then have everyone in the program show off their projects to the rest of the group, and maybe even vote on their favorites! If the library has access to a branch or regional YouTube account, posting videos there could be a fun option, but make sure to have the appropriate media release forms (according to the library's policy) signed by any parents or guardians, before doing so.

A green screen can also work well as an additional activity in other kinds of programs. Having it out as a photo booth with a couple of select backgrounds that match the theme of the library's pop culture programs is often a quick hit. Try stationing the backdrop in a corner beside the games and crafts, or invite people in after a group trivia program.

If there's a larger crowd participating, this activity becomes less about the hands-on learning of technology skills, since you'll need a staff member or teen volunteer to be taking all of the pictures—but, it's still a good introduction to the technology in general. Families can watch as your staff or volunteer swirls the chroma-key around in the Do Ink app, as they have casual conversations with patrons about how the technology works, and even how they can re-create it at home with the green tablecloths and $4 app on their iPads. Try planning this kind of program just before a more focused, hands-on green screen event, so that you can promote it during these casual, quick photo booth lineups. Teens are also sure to love being able to go home with pictures of themselves with their favorite pop culture characters in your Dr. Who, *Hamilton*, or Rick & Morty programs.

Other Cosplay Green Screen Opportunities

Green screen cosplay photo booths are a fun activity for a variety of different themes and seasons, such as Anime Clubs, Halloween, or mini library comic conventions. Is there a local sci-fi convention in your community? Perhaps the library could even bring the green screen kit there, and provide a free green screen booth. Don't forget to take promo for all your nerdy STEM programs while you're at it!

Holiday Family Photo Booth Green Screen (Technology)

While green screens go well with cosplay and holidays like Halloween, they can also be quite fun for families surrounding other holidays, like Christmas. Holiday- or winter-themed backgrounds are extremely useful for a family holiday photo booth. Hosting this program sometime in December will allow families to take family photos in front of wintery, festive backgrounds that they can later use to send out as printed or electronic cards during the holiday season. If this is likely to be a popular event, consider holding registration for the program and booking each family into a different twenty-minute time slot.

Screen Printing Workshops (Technology, Art)

While somewhat messy, screen printing is a fun, adaptable library activity that can incorporate a variety of different themes, holidays, and interests as expressed by the kids, teens, and families in your community. Screen printing programs not only provide youth and adults with the opportunity to get hands-on experience with the tools and technology of printmaking, but they can also provide them with a creative outlet to practice their art skills.

There are a variety of different items and materials that will accept a screen printed image, but for this proposed library program, we'll be focusing on one of the most simple: fabric. This can include T-shirts, pillowcases, tea towels, canvas bags, and so forth.

Collecting Materials

Investing in a screen printing kit for your library can be a moderately expensive process, and, although there are consumables that have expiry dates, a few of the items are certainly reusable throughout the course of many programs. Like many of the other suggestions for more expensive materials, these items could be purchased as a regional kit that is shared and circulated between different branches in your multi-branch system. But keep in mind that you'll want to make sure to book the branch loans for a week or two in advance, as you'll need at least a few days to prepare your screens before the day of your actual program.

You'll need the following items to get you started:

As a first-time screen printer, there are one-stop-shopping options where you can purchase everything you need in one simple kit. Both the Speedball Diazo Ultimate Screen Printing kit and the Speedball Advanced All-In-One Screen Printing kit should run you around US$150, and include everything you need to get started—screen frames, squeegees, inks, emulsion fluids, transparency sheets, and even the lights! You can find these kits on Amazon, or most art supply stores like Michael's, Hobby Lobby, or DeSerres. The individual mandatory components will be broken out below—if you'd like to source your own kit, purchase multiples, or restock on those consumables, the following list should keep you covered. Unless otherwise noted, the following supplies can purchased through the same outlets that were mentioned for the full kits above. Prices are approximate, and subject to vary based upon date and location.

8" × 10" screens ($30 each):

Speedball makes screen frames in both 8" × 10" as well as 10" × 14". Go for the smaller size to save a few dollars—it's still plenty big to allow for a medium-sized image that should fit onto an adult-size T-shirt. Screens can be used over and over again, as long as they are cleaned gently, yet thoroughly, immediately after use. Follow the accompanied Speedball instructions meticulously.

Speedball Photo Emulsion kit ($33):

This is a consumable product, and will last for about three to five screens. Keep in mind that it does normally expire six months after its first use, so you might want to pre-plan your next few screen print programs, or share the product with another branch, to make sure you get your money's worth. The kit includes two solutions: The first is emulsion—the fluid used to burn your photo image onto the screen (which then later allows the ink to pass through the screen onto the fabric in that shape). The second is cleaning fluid (emulsion remover), which allows you to remove the previously burned image, giving you a clean slate to start all over again with your next image. Follow the accompanied Speedball instructions meticulously.

Speedball Drawing Fluid / Screen Filler kit ($30):

This too is a consumable product—but it is to be used as an alternative to the photo emulsion kit. While the photo emulsion kit above will allow you to burn a detailed, computer-printed image onto your screen, this Drawing Fluid / Screen

Filler kit gets you to freehand draw the desired image right onto the screen, with a brush. The blue drawing fluid is used to paint the simple image onto the screen in your desired shape. After this dries, the red screen filler goes on top to block out the rest of the screen. A quick wash and you can see the blue fluid disappearing, leaving that shaped space free for the ink to pass through. As usual, make sure to follow the accompanied Speedball instructions meticulously.

9" Plastic Handle Squeegee ($13):

Used for short run (as opposed to mass quantity manufacturing) print projects, this plastic handle with neoprene blade helps to press your ink through the screen. Since it's recommended not to place images too closely to the edge of a screen frame, the 9" squeegee should work fine with both an 8" × 10" and a 10" × 14" screen.

Speedball Fabric Screen Printing Ink ($10 for an 8-ounce pot):

Make sure to get the screen print ink for fabric (as opposed to the acrylic version). Speedball fabric ink comes in a variety of different options—black, white, and primary colors, as well as neons and glow in the darks. An 8-ounce portion should normally last you for about 150 prints of a small image. Don't forget to scrape and save any of the leftovers left in the corner of your screens, and to close the lid tightly in between uses.

Transparency Film (price varies):

Prices for packs of transparency film seems to vary—you can buy bulk packs of 100 sheets for around $50, but Amazon also has 50-count boxes of Apollo brand for $15. Before setting out to buy a new package of transparency film, check around through your old office supplies, or ask your admin office if it has any kicking around. They were a common office supply in the days of overhead projectors, so it's possible someone in your system has some leftover supplies you could use instead.

Important notes with transparency printing are to account for double copies—print two transparencies of your photo image (for use with the photo emulsion kit) so you can double up on the opacity of your image during screen burning. Any error or hole in the printed ink image will allow ink to pass through your finalized screen, so doubling up on transparencies helps to ensure total blockage.

You'll also want to make sure that you have the correct type of transparency film for your available printer. Some film is meant for laser printers, while others are meant for inkjet. Using the wrong kind of transparency film in your printer can cause a major jamming, and even melting, mishap.

Choosing Your Image

There are a variety of different ways to choose the image for your screen printing project. You'll likely start with an associated program theme—holidays, pop culture, or perhaps something to do with a local festival or club. You'll want to make sure it's a simple image—look for a silhouette or thick black outlines of specific shapes. Avoid fine details and thinner lines, as they are harder to catch in both the photo emulsion burning process, as well as the freehand drawing fluid method.

Finding an image that is not infringing upon copyright is a bit more challenging, but as the library is meant to be an upholder of such values, it is, of course, wise to do so. Try looking through Microsoft clip art, Pixabay, Flickr, or Google Image searches using the Creative Commons search feature.

If your library has a marketing and communications department in your library, it might be able to create a specific silhouette for you from scratch, or it might have access to a variety of subscription-based image galleries that could have the appropriate available licenses.

When in doubt, text is always an easy solution—think about a fun or cute slogan that might work on your fabric project. Make sure to choose a thick, bold font too.

Original Art Pieces

If you're new to screen printing library programs, you'll likely want to get some hands-on experience for yourself, and select, prepare, and test out the printed screen on your own, a day or two before your program. Once you feel more comfortable with teaching the process, however, incorporating the drawing of the screen printed image into a library program can be an excellent way to provide an opportunity for your community members to practice their art skills. Budding graphic designers can create their own fonts for a specific saying or slogan, manga artists can draw fan art of their favorite characters, or digital media artists could create their own unique image.

Of course, since you can usually only place one image on a screen at a time, you will need either a large set of screens, a smaller group of participants, or perhaps an organized schedule of how you will be accepting and incorporating the art pieces into future printing projects, so that everyone gets a chance. Perhaps your monthly Anime Club will have a screen printing night twice a year—given that most library program planning cycles are carried out months in advance, you should have plenty of notice to tell your chosen young artists about their opportunity to shine. Multi-term teen volunteers might also be well suited for this time intensive project.

Burning Images

As mentioned above, when it comes down to burning your images (or hand-filling them with fluid), as a new screen printer, you'll want the hands-on experience to do this yourself. If you're ready to branch out and teach it to others, you could try incorporating it into the learning processes of something like a weeklong day camp or a weekly summer series. Both the photo emulsion and the hand-drawn fluid methods take several hours to dry and set, so they are both multiple-day processes.

Photo Emulsion Print

While the all-in-one screen printing kits above include a specific screen printing bulb and lamp, you can definitely source your own elsewhere. You'll want to follow the explicit Speedball instructions in your photo emulsion kit for the photo burning process, but the basic concept is that the higher the wattage/UV, the quicker the length of burning time. The distance from your light source to your screen will also affect the burn time. You can use a 150-watt bulb found at your local hardware store for a few dollars, but it will take about forty-five minutes to burn, as opposed to your 250 watt, or halogen work lamps, which take around ten to fifteen minutes to burn the image.

There is also the option of buying the separate but more costly Speedball Diazo Light kit, which will run you about $80 on Amazon. While the cost is much higher, it should cut down on your research and experimentation time with trying out different variations of burn wattage, distance, and times.

Hand Drawn

Detailed instructions can be found in the instructions included in the Speedball Drawing Fluid / Screen Filler kits. You'll want to print out your silhouette or thick-text image on a regular piece of paper, and tape it with painter's tape to the back of the screen. You can then use this as a guide to trace the silhouette outline onto the screen with a washable marker.

Remove your guide paper, and you'll then want to prop the screen in a stable position above your working table—the screen should not be touching the table, even if you have a recycled newspaper barrier on top it. While this barrier is smart in terms of cleaning up any drips, you need to make sure that nothing is pressing up against the back of the screen when applying the blue drawing fluid, lest it smudge and spread to unintended places. Ideally you shouldn't have too many drips dropping on your newspaper beneath, though, because you want to use as little fluid as possible. Once quick pass should stain and cover the area—using too much product can cause the fluid to bubble and create air holes, which could create unintended spots in your image. This is another reason to follow the included instructions, which remind you to stir (instead of shaking) each of the fluid bottles, in order to avoid those dreaded air bubbles.

Once your blue image is completely dry, it's time for your single pass of the screen filler. Instructions remind you to coat with one squeegee pass of the red solution—the more passes you make, the more chances you have of flaking off your blue hand-painted image. You'll now want to let your red screen filler dry for about a day—if you go to wash away the blue image fluid from your screen before the red screen filler has fully dried, the red will start to chip away with the blue, ruining your image. Similar to the photo emulsion exposures, this can be a finicky process, so you'll want to start testing out your image creation at least a few days before your program proper. When in doubt, refer to Speedball's specific instructions!

Program Promotion and Planning Elements

Screen printing can be a station activity within a larger program, or it can also work well on its own. It all depends upon your access to staff, planning and prep hours, and volunteer program assistant to help run the event. If you're planning on running the screen printing as the focus activity of your program, you might want to include thematically appropriate coloring sheets, or even blank paper T-shirt templates, giving teens and younger children a creative outlet to occupy their time while waiting in line to have their T-shirt printed. You can start the program with an explanation of all the materials used, and the process of how the image was burned or drawn onto the screen. The tools and process can be reiterated through casual conversation with each person as they step up to the printing station and take their turn at the squeegee.

During your promotional period, you'll want to make sure that your program blurbs advertise the drop-in nature of the program—if you give yourself two hours to get through a lineup of one hundred people, some might show up expecting two hours' worth of program content. You can try to fill the lineup wait times with as many casual crafts and coloring sheets as possible (as seen below), but the first people in and out will likely only be there for a short time. The "drop-in" clause of your promo should help remind people what to expect.

The promotional posters, web ads, and library guide are also an important place to remind your community to bring a piece of fabric. It's safe to proactively choose a palette of darker inks when supply shopping, and to ask patrons to bring a "light-colored T-shirt or pillowcase." T-shirts and pillowcases don't even need to be new—simply light in color, and with a bit of blank space.

Despite your best efforts at fabric-reminder promo, you're still likely to receive a few attendees who "forgot," "didn't notice," or simply happened upon the real-time program while in your branch. If you've got the budget for it, you could purchase a few surplus blank fabric pieces for these special cases. Try Dollar Store blank tea towels, bulk canvas bags, or even just a large scrap of pre-cut fabric portions from the fabric store.

If you have the option of multiple screens/images to choose from, try having a whiteboard outside of your program room, reminding the people in line of their choices. Suggest they arrive with their chosen image, and their T-shirt/pillowcase/bag pre-lined with a layer of recycled newspaper (provided to them by your volunteer or staff crowd controller). This will ensure that the printed ink does not squish through on lighter fabrics, ending up in a mirrored backward image on the other side of their shirt.

You'll definitely want to stick to one color of ink per image; otherwise, you'll be washing your screen in between printings way more than necessary, and thereby increasing the chances of flaking the image off.

Speaking of ink! Staff who are helping out with the actual printing process will want to wear aprons or old T-shirts that they don't mind getting a little extra inked. It can be a messy process!

You'll also want to have an ironing station—you can use a regular clothes iron from home, or perhaps you have one in your craft supplies cupboard for frequent use with a Perler bead kit. Once the image is printed, you'll want to heat set the ink by having a staff member iron over the image. Make sure to have a barrier of parchment paper or cleaner, excess fabric as a barrier between your iron and the ink, and suggest that your new T-shirt owners pop the fabric in the dryer when they get home. Heat setting should ideally help to avoid the ink from fading in future washes, but most customers will understand that this is a free project, carried out by library and craft enthusiasts—most people won't be expecting professional-quality prints.

ALLERGY ALERTS

Each pot of Speedball fabric ink has a listed source of ingredients, which you can make available to your program attendees. Packaging does list ingredients to be certified as non-toxic, but consider the following tips for extra care when there are concerns about allergies:

Given that not everyone can afford to bring in brand new T-shirts to this activity, program attendees might want to wash their T-shirts at home after having placed them in the communal printing frame, as things like pet fur and dander could have been transferred with the shared usage.

A note on the pillowcase prints—encourage these pillows to be used decoratively as opposed to functionally. Speedball ink sensitivity has likely not been tested for prolonged usage of skin-to-direct-ink contact (say, overnight, on a pillow).

Finding Art School Partners

If you're unsure about committing your budget funds to a screen printing kit for your library before really testing out the idea within your community, you could alternatively speak to any local art schools to see if they might have a screen printing class or program that might be interesting in partnering up for a free program at your branch. This could give their students a chance to practice their professional skills, gain some volunteer hours, and promote their program and institution. If they've got the knowledge, experts, and tools, you could offer to at least supplement the inks (based upon their recommendation).

More information about partnering up with local community groups and organizations can be found in chapter 9.

Screen Printing Program Themes

Choosing images for a screen printing project will normally expand into the planning process of choosing a theme. Depending upon how busy the program is expected to be, the screen printing program can be simply a drop-in event where people wait in line to get a hands-on demo of how to print their item of fabric, like a Star Wars screen printing program, where families choose from a variety of different text-based slogans like #lightside or #darkside, in addition to a Darth Vader helmet icon digitally drawn by staff. Star Wars coloring sheets wait on the sidelines to occupy younger children while waiting for their turn at the screens.

Examples of screen printing stations as a part of a larger program include the Keshen Goodman Public Library where a teen-drawn Pokémon image was printed on tees during the height of Pokémon Go in summer 2016—Pokémon Go lures were dropped at the Pokestop just outside the library in order to attract more players to the event. A Halloween carnival in fall 2017 saw families arriving with pillowcases to print onto for their treat bags—hand-drawn pumpkin images and clip art ghosts left on many a candy tote, among the Halloween slime, and candy apple pop making activities.

Figure 8.1. Screen printing supplies

Collection Items

Plenty of library staff have long used their programs as an additional way to promote their collection by incorporating a display of books that are topical to your event's theme. Checking out one of these displayed materials is also an opportunity for teens and families to continue their learning and experimentation from home after the event. Below is a quick list that you might find useful for your own screen printing program research (particularly the details of creating your own exposure lamp) or even just as a useful addition to your YA non-fiction collection.

- Cossu, Matteo, and Claire Dalquié. *Silkscreen Basics: A Complete How-to Handbook*. Berkeley, CA: Gingko, 2012.
- Dillon, Jamie, Nick Paparone, and Luren Jenison. *Print Liberation: The Screen Printing Primer*. Cincinnati, OH: North Light Books, 2008. Lewis, Karen. *Screen Printing at Home*. New York: F & W Media, 2014.
- Doh, Jenny. *Print Collective: Screenprinting Techniques & Projects*. New York: Sterling, 2013.
- Isaacson, John. *Do-It-Together Screen Printing*. Bloomington, IN: Microcosm, 2007.
- Lévy, Marion, Véronique Georgelin, and Pauline Ricard-André. *Screen Your Stuff: A Fun, Funky Introduction to Silk-Screening Your Tees, Totes, Towels, and More*. New York: Watson-Guptill, 2008.
- Lewis, Karen. *Screen Printing at Home*. New York: F & W Media, 2014.

Escape Rooms (Science, Technology, Engineering, Math)

In Katie O'Reilly's 2016 "Libraries on Lockdown" article for *American Libraries*, she explains that "escape rooms have taken off, in a big way."[5] Citing the 2,800 escape rooms that launched around the world from 2010 to 2015 alone, she argues that it's no wonder that "youth librarians are getting into the spirit of escapism" with these team-building, logic-muscle-flexing activities.[6] Library escape rooms can be a fun and exciting way to help kids, teens, and families to practice their STEM skills, by solving clues and puzzles that open locked boxes in order to solve a riddle and hypothetically "escape" from the impending fantasy disaster that looms ahead.

Escape Room Planning

Libraries looking to start escape room programming should do some local research by attending any local commercial escape rooms, to mine for interesting ideas. O'Reilly even suggests partnering with local escape rooms, who might even "lend props or offer to help plan the event, free of charge, if they get to promote their escape rooms at the library event."[7] Libraries can build their own escape room kits by including things from local hardware stores like lockable boxes and different types of locks: number or letter combinations, keys, or even color combo locks. Invisible ink and a UV flashlight are also a common component, and since you're in a library, it's a perfect place to try the old hollowed-out-book hiding place trick (just make sure to use a discarded item).

Libraries can also purchase a pre-planned kit from Breakout EDU, which allows for the "facilitation of games where players use teamwork and critical thinking to solve a series of challenging puzzles in order to open the locked box" by including all the necessary items (such as locks, hasps, UV lights, etc.) to play "over 350 games" in the "classroom environment" for US$125.[8] While the kits are marketed for classroom use, libraries all over North America are purchasing them for public library programs, as it's perfectly applicable for a library program group setting.

When planning an escape room from scratch, be sure to have access to all of the necessary items for hands-on testing. Flowcharts will help with the logical progression of each clue set—there are often multiple levels of clues to open one particular box, so be sure to document the planned progression thoroughly.

When setting a customizable lock combination to a particular code that coordinates with your theme or clues, be diligent about documenting this change somewhere that is accessible to all who might use the kit. If the combinations change repeatedly and are lost, the lock will no longer be useful.

Escape rooms are also well suited to theme incorporation—be it pop culture, libraries, or holidays, the possibilities for background stories are endless! Specific clues can also incorporate a variety of STEM skills, such as solving math equations or counting repetitive items, or even testing STEM knowledge trivia.

Commercial escape rooms are run by a registered booking process, where groups sign up for a particular hour time slot. Library escape rooms can work much the same: as a daylong event, where families register to run through in fifteen- or thirty-minute intervals. Alternatively, a single hour-long event where multiple groups can separate and work on different clue stations simultaneously to each other is another option. The hour-long event works well if each clue station provides a specific extra riddle, such as a letter—participants can then complete the clue stations in any order, and they'll have to unscramble the given letters to give a secret password to the library host to escape before the end of the hour.

ESCAPE ROOM TIPS

Be sure to test the escape room clues before hosting the actual program—ask teen volunteers or other library staff to try things out and let the programmer know whether things seem too easy or too difficult.

Be sure to remind participants that the actual doors to the room are not locked down, which would be a fire hazard. Anybody can leave the room whenever they wish to do so, just by opening any of the doors.

Be sure to lay out any rules for participants before they enter the game: things that are off limits and shouldn't be touched (e.g., "The food cupboards are locked for a reason; they are not a part of the game, so please do not yank on my locked cabinets at the front of the room").

Success or failure photo booth: If the escape room incorporates people and families of all ages, they might be more open to taking a silly "We didn't make it out in time!" group photo, but escape rooms focused on younger children only might want to focus on the "We Escaped!" celebratory photo only.

Popin' Cookin' Escape Lab (Science, Technology, Engineering, Math)

Keshen Goodman Public Library held an Anime Club Popin' Cookin' Escape Lab for their Teen Anime Club in the summer of 2017. Teens had to solve anime-themed puzzles, basic mathematical equations, and a Dewey Decimal scavenger hunt to find a hollowed-out manga that held the key to a locked box. Teens worked in teams to solve three clue sets—each of which opened to provide a DIY Japanese candy making kit from Kracie: Popin' Cookin', Gummy Land, and Nerunerune. Teens had to work as a team to create the DIY candy kits by following the picture-based instructions in order to create

Figure 8.2. Popin' Cookin': Escape Lab clue station

their candy meal, gummies, or edible soda slime well enough to have a picture taken of the finished product before moving on to the next clue.

The team that documented completed pictures of all three candy kits first was the winner. Interestingly enough, the winning team consisted of older teens, who found the thought of tasting the DIY candy kits somewhat repulsive, and flew through the instructions. A team of younger teens came in last place because of their meticulous attention to re-creation detail, and their enjoyment of stopping to taste each kit.

Virtual Reality (Technology, Engineering)

Modern-day public libraries are often in the game of acquiring new and innovative technology in order to bring a hands-on experience with expensive digital equipment to community members of all ages, who might otherwise not have access to such high-end learning environments. Virtual reality (VR) is an excellent example of technology currently being purchased by libraries—one that although is now being marketed for at-home use, is still out of reach for the average consumer due to the high price point. Ted Belke, the services specialist for Toronto Public Library's Service Innovation / Learning, Innovation, and Resource Planning Department, explains that although virtual reality can be a "very effective tool in teaching STEM skills through educational and simulation software," that was not, in fact, the primary consideration in the implementation and use of virtual reality equipment at Toronto Public Library. Belke instead sees the "opportunity to access and learn about virtual reality technology through hands on experience" as a way to "build digital literacy skills."[9] The Toronto Public Library's VR workshops include "information about the history of VR, how the technology works, current uses of VR, and the potential future applications of Virtual Reality (and Augmented Reality)."[10]

The Toronto Public Library has six Digital Innovation Hubs located at various branches across the system, which are "learning and creation spaces" that foster, support, and inspire the "development of knowledge about new and emerging digital technology."[11] These hubs are equipped with "high end PCs and Macs with a variety of software, including Adobe Creative Suite, audio and video editing, 3D design, and document/photo scanning," and so, "adding Virtual Reality equipment to these spaces," Belke says, "was a natural step given their focus on expanding access to new technology."[12]

Virtual Reality Equipment

The Toronto Public Library (TPL) uses HTC Vive headsets running on a mix of Alienware desktops and laptops. One of the main considerations at the time of purchase, says Belke, was that "the Oculus Rift did not include motion-tracking controllers."[13] In combination with research and user reviews, TPL management decided that the HTC Vive was the most suitable system for their library because they saw it as the "most advanced and immersive system available." But if Belke were to be making a purchase decision now, he says, he thinks it would be a "tossup between the Vive and Oculus."[14] Libraries looking to purchase VR equipment in the near future should conduct their own market research based upon their budget and equipment needs, while looking for help from any local VR experts who might offer suggestions.

At present TPL has been using its VR equipment to offer drop-in demonstration programs to the public, but will be offering bookable usage by the public in early 2018. Staff are currently "in the process of developing workshops that will focus on content creation such as VR game design and 360 filmmaking."[15] Popular demos on the HTC Vive have been "Tiltbrush," which is often a "favorite to demo with first time users," due to its intuitive design and ability to "simplify the experience by only providing one controller to paint," or, experiences like "Google Earth and the Blu," which are also "great immersive titles that require little experience to enjoy right away."[16]

Belke encourages other libraries who are looking into bringing virtual reality to their own systems to research "the equipment and software available for each type of headset," noting that it is also "worth keeping an eye on what new equipment is waiting around the corner," such as the Oculus Go headset, which is due to be released in 2018, and should "bring costs down significantly and reduce some of the space and setup requirements compared to the HTC Vive and Oculus Rift."[17]

Virtual Reality Programming

Instead of requiring a signed terms of use waiver, TPL staff ensure that all VR equipment usage is "supervised and a verbal statement about safety is given before people put on the headset."[18] Children twelve and under are required to have adult supervision to use the headset, which is limited to between five and fifteen minutes maximum. In terms of adult accompaniment, while TPL's VR programming has attracted users of all ages, the demographic "does skew younger"; however, "generally, the parents who accompany their children to programs and events are equally engaged and participate" even though, Belke hypothesizes, they probably would not have attended "on their own."[19]

A common concern with newer, costly technology like virtual reality is often how this solitary, headset-wearing experience will fit into the library setting. Belke recommends using a "large TV or projector to display what the VR participant is viewing" in order to keep the larger group more engaged.[20]

If it's possible, leaning on community partners to further explore the potential of virtual reality programming should also benefit the library and its community in its adopting of this technology.[21] The Toronto Public Library launched its VR programming with their innovator in residence, VR filmmaker Elli Raynai. This twelve-week residency saw Raynai providing public workshops, lectures, and one-on-one bookings related to various aspects of VR technology and 360-degree filmmaking, Belke says. He also provided staff training to TPL's Digital Innovation Hub staff who would be receiving VR equipment at their own locations. This is an excellent example of how TPL is filling in any gaps in staff competencies, particularly with regard to developing VR game design workshops, which is something they are actively developing relationships with community partners in order to achieve.[22]

Makedo: Cardboard Cities (Technology, Art, Engineering)

Makedo is a "cardboard construction system for 21st century thinking, making and play" that involves plastic tools and supplies such as reusable screws, cardboard saws, and screwdrivers, intended to aid with the construction of cardboard creations.[23]

A Makedo "Classroom Pack" is sold for US$235 on its website, and comes with twenty Safe-Saws, twenty screwdrivers, and a large quantity of different-size screws. "Event Packs" offer two classroom packs for US$440, which might sound like a steep programming cost, but it is well worth the money in reusability. Cardboard materials are often easily sourced from library and staff recycling when programming staff sends a note out a few weeks early for staff to start saving any cardboard scraps for this upcoming program.

Cardboard Cities programs are quite simple—libraries need only provide the Makedo tool kits, along with a variety of cardboard scraps, and the children and families will use their imaginations from there! One end of the gray Safe-Saw is used to safely saw the cardboard into smaller pieces, while the other is used to poke holes in areas that require a screw. The yellow screwdriver hooks onto one of the blue screws (small or XL in size), and is used to twist it into the holes to join the two pieces of cardboard together.

Makedo explains on its website that "children learn by doing, creating, experimenting, failing and maybe succeeding" but, it warns "that's not [what is] essential."[24] The limitless possibilities of a child's Makedo creations "then open the door to imaginative play where the child is protagonist in a hack-able world of their own making."[25] They're also thereby practicing the principles of hands-on learning and engineering design.

The Makedo community website has plenty of ideas to get inspired for cardboard creations—child-size houses, cars, airplanes, hats, swords, armor, and much more. Children learn best and are most creative, however, when they are given a blank slate. Family-targeted Cardboard Cities programs will see adults and children working together to make their unique creations.

MAKEDO TIP!

Screws are reusable again and again, so prior to the start of the program, remind participants that while they can take their cardboard pieces home, all tools, including the screws, will need to stay at the library, so that other children and families can continue to experiment with them. Children who want to take their creations home will need to remove the blue screws, but—if library programmers have some cavatappi (corkscrew) pasta on hand—the blue screw can be replaced with this option for a bit more careful, temporary play at home.

Key Points

Library STEM programs can be tailored for all ages and communities. Creating all-ages programs will broaden the possible program audience, ensuring that people of all ages and family sizes feel comfortable attending these events.

Libraries should work to find local comic shop partners in order to start annual Free Comic Book Day celebrations, which can bring new patrons into the branch and highlight any graphic novel and comic collections, while also providing a unique pop-culture-laden avenue for STEM programming, such as costume creation stations, cosplay costume contests, build and smash superhero walls, and cosplay green screen photo booths.

With the US$3.99 Do Ink Green Screen app, libraries and even families at home can create their own green screen photo booth. Professional, fold-down chroma-key green screen backgrounds can be purchased from Amazon, but a large, ironed sheet of blue or green fabric, or even a plastic green or blue tablecloth, will also work too.

Be sure to have the copyright for any images you are using and reproducing in any design programs such as screen printing or green screen photo booths.

While somewhat messy, screen printing is a fun, adaptable library activity that is suitable for pop culture, holiday, and many more themes. These programs provide children, teens, and families with a hands-on experience with the tools and technology of printmaking, as well as a creative outlet to practice their art skills. Screen printing kits can be sourced in multiple parts, or as completed beginner kits from local craft and art stores like Michael's, Hobby Lobby, and DeSerres.

Figure 8.3. Makedo supplies

Escape rooms are a creative way to incorporate each STEM skill set into their customizable questions, riddles, and clues. Libraries can make their own kits for these programs by sourcing lockable boxes and different combination locks from local hardware stores, or they can purchase a pre-made classroom kit that includes more than 350 game options, from BreakoutEDU.com.

Libraries can seek partnership support from local virtual reality experts when looking to research the best VR equipment for their budgetary needs while also filling in any gaps in staff competencies.

The Makedo construction kits are a reusable, creative way to have children practice their engineering design skills, all with only the inclusion of some cardboard scraps. Be sure to remove any blue screws from projects that will be taken home, so that the program can run again and again. Corkscrew pasta will even work as a temporary replacement screw for kids who are looking to take their creations home to play with for a few more hours.

Notes

1. Heather Love Beverley in discussion with the author, November 2017.
2. Heather Love Beverley in discussion with the author, November 2017.
3. "Home Page," Free Comic Book Day, accessed December 10, 2017, http://www.freecomicbookday.com/.
4. "Home," Do Ink, accessed December 10, 2017, http://www.doink.com/.
5. Katie O'Reilly, "Libraries on Lockdown," *American Libraries* 47, nos. 9/10 (2016): 14.
6. O'Reilly, "Libraries on Lockdown," 14.
7. O'Reilly, "Libraries on Lockdown," 15.
8. "About," Breakout EDU, accessed December 10, 2017, https://www.breakoutedu.com/about.
9. Ted Belke in discussion with the author, December 2017.
10. Ted Belke in discussion with the author, December 2017.
11. Ted Belke in discussion with the author, December 2017.
12. Ted Belke in discussion with the author, December 2017.
13. Ted Belke in discussion with the author, December 2017.
14. Ted Belke in discussion with the author, December 2017.
15. Ted Belke in discussion with the author, December 2017.
16. Ted Belke in discussion with the author, December 2017.
17. Ted Belke in discussion with the author, December 2017.
18. Ted Belke in discussion with the author, December 2017.
19. Ted Belke in discussion with the author, December 2017.
20. Ted Belke in discussion with the author, December 2017.
21. Ted Belke in discussion with the author, December 2017.
22. Ted Belke in discussion with the author, December 2017.
23. "What Is Makedo," Makedo Cardboard Construction, accessed December 10, 2017, https://www.make.do/pages/what-is-makedo.
24. "What Is Makedo."
25. "What Is Makedo."

CHAPTER 9

The Power of Partnerships

IN THIS CHAPTER

- ▷ Community engagement
- ▷ STEM programming with local guests

Community Engagement

LIBRARIES ALL AROUND THE GLOBE are offering STEM programming in coordination with local and national programs, organizations, or educational institutions to bring the unique expertise (and costly equipment) of the community to free, engaging library STEM activities for all ages. Partnerships truly are such an excellent fit for STEM programming specifically, because these events aren't "just about STEM" but are also about "people and connections."[1] The vitality of the library itself can be "partially sustained by its partnerships,"[2] and libraries that create these vital civic relationships can also help to increase their STEM programming offers, thereby developing their community toward a brighter future.

Perfectly suited to become involved with "promoting civic engagement in their communities," libraries can join forces with the "many organizations and institutions already committed to strengthening participation in democracy," such as organizations and individuals who have similar missions and goals of helping the community.[3] Forging new relationships with local makerspaces, universities, and other like-minded organizations can provide "expertise, financial support, experience," and "good public relations" to public libraries.[4] Paul Dusenbery and Keliann LaConte, organizers of the 2015 Public Libraries and STEM Conference, suggest that public libraries need come together with the professionals who are engaged in "evaluation, funding, and policy," such as individuals from "related [library] associations; STEM leaders from informal science education institutions, universities, and research institutions," to create strong STEM partnerships for the benefit of the community,[5] which will allow them to "accomplish more together than alone."[6]

Building relationships with community partners in order to provide further STEM learning experiences can also provide libraries and their neighborhoods with the benefits from having "access to the richness of [their] world" through their combined, local knowledge, be it in STEM fields or otherwise.[7] The information found below provides different examples of community partnerships made between public libraries and civic or educational organizations in order to better offer more unique or costly STEM programming initiatives in their neighborhoods.

Candice Blackwood, the Teen Services librarian at the Nepean Centrepointe Branch of Ottawa Public Library, provides examples of several STEM-based partnerships in her branch, including:

- Customers from their own makerspace who have led programs such as Introduction to Inkscape (a free software that customers use frequently to design jobs for the laser cutters)
- Vendors who have led programs on the use of 3D scanners (for both customers and staff)
- A local robotics group that has led Raspberry Pi programs and developed and trained staff on Arduino Programs
- Students from Carleton University who have offered programs as required by their research grants[8]

Local Guests

Starting the partner relationship can be simple: Dusenbery says that "the easiest thing to do is ask!"[9] Librarians can pick up the phone and call the researched organizations or groups they think might be a good fit for a potential library partner. Most public benefit institutions (like zoos and museums) "have a mandate to do local community outreach," and will be thrilled to visit flexible venues like libraries, especially in the wake of rigid school curricula programming.[10] Local community college and university staff are also likely candidates to be available for "talks based on their current research," but libraries should make sure to "make it fun," since "scientists get a lot of requests to do lectures."[11] Programming staff should pitch to include a hands-on activity or incorporate a unique twist with the requested visit. This will ideally offer more incentive for both the visiting scientist as well as potential program attendees. Dusenbery also recommends having a specific program idea in mind when approaching STEM professionals as partners, but also being flexible and open to their own ideas if partners have their own suggestions.[12] Communication will be important in any community partnership—libraries should make sure to listen to their partner's ideas, mandates, and needs, while also explaining the library's own resources, policies, and community knowledge.

Paleontology Partners

Heather Love Beverley, the Children's Services assistant manager at the Cook Memorial Public Library District, provides an example of a strong community partnership with local colleges, where professors speak to patrons via Skype at their "Science Explorers" programs.[13]

The most notable partnered event was the paleontology theme that was held for children in grades 1–3, and featured two paleontologists from the local university who Skyped with their participants. The paleontologists "described their work, how dig sites were found and managed, and answered a multitude of questions from an enraptured audience."[14] The paleontologists also even kindly lent the branch "a small sampling of tools that they used in the field, as well as 3D printed replicas of fossils" for the children to look at and touch, which, Love Beverley explains, added "weight to what they heard in the skype session." Programmers followed this talk with a "mini dig for (toy) dinosaurs, using dried cornstarch and water with dinosaurs embedded in the mixture."[15]

Kids Embroidery Group (Technology, Art)

Libraries can reach out to local hobby groups such as knitting, crochet, or cross-stitching clubs to teach children the fiber arts. The creation processes of coding and fiber art projects have similarities in their architectural and troubleshooting natures,[16] but fiber art programs also hold their own strengths in teaching children to work with simple tools while allowing them to express their creative and artistic skills.

If the library's local fiber artist groups are made up of seniors, they might have a more flexible schedule to organize library programs—they could perhaps even come in on a school day to help with a class visit program.

Depending upon the size of the group, teen volunteers or extra staff people may be necessary to help younger children complete their projects. The Keshen Goodman Public Library in Nova Scotia hosts a quarterly Kids Embroidery Group program that registers a dozen children ages five through twelve. A local stitching group creates and prepares thematic projects (seasonal- or holiday-themed embroidered bookmarks, cards, or wall hangings) and brings one experienced adult stitcher to help each individual child with his or her 1.5-hour-long project. This inter-generational program also allows senior community members to meet and interact with young children.

University-Led Science Camps (Science, Technology)

Nearby colleges and universities might not only have STEM professionals willing to lecture and lead programs—they might also have not-for-profit outreach groups that will be willing to partner with public libraries. Dalhousie University has a not-for-profit initiative that promotes "science, engineering, technology and mathematics (STEM) to youth from 5 to 18 years of age" by offering exciting and innovative "workshops, summer camps, clubs, and community events throughout Atlantic Canada" that aim to provide children and teens with exciting STEM experiences in hopes that they "nurture a lifelong love of exploration, creativity, and academic achievement."[17]

Dalhousie's SuperNOVA is sponsored by ACTUA, "Canada's largest STEM outreach organization," which consists of a network of thirty-six participating universities and colleges across the country.[18] ACTUA's website lists all thirty-six partnering institutions sorted by province. Canadian public libraries can use this to see if there are any applicable ACTUA programs in their area.

Local Makerspace Demos (Technology, Engineering)

Local makerspaces are excellent resources of new tech equipment, and might be willing to visit public libraries to expand community STEM skills gadget knowledge. For example, in 2013, the Brooklyn Public Library in New York partnered with community technology organizations to host a program called "Storymaker Maker Party," which saw children creating narratives using computer programming, stop-motion animation, circuits, and robotics.[19] Makerspaces will likely have it in their own mandates to complete community outreach, and will also benefit from the increased exposure and promotion of their services.

Mad Science (Science)

Mad Science rightfully markets itself as the "STEM 'Edu-Tainment' Experts," who are available to local libraries for bookings of their special event shows that can include dry ice storms, floating hovercrafts, foam factories, super bouncy balls, magic mud, explosions, and so much more.[20] This STEM show is sure to delight library users young and old, and although the special events do come at a program performer fee, they are well worth it for a special event during high programming times such as March Break and Summer Reading Clubs. The local Mad Science "Spin, Pop, BOOM!" show performed in Halifax Public Libraries in 2016/2017 elicited many screams and shouts of laughter and glee, with children often commenting on their own surprise at how the library allowed someone to create explosions inside the branch.

Mad Science boasts hosting STEM shows, workshops, and programs to over "6.5 million children in 25 countries across 5 continents."[21] Libraries can look for their local Mad Science location in the top left corner of the MadScience.org website.

Library Lemonade with Lemon Dogs (Science)

Halifax Public Libraries' 2017 "Tastes Like Home" initiative made use of their awarded provincial 150 Forward grant funds to celebrate food culture in Nova Scotia through cooking programs, gardening workshops, and food lectures. During this celebratory program roster, the Keshen Goodman Public Library partnered with a local lemonade stand and canteen, Lemon Dogs, for the "Library Lemonade with Lemon Dogs" program. Lemon Dogs brought their staff and hand-pressed lemonade equipment to demonstrate to children how they made their unique and funky flavored drinks.

As partners, Lemon Dogs and the library worked together during program planning to organize three special storybook-themed flavored lemonades: the magical color-changing "Hermione," the fruit-flavor-laden "The Very Hungry Caterpillar," and the honey-and-pansy-flavored "Matilda"—this was an excellent melding of shared ideas. The library brought forth the idea of storybook-themed flavors, and as the flavor and lemonade experts, Lemon Dogs came up with the specific titles and flavors.

More than one hundred children and families were drawn into the program by the promise of free lemonade tastings. Lemon Dogs explained the science of a lemon's acidity, and how they make this sour liquid sweet and drinkable, all before allowing each child to taste a two-ounce sample of each of the three storybook flavors (from a large quantity of two-ounce portion cups, procured by the library during program planning time). Children then voted on their favorite flavor by writing their name and phone number on a piece of

Figure 9.1. Library Lemonade with Lemon Dogs

paper and depositing them in the marked papier-mâché lemon. The lemonade with the most votes would bequeath a full bottle of a drawn entrant's favorite drink to take home. Lemonade crafts and Makey Makey lemon pianos attached to lemonade-themed Scratch games rounded out the event (bonus STEM inclusions!).

Lemonade science need not be a partner program, however; if the library is unable to find a local lemonade expert with whom to partner, it could still adapt a version of this program idea by focusing on something more like the lemonade science project offered by Education.com in the "Further Reading" section below. Happy puckering!

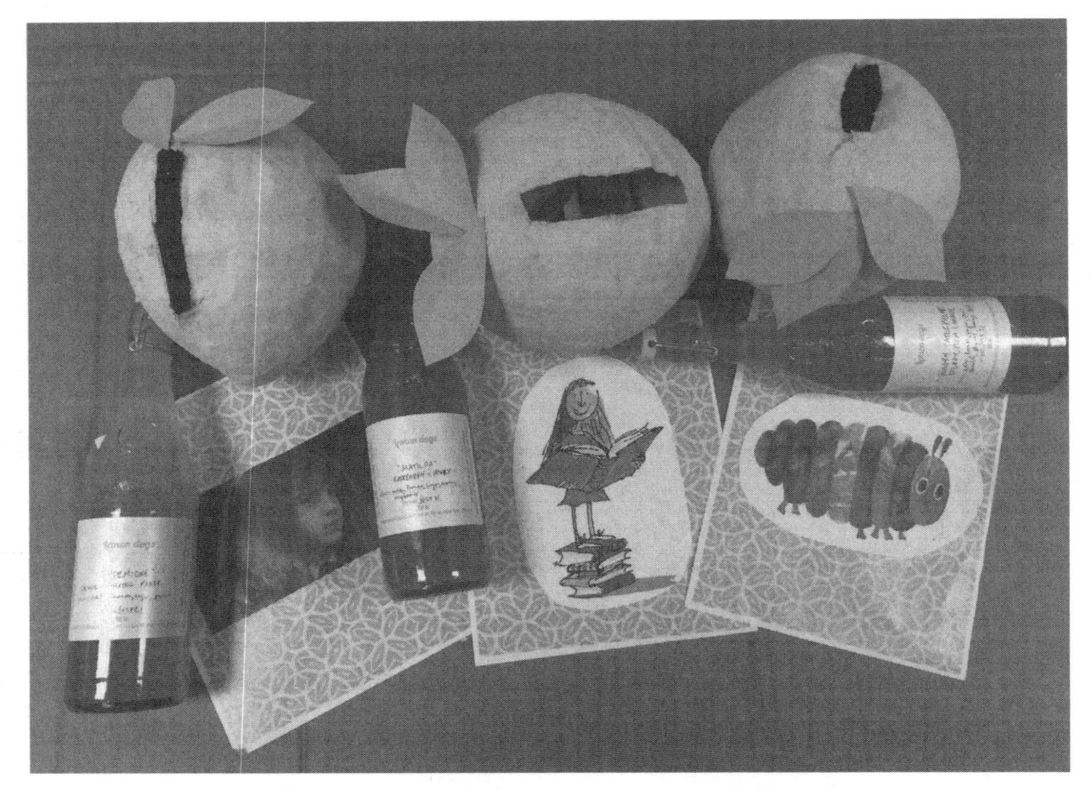

Figure 9.2. Library Lemonade with Lemon Dogs: voting lemons

Key Points

Libraries are well suited to promote civic engagement in their communities by joining forces with the STEM professionals engaged in evaluation, funding, and policy. The individuals can often be found in local associations, local hobby groups, science education institutions, universities, or research institutions. Partnering will allow both libraries and community organizations to "accomplish more together than alone."[22]

Librarians should research local organizations that have similar mandates and goals and reach out to them directly, making sure to have a program idea in mind, while also being adaptable to a partner's suggested ideas.

Local organizations like university not-for-profit outreach groups, Mad Science, or even local hobby groups or restaurants can all make willing and unique library STEM programming partners, but library staff will need to be willing to communicate and build relationships with them in order to do so.

Notes

1. "Public Libraries and STEM: An Interview with Paul Dusenbery and Keliann LaConte," *Young Adult Library Services* 14, no. 2 (2016): 12.

2. Bruce Massis, "Library Partnerships: A Key to Growth," *New Library World* 114, nos. 11/12 (2013): 552.

3. Nancy Kranich, "Civic Partnerships," *Resource Sharing & Information Networks* 18, nos. 1/2 (2005): 98.
4. Kranich, "Civic Partnerships," 98.
5. "Public Libraries and STEM," 11.
6. "Public Libraries and STEM," 12.
7. "Public Libraries and STEM," 12.
8. Candice Blackwood in discussion with the author, November 2017.
9. "Public Libraries and STEM."
10. "Public Libraries and STEM."
11. "Public Libraries and STEM."
12. "Public Libraries and STEM."
13. Heather Love Beverley in discussion with the author, November 2017.
14. Heather Love Beverley in discussion with the author, November 2017.
15. Heather Love Beverley in discussion with the author, November 2017.
16. Anna Ossowski, "What Does Cross Stitch Have to Do with Programming? More Than You Think," Opensource.com, January 3, 2017, accessed December 11, 2017, https://opensource.com/article/17/11/traditional-arts-crafts-code-programming.
17. "About SuperNOVA," SuperNOVA at Dalhousie University, accessed December 11, 2017, http://www.supernova.dal.ca/about/.
18. "About," ACTUA, accessed December 11, 2017, http://actua.ca/en/about.
19. Meredith Farkas, "Making for STEM Success," *American Libraries* 46, no. 5 (2015): 27.
20. "Education Wrapped in Entertainment!" Mad Science Group, accessed December 11, 2017, http://madscience.org/.
21. "Education Wrapped in Entertainment!"
22. Farkas, "Making for STEM Success," 27.

Further Reading

Education.com. "Make Your Own Fizzy Lemonade." Science Project. October 1, 2014. Accessed December 11, 2017. https://www.education.com/science-fair/article/make-fizzy-lemonade/.

Ossowski, Anna. "What Does Cross Stitch Have to Do with Programming? More Than You Think." Opensource.com. January 3, 2017. Accessed December 11, 2017. https://opensource.com/article/17/11/traditional-arts-crafts-code-programming.

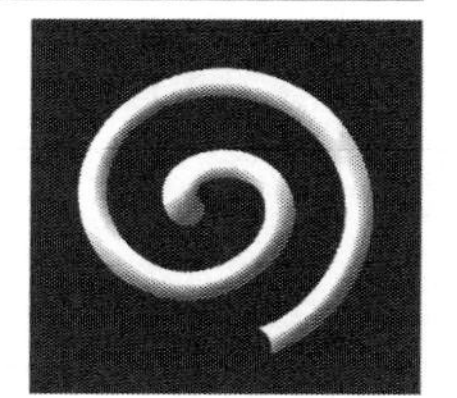

CHAPTER 10

Breaking Down Barriers

STEM Skills for Underserved Populations

IN THIS CHAPTER

- ▷ Newcomer STEM programs
- ▷ Girls in STEM
- ▷ LGBTQ+ in STEM

WHILE THE PREVIOUS CHAPTERS detail a variety of STEM programming for people of all ages, it should be noted that there are certain populations for whom STEM skills are not so easily accessible. In each community, state, province, or country, there will be communities of people who are underrepresented in the STEM career fields for a variety of different factors.

Public libraries can start trying to eliminate the barriers to service for these underserved communities in their areas by building trusting relationships with these groups. This will ideally lead to the library providing them with the appropriate knowledge and hands-on experience to start stimulating an interest in STEM-related careers. Preparing community members to excel in STEM is "crucial to ensuring that [they] have access to these and other STEM occupations in the future,"[1] but also for those individuals who don't end up in STEM careers, even just the beneficial critical thinking and problem-solving skills that go hand in hand with STEM studies should provide them with a more successful future. The Council for Canadian Academies warns Canadians that the implications of any "serious disparities" in underrepresented communities in the STEM fields are "costly for society, the economy, science, and innovation," and that by "attracting individuals with diverse perspectives, experiences, and ideas," a wider talent pool can "reveal deeper assets."[2]

Women, minorities, indigenous peoples, LGBTQ+, and people from rural or low-income communities have all faced barriers to accessing STEM programming. It is important for public libraries to find the underserved communities within their area, and to work toward building better relationships with them, so that these community members may eventually trust the library enough to ask for what it is they might need.

Librarians can approach local underserved community, cultural, or advocacy groups to start relationship building and see if these communities have access to STEM programming. Staff should likewise remain flexible, open to new ideas, and willing to work with the community group based upon their needs. If the library is not an appropriate venue for such programming, consider planning something that will work well in an off-site, outreach capacity that staff can bring directly to a particular meeting spot of this group, if the library has been invited. Offering to provide off-site programming directly in any meeting places of these underrepresented communities can not only go a long way into saving them the cost of travel, it can also help to "break down any negative connotations about STEM" by offering this programming in a "familiar and comfortable local setting."[3]

Newcomer STEM Programs

Public libraries would also be wise to do as SuperNOVA, the not-for-profit STEM programming initiative of Dalhousie, does, and "tailor" their outreach programming "to each audience, as a way of maximizing impact."[4] For example, when providing STEM programming to newcomers, or people whose first language isn't English, program plans should be calculated to incorporate this need, and to allow for some additional time with each activity in the event that things take longer to explain. Programming staff could also make use of any bilingual teen volunteers or staff on hand, if they have any, to help translate and communicate. Staff can also make sure to use plainer language, and to be prepared to use synonyms to help explain certain concepts.

SuperNOVA Science Camp for Newcomers

Dalhousie University's SuperNOVA STEM programming initiative promotes "science, engineering, technology and mathematics (STEM) to youth from 5 to 18 years of age" by offering exciting and innovative "workshops, summer camps, clubs, and community events throughout Atlantic Canada" that aim to provide children and teens with exciting STEM experiences in hopes that they "nurture a life-long love of exploration, creativity, and academic achievement."[5]

In order to meet their mandate of serving underrepresented demographics in STEM, SuperNOVA partnered with the Keshen Goodman Public Library for Newcomer Science Camps over the March Break week off school in 2015 and 2016. The library provided the free space, promotion, and program registration, while SuperNOVA supplied all of the staff, program plans, and STEM supplies. Children made alien eggs, binary code bracelets, Popsicle stick catapults, Mentos bottle rockets, and more. There was a large interest for this program in the library's community—both years the twenty-spot registration list filled up with an additional waiting list full of people hoping to take the spot of someone who might cancel.

Libraries should be prepared to advocate for the need of programming intended for underrepresented demographics, lest they get any complaints that this specific community is "taking away" programming options from the "rest of the community." Having a frank discussion with unhappy customers about the need for such programming in an attempt to eliminate additional barriers that this community might be experiencing can be a difficult discussion to have, but it is important to commit and advocate on behalf of the community that the library is seeking to help.

It is useful to allow people to self-identify as a part of the underrepresented community. Libraries are about being open and to anyone and everyone, so if individuals feel that they are new enough to your community to warrant coming to a "newcomer" program, let them in. During the registration process for SuperNOVA Science Camp for Newcomer Youth, plenty of registrants seemed worried that they weren't "new enough":

We moved here three years ago

Three months ago

Ten years ago

Information desk staff were instructed to respond to these requests explaining that, by the family's own definition, if they were new to Canada, they were welcome into the program. Either way, library staff should be prepared to offer other upcoming programming options that might suit customers' needs, if they are upset that the current demographic-focused STEM program does not meet their own identity.

Girls in STEM

The Council of Canadian Academies reports that only "29.6% of individuals with a post-secondary STEM credential and 26.9% of those employed in a STEM-intensive occupation in Canada are women."[6] Libraries and STEM organizations around the world are responding to similar situations of lacking female perspectives by trying to engage young women in STEM skill interests and learning.

For example, the Fayetteville Free Library in New York offered a weeklong Library Geek Girl Camp in 2014 where girls participated in fun science activities and met women working in the sciences.[7] Girls-only library programming should be open to anyone who identifies as female, and should aim to promote a safe space where young women can explore, experiment, and take pride in their intelligence and passions.

LGBTQ+

Although the National Science Foundation releases regular reports on the "state of women, minorities, and persons with disabilities in STEM fields," it does not include lesbian, gay, bisexual, transgender, and queer or questioning (LGBTQ+) people in its research. This, Barbara Moran argues in her 2017 Boston University Research article, can lead to a "sense of invisibility among LGBTQ+ scientists."[8] Manil Suri hypothesizes in his 2015 *New York Times* article that LGBTQ+ people are likely invisible in the STEM world because of the nature of STEM culture being so "problem-focused," that by extension, being "too expressive of personal identity can be viewed as running counter to scientific neutrality."[9] Suri urges LGBTQ+ STEM professionals to "come out not just to colleagues, but to students—some of whom will need role models," while also reiterating the critical need for STEM culture to "rein in the pressure to separate professional and personal identities" and to view its workers "more holistically," making sure to welcome "their interests and differences as sources of enhanced resourcefulness."[10]

Public libraries can stimulate STEM skill interests in LGBTQ+ communities while helping to increase the exposure of queer scientists by partnering with any local LGBTQ+ youth or ally programs that might know a STEM professional in the community who is willing to come and speak to youth. Libraries might want to bring STEM equipment off-site to any local LGBTQ+ organizations or Gender & Sexualities Alliance meetings. These groups might feel more comfortable in their well-known off-site safe spaces, but they should also be welcomed into the library: the key is to ask the partnering group as to what they would prefer.

Local Pride Week celebrations could include some STEM programming components, but be sure to focus on any marginalized community year-round as opposed to their one week or month that local government emphasizes the importance of their history and culture.

Key Points

Libraries should be adaptable and willing to plan STEM programs as outreach events off-site, which can go a long way into saving community members the cost of travel, while also helping to break down any negative connotations about STEM by offering events in comfortable local settings.

Libraries should also make sure to tailor their STEM programs to each unique audience in order to maximize impact.

Women, minorities, newcomers, indigenous peoples, LGBTQ+, and people from rural or low-income communities have all faced barriers to accessing STEM programming. It is important for public libraries to find whichever underserved populations live within their communities in order build better relationships, allowing these community members to eventually trust the library enough to ask for what it is they might need in regard to STEM skills.

Be sure to focus on any marginalized community year-round, instead of only during the one week or month that local government emphasizes the importance of their history and culture.

Notes

1. Jacqueline Leonard, Alan Buss, Ruben Gamboa, Monica Mitchell, Olatokunbo Fashola, S. Hubert, and Tarcia Almughyirah, "Using Robotics and Game Design to Enhance Children's Self-Efficacy, STEM Attitudes, and Computational Thinking Skills," *Journal of Science Education and Technology* 25, no. 6 (2016): 876.

2. Council of Canadian Academies, Expert Panel on STEM Skills for the Future. *Some Assembly Required: STEM Skills and Canada's Economic Productivity*. 2015. Accessed November

27, 2017. http://www.scienceadvice.ca/uploads/ENG/AssessmentsPublicationsNewsReleases/STEM/STEMFullReportEn.pdf: xvi.

3. Alexandra Fenton, *SuperNOVA Annual Report*, Dalhousie University, Halifax, NS, 2016, 16.

4. Fenton, *SuperNOVA Annual Report.*

5. "Home," SuperNOVA at Dalhousie University, accessed December 10, 2017, http://www.supernova.dal.ca/.

6. Council of Canadian Academies, *Some Assembly Required.*

7. Meredith Farkas, "Making for STEM Success," *American Libraries* 46, no. 5 (2015): 27.

8. Barbara Moran, "LGBTQ+ Issues in STEM Diversity," Boston University Research, June 15, 2017, http://www.bu.edu/research/articles/lgbt-issues-stem-diversity/.

9. Manil Suri, "Why Is Science So Straight?" *New York Times*, September 4, 2015, accessed December 10, 2017, https://www.nytimes.com/2015/09/05/opinion/manil-suri-why-is-science-so-straight.html.

10. Suri, "Why Is Science So Straight?"

Further Reading

Genders & Sexualities Alliance Network. "Our Approach." Accessed December 10, 2017. https://gsanetwork.org/about-us.

GLSEN. "Why (and How) STEM Curriculum Needs to Be LGBT Inclusive." Accessed December 10, 2017. https://www.glsen.org/blog/why-and-how-stem-curriculum-needs-be-lgbt-inclusive.

LGBT STEM. "LGBT STEM." Accessed December 10, 2017. https://lgbtstem.wordpress.com/.

National Organization of Gay and Lesbian Scientists and Technical Professionals. "NOGLSTP—National Organization of Gay and Lesbian Scientists and Technical Professionals." Accessed December 10, 2017. http://www.noglstp.org/.

Out in Science, Technology, Engineering, and Mathematics. "Diversity Innovates." Accessed December 10, 2017. https://www.ostem.org/.

Scholastic. "Girls Rock STEM." Accessed December 10, 2017. https://www.scholastic.com/teachers/articles/teaching-content/girls-rock-stem/.

Singh, Sandra, Working Together Project, Issuing Body, and Canadian Electronic Library, Distributor. *Community-Led Libraries Toolkit: Starting Us All down the Path toward Developing Inclusive Public Libraries.* DesLibris. Documents Collection. Vancouver, BC: Working Together, 2008.

Yoder, Jeremy. "Queer in STEM." Queer in STEM. November 22, 2016. Accessed December 10, 2017. http://www.queerstem.org/.

CHAPTER 11

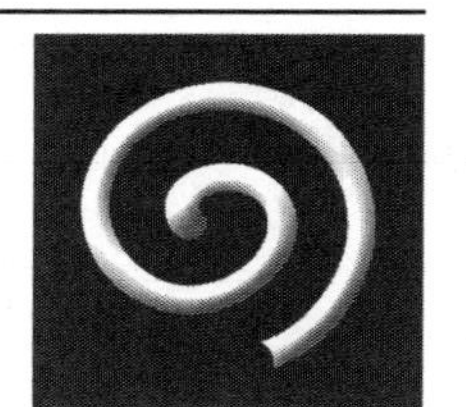

Passive STEM Programming

IN THIS CHAPTER

- ▷ Play areas
- ▷ Info desk terrariums
- ▷ Science Career Day displays
- ▷ Circulating STEM equipment
- ▷ Tethered iPads

PASSIVE LIBRARY PROGRAMS are a way to provide simple, engaging activities or services to the library's community, anywhere in the branch, whenever it is open. While proper programs require a set time, room space, promotions, and staff facilitation, passive programs avoid these needs, and can therefore be more cost effective and flexible in nature. Of course, passive programs aren't meant to replace fully planned and hosted programs, but they can often be used to supplement them. Some passive programs might even work well as a way to promote a more explicit program on a particularly related topic in-branch.

Emily T. Wichman explains in her 2012 *Librarian's Guide to Passive Programming: Easy and Affordable Activities for All Ages* how passive programs are "desirable because they encourage patrons to linger in [the] library" while also allowing them to "customize their interactions" with the branch.[1] Wichman's passive programming guide is a great resource for libraries who want to further learn how to adopt more passive programming in their branches, and is recommended in the "Further Reading" section below.

Libraries all over are already incorporating STEM-based passive programming onto their library floors. Heather Love Beverley, the Children's Services assistant manager at the Cook Memorial Public Library District, provides an excellent example of this with her library's portable "Hands-On Science Museum" that is periodically moved out into the children's department, which consists of a variety of exploratory stations where children and caregivers can explore things like magnets, light painting, weighing and measuring, counting, and building structures.[2] Love Beverley explains that the nature of the "Hands-On Science Museum" is flexible, and the library can choose whether to put all of the museum out for special occasions, or perhaps just one or two activities out in the children's area for a fun surprise.[3]

Trina Orchard, a customer service clerk in Children's Services at the Lethbridge Public Library in Alberta, also uses passive science experiments in her library, and remarks that they're "a great way to make science a daily part of the library."[4] She writes that "crystal gardens and plant terrariums" can make excellent attractions that "young visitors can come and watch change over time." Passive science programs are also an "excellent way to draw people's attention to science books in the collection."[5]

The passive programming ideas below also incorporate basic STEM skill exposures or supplements that should also ideally encourage patrons to engage in their own problem-solving conversations surrounding the chosen theme.

Play Areas

A library's children's play area is ripe with possibilities for passive STEM programming opportunities. Consider acquiring some of the following equipment and supplies in order to encourage STEM-based learning on the library floor, during all open hours.

Light Cubes (Science, Engineering, Art)

The Roylco Light Cube is a portable, 16" × 16" × 16" foot cube that lights up, flashes, and changes color. Preschoolers can stand or kneel at the cube and "engage in focused, quiet play" while using the cube for "examining transparent and opaque objects" such as beads, x-rays, optical illusion sheets, transparent blocks, and paint scrapers, which can "add interest to counting, sorting, sequencing and building activities."[6]

Sand and water tables are a popular sensory, STEM play source that are common in day cares, but they can be a bit messy in carpeted and book-laden areas. The light cube is an easier-to-clean sensory experience that can still supplement STEM learning.

They can be purchased from Amazon.com, Discount School Supply, Scholar's Choice, or Wintergreen, and run for about C$220 for the cube, or C$50 for an accessory kit.

LEGO/DUPLO Tables (Engineering)

DUPLO and LEGO tables will bring the open block building play programs right to the library play area. Preschool play areas are better suited for the DUPLO versions, although a school-age area of the library could certainly make great use of a LEGO table too. These wooden tables topped with DUPLO or LEGO bases allow children to build and design block worlds right on the table. Higher-end versions will even include space for plastic drawers beneath the base as a place to store the bricks. These tables can be purchased at most library furniture supply

Figure 11.1. Transparent building blocks

stores like Brodart and Carr McLean, as well as school supply stores like Discount School Supply, Scholar's Choice, and Wintergreen.

Magnetic Mural Walls (Science, Engineering, Art, Math)

Libraries that have the permission and ability to paint their children's play area walls could lay a coat of magnetic paint on underneath a happy, colorful mural. Having various larger magnetic supplies out in this area will allow children a hands-on experience with magnetism as they slap sight words, large foam numbers, Magformer 3D building blocks, or even series of gears onto the mural.

Info Desk Terrariums (Science, Art)

Both DuneCraft's and Faber-Castell's Creativity for Kids' Grow series of terrariums and garden crafts can be a fun biology experiment to bring to the library's information desk. Dunecraft offers tiny desk-terrarium-sized winter wonderland pine forests, fairy gardens, and carnivorous creation kits, all including real, live plants that grow within weeks.[7] Faber-Castell's Creativity For Kids' Grow line of desk-sized planters and terrariums includes fairy and sparkle butterfly gardens, pizza gardens, and even an old-school macramé terrarium that can help kids "express their artistic side with these crafts while still learning how to tend to their growing plants."[8]

These products are designed to have children plant seeds and decorate the surrounding packaging, which incorporates both artistic and science learning. Since the plants

Figure 11.2. The Turn & Learn Magnetic Gears can be purchased from LakeshoreLearning.com for US$29.99.

take weeks to grow, this makes an excellent passive STEM program. Librarians can invite children who are in the branch to decorate and help plant the seeds when it is time to start the project. Staff should encourage children to come back and check up on the progress over the next few weeks.

If there is space, the terrarium would ideally live in a visible spot on the information desk, so as to attract attention from passersby. Info staff can ask any visiting children if

Figure 11.3. Dunecraft terrarium made by children at Keshen Goodman Public Library, in Halifax, Nova Scotia

they would like to help water the plants, if there are any around the branch each time it is necessary to do so. This will, again, ideally encourage them to check up on the progress of the plant growth.

Information staff should be prepared to interact with any children and families who inquire about the project and explain what it looked like on the first day, what kinds of things are planted, and ask children what they are able to see inside, encouraging them to check in on the progress the next time they visit.

The Keshen Goodman Public Library in Halifax, Nova Scotia, planted and decorated a Dunecraft sparkle "Butterfly Glamour Garden" terrarium with the children at their Summer Reading Club Kick-Off Carnival in June 2015. By the end of the summer when the plants started to outgrow the terrarium, staff noticed that one particular young girl kept a keen eye on its progress, all summer, and they offered it to her to take home for continued care. The young girl happily accepted and took the project home for the rest of its growth, come September.

Should there be multiple children interested in the idea of taking the terrarium home for replanting at the end of the terrarium growth period, libraries could hold a contest—perhaps where children draw their own terrariums full of different plant life and stages, and one of these could be selected to take the terrarium home, once it outgrows the library space.

Celebrate a Science Career Day

Library collections are often full of STEM-themed materials, plenty of which can be used for highlighting specific areas with displays. Displays could be more generically based on particular areas within STEM fields, but connecting it to a real-world event like a local Science Career Day will give the day more meaning. Libraries can try tying this into National Engineers Week, or perhaps a local university is hosting a Medical Careers Day; public library displays could be made for both adult and youth with related fiction and non-fiction titles from the branch's collection.

Circulating STEM Equipment

Libraries aren't only in the business of circulating books. Types of circulating items have grown wildly over the past decade of public library service here in North America. Lending STEM equipment as a part of a library's circulating collection can be a unique way to give STEM skill exposure and supplement to children, adults, and families, who can take these tools and supplies and practice with them in the comfort of their own homes.

The circulating of new supplies or equipment can require putting some extra thought into the unique borrowing policies and procedures that come along with borrowing time, replacement fees, and return methods for items that don't traditionally fit into book drops. Libraries are still managing to break down barriers, however, in order to offer unique items to lend to their community members. Below are some examples of STEM-based equipment being lent in public libraries around North America:

Avondale Public Library, Arizona:
Telescopes, binoculars, magnifiers, Snap Circuits, model brains, and model hearts.[9]

Austin Public Library, Texas:
Sunlight calculators, water saver usage meters.[10]

Reading Public Library, Massachusetts:
Infrared thermometers, Spheros, Ozobots, Cubetto, KEVA planks, and Makey Makeys.[11]

Ann Arbor District Library, Michigan:
Arduino starter kits, digital microscopes, digital oscilloscopes, sound meters, metal detectors, and globes.[12]

Ottawa Public Library:
Instrument collection: guitars, keyboards, mandolins, percussion items.[13]

Tethered iPads (Technology)

Incorporating tethered iPads onto the library floor, and even into a children's play area, is a great way to expose people to technology skills they may not yet have access to. Although some families may have access to such technology at home, others may not be within the economical means to do the same. Like with any unique or expensive material or equipment, the public library is often perfectly positioned to house a local collection for free access to its community members.

Libraries will want to research which tethers and theft-proof iPad cases will work best for their branches. The Kensington SafeGrip Security Case is a popular choice for children's play areas, due to its sturdy protection against drops and bumps, and is sold on Amazon.com for US$21.

Preschool App Usage and Recommended Screen Time Usage

Keep in mind that if you're planning on bringing iPads into your preschool play area or any type of program with young children, you may experience some amount of backlash. Libraries should be prepared to present your suggestions and research to any concerned parents, while making sure to defer to their right to make any decisions for their children. By no means should libraries be suggesting how they should parent their preschooler, but, staff may want to have a researched explanation ready to advocate for their decisions to incorporate children's apps and technology in their play areas.

While the use of iPads exposes patrons to technology use in general, the apps selected for this resource can also be STEM themed as well. Although, much the same as how libraries would defend the inclusion of a "banned book" into their collection, they'll want to reference journals and professional educational sources that led them to choosing any particularly preschool-focused particular apps for the children's area if it's ever challenged by a community member. Common Sense Media is a good place to get one's bearings about age appropriateness of books as well as apps and DVDs, but selectors should keep in mind that these are largely crowdsourced collections of opinions from members of the public.

Libraries can also refer inquiring families to the American Academy of Pediatrics or the Canadian Paediatric Society's recommended screen time suggestions, which give the recommended amount of screen time usage by age. Adults can use this if they're looking for some help deciding how to help monitor the amount of time they might like to allow for their child to engage with screenplay.

Key Points

Passive programs can supplement program-specific STEM activities by providing casual access to STEM equipment and supplies on the library floor during open hours. This can also save on staff time and budgetary resources, as they are unfacilitated, and meant to be shared first come first serve, as a community group.

Children's play areas are ripe with possibilities for passive STEM library programming opportunities. Libraries can implement things like light cubes, DUPLO tables, and magnetic mural walls in order to encourage STEM-based learning on the library floor, during all open hours.

Libraries can invite visiting children to decorate terrariums or planter kits, help plant their seeds, and even to come back and check up on the progress over the next few weeks while plants and flowers bloom from a visible spot at the information desk. Dunecraft and Faber Castell offer easy DIY kits that are cheap and perfect for such library activities.

Libraries can purchase a collection of unique STEM kits and equipment for circulating within the community. This allows access to STEM learning items that patrons may not otherwise have the means to experience, particularly from the comfort of their own homes.

On-floor, tethered iPads can be an additional technology available to visiting library patrons, when paired with the right cases and tether locks that work best for a branch's physical environment. Library staff should be prepared to answer any complaints or challenges about their inclusion to the library environment, especially if they are being placed near a children's area. Referring to Common Sense Media and pediatric societies' screen time usage recommendations should help provide them with knowledge to pass on to inquiring parents.

Notes

1. Emily T. Wichman, *Librarian's Guide to Passive Programming: Easy and Affordable Activities for All Ages* (Santa Barbara, CA: Libraries Unlimited, 2012), xii.
2. Heather Love Beverley in discussion with the author, November 2017.
3. Heather Love Beverley in discussion with the author, November 2017.
4. Trina Orchard in discussion with the author, November 2017.
5. Trina Orchard in discussion with the author, November 2017.
6. "Roylco Educational Light Cube," School Specialty, accessed December 10, 2017, https://www.schoolspecialty.com/educational-light-cube-1489664.
7. "DuneCraft.com: Bring Learning to Life!" DuneCraft.com, accessed December 10, 2017, http://www.dunecraft.com/.
8. "Grow," Faber-Castell, accessed December 10, 2017, http://www.fabercastell.com/creativity-for-kids/products/categories/grow.
9. "Beyond Books Collection," Avondale Library, accessed December 10, 2017, http://www.avondalelibrary.org/books-media/beyond-books-collection.
10. "Search: BiblioCommons," Austin Public Library, accessed December 10, 2017, https://austin.bibliocommons.com/v2/search?query=equipment&searchType=smart.

11. “Library of Things,” Reading Public Library, accessed December 10, 2017, http://www.readingpl.org/discover/library-of-things/.

12. “Unusual Stuff to Borrow,” Ann Arbor District Library, accessed December 10, 2017, http://www.aadl.org/catalog/browse/unusual.

13. “Musical Instruments,” Ottawa Public Library, accessed December 10, 2017, https://biblioottawalibrary.ca/en/instruments.

Further Reading

Wichman, Emily T. *Librarian's Guide to Passive Programming: Easy and Affordable Activities for All Ages*. Santa Barbara, CA: Libraries Unlimited, 2012.

Appendix

Must-Read Blogs and Sites

- Community STEPs—STEM Activities for Public Programs
  http://www.supernova.dal.ca/community-steps/
- Kitsap Regional Library—Make Do Share—Guide for STEM with Youth
  http://www.krl.org/makedoshare/ourguide
- littleBits Education—Powerful STEAM Learning. Simplified.
  https://littlebits.cc/education
- Minecraft Education Edition
  https://education.minecraft.net/how-it-works/in-the-classroom/
- Programming Librarian—STEM
  http://www.programminglibrarian.org/tags/stem
- The Show Me Librarian—All Things STEM
  https://showmelibrarian.blogspot.ca/p/all-things-steam.html
- STAR_net—Science-Technology Activities & Resources for Libraries
  https://www.starnetlibraries.org/
- STEM in Libraries
  https://steminlibraries.com/
- STEMRead
  http://www.stemread.com/
- Wonder Education Community—Learning Resources for Dot and Dash Robots
  https://education.makewonder.com/
- YALSA STEAM Programming Toolkit
  http://www.ala.org/yalsa/steam-toolkit
- YALSA STEM Resources Wiki
  http://wikis.ala.org/yalsa/index.php/STEM_Resources

Professional Collection Items

Miller, John, and Chris Fornell Scott. *Unofficial Minecraft Lab for Kids: Family-Friendly Projects for Exploring and Teaching Math, Science, History, and Culture through Creative Building*. Beverly, MA: Quarry, 2016.

Pandora, Cherie P., and Kathy Fredrick. *Full STEAM Ahead: Science, Technology, Engineering, Art, and Mathematics in Library Programs and Collections*. Santa Barbara, CA: Libraries Unlimited, 2017.

Pichman, Brian. *Technology for Makerspaces*. New York: McGraw-Hill Education, 2018.

Must-Watch YouTube Series

- ASAP Science
  https://www.youtube.com/user/AsapSCIENCE/videos
- Buzz Feed—Talk Nerdy to Me
  https://www.youtube.com/user/talknerdytomeHP/videos
- Crash Course: Playlists for Biology, Chemistry, Computer Science, Anatomy and More!
  https://www.youtube.com/user/crashcourse/playlists
- Crash Course Kids: Playlists for Engineering, Space, Life, Earth, and Physical Sciences
  https://www.youtube.com/user/crashcoursekids/playlists
- Minute Physics
  https://www.youtube.com/user/minutephysics/videos
- Sci Show
  https://www.youtube.com/user/scishow/videos
- This Is Chemistry—American Chemical Society
  https://www.youtube.com/user/ACSReactions/videos

Bibliography

ABRA Electronics. "ABRA Electronics Corp." Accessed December 11, 2017. https://abra-electronics.com/.

ACTUA. "About." Accessed December 11, 2017. http://actua.ca/en/about.

Allain, Rhett. "Let's Explore the Physics of Rotational Motion with a Fidget Spinner." Wired. August 17, 2017. Accessed December 11, 2017. https://www.wired.com/2017/05/physics-of-a-fidget-spinner/.

Amazon Canada. "Learning Resources Classroom Magnet Lab Kit, Magnets." Magnets. Accessed December 10, 2017. https://www.amazon.ca/dp/B000ENW5ZG/ref=sspa_dk_detail_6?psc=1.

Amazon.com. "Fotodiox 5' x 7' Collapsible Chromakey Green Blue 2-in-1 Background Panel and Support Stand: Photo Studio Backgrounds." Camera & Photo. Accessed December 10, 2017. https://www.amazon.com/Fotodiox-Collapsible-Chromakey-Background-Support/dp/B003Y2KSC6/ref=sr_1_15?ie=UTF8&qid=1511894715&sr=8-15&keywords=chromakey.

———. "Kensington SafeGrip Security Case for iPad with Stylus—Sunshine—K67796AM: Computers & Accessories." Computers & Accessories. Accessed December 10, 2017. https://www.amazon.com/Kensington-SafeGrip-Security-Case-Stylus/dp/B00AQKSVDW.

Anderson, Janna, and Lee Rainie. "The Future of Truth and Misinformation Online." Pew Research Center: Internet, Science & Tech. October 19, 2017. Accessed December 10, 2017. http://www.pewinternet.org/2017/10/19/the-future-of-truth-and-misinformation-online/.

Anderson, Monica, Paul Hitlin, and Michelle Atkinson. "Wikipedia at 15: Millions of readers in Scores of Languages." Pew Research Center. January 14, 2016. Accessed December 10, 2017. http://www.pewresearch.org/fact-tank/2016/01/14/wikipedia-at-15/.

Anderson, Monica, and Andrew Perrin. "Technology Use among Seniors." Pew Research Center: Internet, Science & Tech. May 17, 2017. Accessed December 10, 2017. http://www.pewinternet.org/2017/05/17/technology-use-among-seniors/.

Ann Arbor District Library. "Unusual Stuff to Borrow." Accessed December 10, 2017. http://www.aadl.org/catalog/browse/unusual.

Austin Public Library. "Search: BiblioCommons." Accessed December 10, 2017. https://austin.bibliocommons.com/v2/search?query=equipment&searchType=smart.

Avondale Library. "Beyond Books Collection." Accessed December 10, 2017. http://www.avondalelibrary.org/books-media/beyond-books-collection.

Banks, Marcus. "Fighting Fake News." *American Libraries Magazine*, December 27, 2016. Accessed December 10, 2017. https://americanlibrariesmagazine.org/2016/12/27/fighting-fake-news/.

Basham, James D., Maya Israel, and Kathie Maynard. "An Ecological Model of STEM Education: Operationalizing STEM for All." *Journal of Special Education Technology* 25, no. 3 (2010): 9–19.

Berkeley Public Library. "Planning." Accessed December 11, 2017. https://www.berkeleypubliclibrary.org/about/planning.

Best Buy. "Community Grants." Accessed November 20, 2017. https://corporate.bestbuy.com/community-grants-page/.

Billboard. "Musical.ly Acquired by Chinese Startup for $800 Million." November 10, 2017. Accessed December 10, 2017. https://www.billboard.com/biz/articles/news/legal-and-management/8031196/musically-acquired-by-chinese-startup-for-800-million#print.

Boylan, Wendy. "Why and When to Turn to Grant Seeking." *Public Libraries* 52, no. 6 (2013): 26–28.

Breakout EDU. "About." Accessed December 10, 2017. https://www.breakoutedu.com/about.

"Bytedance and Musical.ly Announce Agreement to Merge." PR Newswire. Accessed December 10, 2017. https://en.prnasia.com/releases/apac/Bytedance_and_Musical_ly_Announce_Agreement_to_Merge-193715.shtml.

Canada Post. "Canada Post Community Foundation Grant Process." Accessed December 11, 2017. https://www.canadapost.ca/web/en/pages/aboutus/communityfoundation/criteria.page.

Canadian Paediatric Society. "Screen Time and Young Children: Promoting Health and Development in a Digital World." Accessed December 10, 2017. https://www.cps.ca/en/documents/position/screen-time-and-young-children.

Casey, Beth M., Nicole Andrews, Holly Schindler, Joanne E. Kersh, Alexandra Samper, and Juanita Copley. "The Development of Spatial Skills Through Interventions Involving Block Building Activities." *Cognition and Instruction* 26, no. 3 (2008): 269–309.

Chalufour, Ingrid, and Karen Worth. *Building Structures with Young Children*. 1st ed. The Young Scientist. St. Paul, MN: Redleaf, 2004.

Cohen, Lynn E., and Janet Emmons. "Block Play: Spatial Language with Preschool and School-Aged Children." *Early Child Development and Care* 187 (2017): 967–77.

Comic Shop Locator. "There's a Lot to See and Do at Your Local Comic Shop!" Accessed December 10, 2017. https://www.comicshoplocator.com/storelocator.

Common Sense Media. "App Reviews—Kids Apps." Ratings, Reviews, and Advice. Accessed December 10, 2017. https://www.commonsensemedia.org/app-reviews.

Council of Canadian Academies, Expert Panel on STEM Skills for the Future. *Some Assembly Required: STEM Skills and Canada's Economic Productivity.* 2015. Accessed November 27, 2017. http://www.scienceadvice.ca/uploads/ENG/AssessmentsPublicationsNewsReleases/STEM/STEMFullReportEn.pdf.

Council on Communications and Media. "Media and Young Minds." *Pediatrics*, October 21, 2016. Accessed December 10, 2017. http://pediatrics.aappublications.org/content/early/2016/10/19/peds.2016-2591.

Do Ink. "Home." Accessed December 10, 2017. http://www.doink.com/.

Donegan-Ritter, Mary. "STEM for All Children: Preschool Teachers Supporting Engagement of Children with Special Needs in Physical Science Learning Centers." *Young Exceptional Children* 20, no. 1 (2017): 3–15.

DuneCraft. "DuneCraft.com: Bring Learning to Life!" Accessed December 10, 2017. http://www.dunecraft.com/.

Eberhart, George M., ed. *The Whole Library Handbook 5: Current Data, Professional Advice, and Curiosa.* 5th ed. Chicago: American Library Association, 2014.

Elmer's. "Elmer's Slime." Parent Craft Projects. Accessed December 11, 2017. http://elmers.com/slime.

Faber-Castell. "Grow." Accessed December 10, 2017. http://www.fabercastell.com/creativity-for-kids/products/categories/grow.

Farkas, Meredith. "Making for STEM Success." *American Libraries* 46, no. 5 (2015): 27.

Fenton, Alexandra. *SuperNOVA Annual Report*. Dalhousie University, Halifax, NS, 2016, 2–16.

Frank, Flo, and Anne Smith. *The Community Development Handbook: A Tool to Build Community Capacity*. 1999. Accessed November 29, 2017. http://publications.gc.ca/collections/Collection/MP33-13-1999E.pdf.

Free Comic Book Day. "Home Page." Accessed December 10, 2017. http://www.freecomicbookday.com/.

Fun-A-Day! "This Is Such an Awesome Star Wars LEGO Science Idea!" April 26, 2017. Accessed December 11, 2017. https://fun-a-day.com/star-wars-lego-science/.

Government of Canada. "Information Update—Health Canada Advises Canadians to Avoid Homemade Craft and Pesticide Recipes Using Boric Acid." Recalls and Safety Alerts. Accessed December 10, 2017. http://www.healthycanadians.gc.ca/recall-alert-rappel-avis/hc-sc/2016/59514a-eng.php.

The Green Head. "Lay-N-Go—Activity Mat and Storage Bag." December 23, 2014. Accessed December 11, 2017. https://www.thegreenhead.com/2012/04/lay-n-go-activity-mat-storage-bag.php.

Grubbs, Michael. "Robotics Intrigue Middle School Students and Build STEM Skills." *Technology and Engineering Teacher* 72, no. 6 (2013): 12–16.

Hembree, Diana. "Fidget Spinner Choking Hazard Alarms Parents, but Fire Hazards Top Recall List." *Forbes*, July 21, 2017. Accessed December 11, 2017. https://www.forbes.com/sites/dianahembree/2017/06/01/fidget-spinner-choking-hazard-alarms-parents-but-fire-and-shock-risks-top-this-months-recall-list/#5a1e48a317c7.

IncredibleScience. "7 DIY LEGO Hand Spinner Fidget Toys! How to Make Spinners!" YouTube video, 10:34. April 17, 2017. Accessed December 11, 2017. https://www.youtube.com/watch?v=OhJL8dtcLhk.

Indigo Books & Music. "Canada's Biggest Bookstore: Buy Books, Toys, Electronics, Paper Stationery, Home Decor & More." Accessed December 10, 2017. https://www.chapters.indigo.ca/en-ca.

Institute of Museum and Library Services. *Public Libraries in the United States Survey: Fiscal Year 2012*. December 2014. https://www.imls.gov/assets/1/AssetManager/PLS_FY2012.pdf .

Johnson, Abby. "Preschool STEM Lab." *Library Journal* 141, no. 7 (2016): 7.

Jolly, Anne. "STEM vs. STEAM: Do the Arts Belong?" *Education Week Teacher*, April 29, 2016. Accessed December 10, 2017. https://www.edweek.org/tm/articles/2014/11/18/ctq-jolly-stem-vs-steam.html.

Karp, Tanja, and Patricia Maloney. "Exciting Young Students in Grades K–8 about STEM through an Afterschool Robotics Challenge." *American Journal of Engineering Education* 4, no. 1 (2013): 39–54.

KEVA Planks. "Home." Accessed December 10, 2017. http://www.kevaplanks.com/.

Kinney, Bo. "The Internet, Public Libraries, and the Digital Divide." *Public Library Quarterly* 29, no. 2 (2010): 104–61.

Kranich, Nancy. "Civic Partnerships." *Resource Sharing & Information Networks* 18, nos. 1/2 (2005): 89–103.

Lakeshore Learning Materials. "Shop by Category." Accessed December 10, 2017. https://www.lakeshorelearning.com/.

Landau, Herbert B. *Winning Library Grants: A Game Plan*. Chicago: American Library Association, 2011.

LEGO.com. "LEGO Group." May 22, 2017. Accessed December 11, 2017. https://www.lego.com/en-us/videos/themes/lego-system/fidgetspinners-may23-6dd74497c7844f0e-ae15386d97647911##sp=22.

LEGO Education. "LEGO Education." Accessed December 11, 2017. https://education.lego.com/en-us.

Lemon Dogs Tacos & Lemonade. "Halifax Tacos, Freezies, Popsicles, Lemonade Street Food." Accessed December 11, 2017. http://lemon.dog/.

Leonard, Jacqueline, Alan Buss, Ruben Gamboa, Monica Mitchell, Olatokunbo Fashola, S. Hubert, and Tarcia Almughyirah. "Using Robotics and Game Design to Enhance Children's Self-Efficacy, STEM Attitudes, and Computational Thinking Skills." *Journal of Science Education and Technology* 25, no. 6 (2016): 860–76.

Li, Yanyan, Zhinan Huang, Menglu Jiang, and Chang Ting-Wen. "The Effect on Pupils' Science Performance and Problem-Solving Ability through Lego: An Engineering Design-Based Modeling Approach." *Journal of Educational Technology & Society* 19, no. 3 (2016): 143–56.

Library Pipeline. "Innovation in Libraries Grant." Accessed December 11, 2017. https://www.librarypipeline.org/innovation/innovation-microfunding/.

Littlecodr. "Home." Accessed December 10, 2017. http://littlecodr.com/.

Louisekool. "Quality Furniture, Materials for Child Care and Education." Accessed December 10, 2017. http://www.louisekool.com/.

lucybarrow. "Star Wars Day 2014—MaKey MaKey Version." Accessed December 1, 2017. https://scratch.mit.edu/projects/19662631.

Mad Science Group. "Education Wrapped in Entertainment!" Accessed December 11, 2017. http://madscience.org/.

Makedo Cardboard Construction. "What Is Makedo." Accessed December 10, 2017. https://www.make.do/pages/what-is-makedo.

"Make, Do, Share: Sustainable STEM Leadership in a Box; An Interview with Shannon Peterson." *Young Adult Library Services* 14, no. 3 (2016): 13–16.

Makey Makey. "Makey Makey: Buy Direct." Accessed December 11, 2017. https://www.makeymakey.com/.

Massis, Bruce. "Library Partnerships: A Key to Growth." *New Library World* 114, nos. 11/12 (2013): 550–53.

Meyer, Leila. "Higher Stem." *School Library Journal*, April 1, 2017, 28.

Moomaw, Sally, and Jaumall A. Davis. "STEM Comes to Preschool." *Young Children* 65, no. 5 (2010): 12–14.

Moores, David C. "We're All About Educational Supplies." SPECTRUM Nasco. Accessed December 11, 2017. https://spectrum-nasco.ca/catalogpc.htm?Category=ES—LEGO EDUCATION.

Moran, Barbara. "LGBTQ+ Issues in STEM Diversity." Boston University Research. June 15, 2017. http://www.bu.edu/research/articles/lgbt-issues-stem-diversity/.

Murphy, Pat. *Lego Chain Reactions: Design and Build Amazing Moving Machines*. Palo Alto, CA: Klutz, 2014.

Musical.ly. "For Parents." Support. November 15, 2017. Accessed December 10, 2017. https://support.musical.ly/knowledge-base/for-parents/.

National Archives and Records Administration. "Remarks by the President in State of Union Address." January 25, 2011. Accessed December 10, 2017. https://obamawhitehouse.archives.gov/the-press-office/2011/01/25/remarks-president-state-union-address.

National Science Teachers Association. "NSTA Position Statement: Early Childhood Science Education." Accessed December 10, 2017. http://www.nsta.org/about/positions/earlychildhood.aspx.

NDS Queensland. "NDS Queensland State Conference 2007—Keynote Address." YouTube, 9 videos. Accessed December 11, 2017. https://www.youtube.com/playlist?list=PLD1204DAE4DCD8B42.

Nicholson, Simon. "The Theory of Loose Parts: An Important Principle for Design Methodology." *Studies in Design Education Craft and Technology* 4, no. 2 (1972): 5–14.

O'Reilly, Katie. "Libraries on Lockdown." *American Libraries* 47, nos. 9/10 (2016): 14–15, 17.

Ossowski, Anna. "What Does Cross Stitch Have to Do with Programming? More Than You Think." Opensource.com. January 3, 2017. Accessed December 11, 2017. https://opensource.com/article/17/11/traditional-arts-crafts-code-programming.

Ottawa Public Library. "Musical Instruments." Accessed December 10, 2017. https://biblioottawa library.ca/en/instruments.

PancakeBot. "Print Your Pancakes." Accessed December 10, 2017. http://www.pancakebot.com/tutorials.

Party Delights. "Make Your Own Banana Minion." 2015. Accessed December 1, 2017. http://blog.partydelights.co.uk/wp-content/uploads/2015/01/minion-banana-printable.pdf

PBS. "Gooey Gak!" February 21, 2013. Accessed December 10, 2017. http://www.pbs.org/parents/crafts-for-kids/gak-attack/.

People Power Press USA. "Custom Buttons, Button Machines and Supplies." Accessed December 10, 2017. https://peoplepowerpress.net/.

Peterson, Shannon. "Sowing the Seeds of STEM." *Young Adult Library Services* 10, no. 2 (2012): 8.

Picard, Caroline. "Parents Everywhere Are Worried about DIY Slime After Multiple Kids Are Burned." *Good Housekeeping*, April 4, 2017. Accessed December 10, 2017. http://www.good housekeeping.com/life/parenting/news/a43500/slime-safety/.

Pietrowski, Amy. "The History of STEM vs. STEAM Education (and the Rise of STREAM)." *EdTech*, August 14, 2017. Accessed December 10, 2017. https://edtechmagazine.com/k12/article/2017/08/history-stem-vs-steam-education-and-rise-stream.

"Pop Literacy." SLJ ISTE Webcast Series. *School Library Journal*, November 21, 2016. Accessed December 11, 2017. http://www.slj.com/2016/11/industry-news/pop-literacy-slj-iste-web cast-series/.

Primo Toys. "Cubetto: A Robot Teaching Kids Code & Computer Programming." Accessed December 10, 2017. https://www.primotoys.com/.

Prince, April Jones, and François Roca. *Twenty-One Elephants and Still Standing*. Boston: Houghton Mifflin, 2005.

Programming Librarian. "Fake News: A Library Resource Round-Up." October 20, 2017. Accessed December 10, 2017. http://www.programminglibrarian.org/articles/fake-news-library-round.

———. "Robot Storytime: Coding for Preschoolers." July 27, 2017. Accessed December 10, 2017. http://www.programminglibrarian.org/blog/robot-storytime-coding-preschoolers.

Project Outcome. "Home." Accessed December 11, 2017. https://www.projectoutcome.org/home.

"Public Libraries and STEM: An Interview with Paul Dusenbery and Keliann LaConte." *Young Adult Library Services* 14, no. 2 (2016): 10–13.

Reading Public Library. "Library of Things." Accessed December 10, 2017. http://www.readingpl.org/discover/library-of-things/.

Red Ted Art. "Easy Fidget Spinner WITHOUT Bearings TEMPLATE—How to Make a Tri Fidget Spinner DIY." YouTube video, 14:18. May 7, 2017. Accessed December 11, 2017. https://www.youtube.com/watch?v=0Lthvm6yOvY.

Rohrig, Brian. "The Science of Slime." *Chem Matters*, December 2004, 13–16. https://www.acs.org/content/dam/acsorg/education/resources/highschool/chemmatters/articlesbytopic/solidsliquidsgases/chemmatters-dec2004-slime.pdf.

Royal Academy of Engineering. *The UK STEM Education Landscape.* May 2016. Accessed December 10, 2017. https://www.raeng.org.uk/publications/reports/uk-stem-education-landscape.

Ruzzi, Bree Laverdiere, and Angela Eckhoff. "STEM Resources and Materials for Engaging Learning Experiences." *Young Children* 72, no. 1 (March 2017). Accessed December 10, 2017. https://www.naeyc.org/resources/pubs/yc/mar2017/stem-materials-experiences.

Scholastic. "Girls Rock STEM." Accessed December 10, 2017. https://www.scholastic.com/teachers/articles/teaching-content/girls-rock-stem/.

School Specialty. "Roylco Educational Light Cube." Accessed December 10, 2017. https://www.schoolspecialty.com/educational-light-cube-1489664.

Schreiber, Sarah. "Mom Warns Parents after Her Daughter Reportedly Choked on a Fidget Spinner." *Good Housekeeping*, June 22, 2017. Accessed December 11, 2017. http://www.goodhouse keeping.com/life/parenting/news/a44244/mom-warns-fidget-spinner-choking-hazard/.

Scratch. "Scratch—Imagine, Program, Share." Accessed December 11, 2017. https://scratch.mit.edu/.

Sharma, Dilnavaz. "Does STEM Education Belong in the Public Library?" *Public Libraries* 55, no. 2 (2016): 17–19.

Smith, Aaron. "15% of American Adults Have Used Online Dating Sites or Mobile Dating Apps." Pew Research Center: Internet, Science & Tech. February 11, 2016. Accessed December 10, 2017. http://www.pewinternet.org/2016/02/11/15-percent-of-american-adults-have-used-online-dating-sites-or-mobile-dating-apps/.

Squishy Circuits. "Play · Invent · Learn." Accessed December 10, 2017. http://squishycircuits.com/.

Starbucks Newsroom. "Starbucks New Color and Flavor Changing Unicorn Frappuccino." June 12, 2017. Accessed December 10, 2017. https://news.starbucks.com/news/starbucks-unicorn-frappuccino.

States, Dawn. "Out of the Pickle: Promoting Food Science and STEM in Public Libraries." *Pennsylvania Libraries: Research & Practice* 3, no. 2 (2015): 102–14.

STEMfinity. "STEM Grants." Accessed December 11, 2017. https://www.stemfinity.com/STEM-Education-Grants.

"STEM vs. STEAM: Why the 'A' Makes a Difference." Edudemic. January 21, 2015. Accessed December 10, 2017. http://www.edudemic.com/stem-vs-steam-why-the-a-makes-all-the-difference/.

Stoll, Julia, Ashley Hamilton, Emilie Oxley, Angela Mitroff Eastman, and Rachael Brent. "Young Thinkers in Motion: Problem Solving and Physics in Preschool." *Young Children* 67, no. 2 (2012): 20–26.

StoreBound. "PancakeBot 2.0." Accessed December 10, 2017. http://www.storebound.com/storebound/pancakebot-products/pancakebot-2-0.

SuperNOVA at Dalhousie University. "About SuperNOVA." Accessed December 11, 2017. http://www.supernova.dal.ca/about/.

———. "Home." Accessed December 10, 2017. http://www.supernova.dal.ca/.

Suri, Manil. "Why Is Science So Straight?" *New York Times*, September 4, 2015. Accessed December 10, 2017. https://www.nytimes.com/2015/09/05/opinion/manil-suri-why-is-science-so-straight.html.

Teach with Laughter. "Building Block Fun." February 7, 2014. Accessed December 1, 2017. http://teachwithlaughter.blogspot.ca/2014/02/building-block-fun.html.

Tecre. "Home." Accessed December 10, 2017. https://www.tecre.com/.

Thingiverse. "Bearing-to-HexNut Adapter by kroyster." January 17, 2017. Accessed December 11, 2017. https://www.thingiverse.com/thing:2044157.

———. "Fidget: A Collection by glitchpudding." Last updated August 29, 2017. Accessed December 11, 2017. https://www.thingiverse.com/glitchpudding/collections/fidget/page:1.

Toronto Public Library. *Strategic Plan 2016–2019 : Strategic Plans, Annual Reports & Statistics*. Accessed December 11, 2017. http://www.torontopubliclibrary.ca/about-the-library/strategic-plan/2016-2019/consultation.jsp.

US Bureau of Labor Statistics. "Nearly 8.6 Million STEM Jobs in 2015." Accessed December 10, 2017. https://www.bls.gov/spotlight/2017/science-technology-engineering-and-mathematics-stem-occupations-past-present-and-future/home.htm.

Waldrop, M. "The Science of Teaching Science." *Nature* 523, no. 7560 (2015): 272–74.

Walmart Canada. "Apply for a Donation." Accessed December 11, 2017. https://www.walmartcanada.ca/community-giving/corporate-giving.

Walmart Foundation. "Community Grant Program." Accessed December 11, 2017. http://giving.walmart.com/walmart-foundation/community-grant-program.

Wheatley, Margaret J. *Leadership and the New Science: Discovering Order in a Chaotic World*. 2nd ed. San Francisco: Berrett-Koehler, 1999.

Wichman, Emily T. *Librarian's Guide to Passive Programming: Easy and Affordable Activities for All Ages*. Santa Barbara, CA: Libraries Unlimited, 2012.

Young Adult Library Services Association (YALSA). *Issue Brief #3: Libraries Help Teens Build STEM Skills.* http://www.ala.org/yalsa/sites/ala.org.yalsa/files/content/IssueBrief_STEM.pdf.

Index

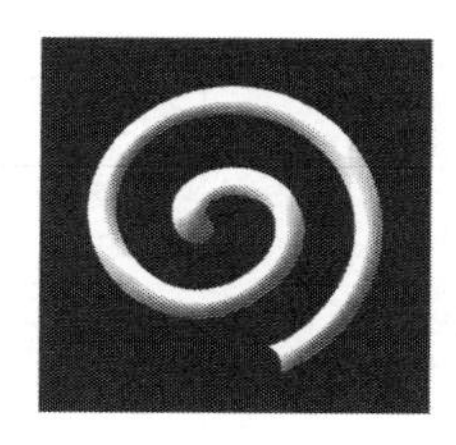

Page references for figures are *italicized*.

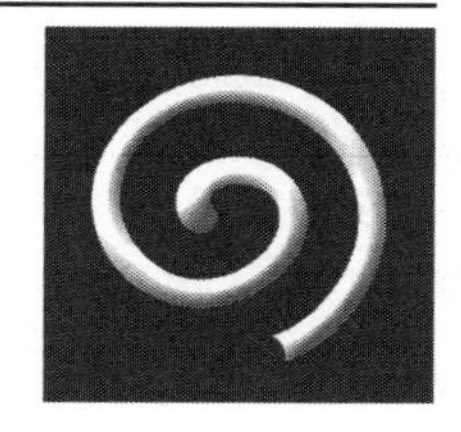

About the Author

Chantale Pard received her master's in library and information science at Western University in 2013. She held positions in a variety of different library settings before settling in at Halifax Public Libraries, where she has been the Youth Services librarian at Keshen Goodman Public Library for more than five years. It is here where she leads a busy and successful team of youth programmers through a variety of classic and pop culture programs at one of the busiest and biggest public libraries east of Montreal. She also runs Keshen Goodman's popular and established Anime Club, which means she is often sought after for advice on anime-themed library programming.